ISLE OF MAN
TRAMWAYS

The crest shown overleaf was used
on I O M T & E P and Manx Electric vehicles
from 1893 to 1956, and is now replaced
by a similar but smaller one. The garter
carrying the motto is red with gold lettering,
edging, buckle, eyelets and endpieces. The
foliage embellishments are in natural colours,
the three legs device appears as of leather,
with steel leg plates, gold knee-pieces and
spurs. The background consists of the car's
varnished teak side-panel

ISLE OF MAN TRAMWAYS

by

F. K. PEARSON
AMIMI, AIRTE

With drawings and maps by S. Broomfield, D. G.
Coakham, ARIBA, J. C. Cooke, P. Hammond, and J. N.
Slater, and an appendix on Tickets by
W. H. Bett, FCII

DAVID & CHARLES : NEWTON ABBOT

7153 4740 3

Set in 10pt Baskerville 1pt leaded
and printed in Great Britain by
Bristol Typesetting Company Limited Bristol
for David & Charles (Publishers) Limited
South Devon House Newton Abbot Devon

Contents

List of Illustrations

LINE ILLUSTRATIONS
IN TEXT

Of the remainder of the illustrations listed above, Mr J. C. Cook provided
those on pages 14, 24, 29, 32, 41, 47, 49, 58, 60, 61, 87, 98, 102, 106,
132, 137, 148, 150, 175, 176, 185, 192, 201, 203, 209, 212, 217, 225,
230, 237, 243, 249, 261, 305, 308, 310, 321, 333, 338, 361, 362, 363,
368, 369 and 370, and Mr D. G. Coakham those on pages 91, 141, 152,
155, 156, 164, 168, 177, 183, 191, 195, 210, 213, 220, 227, 231, 248,
266, 267, 313, 364, 365, 366, 367 and 368. Mr. S. Broomfield (additionally)
provided 219 and 221, the Author the remaining twenty-nine items.

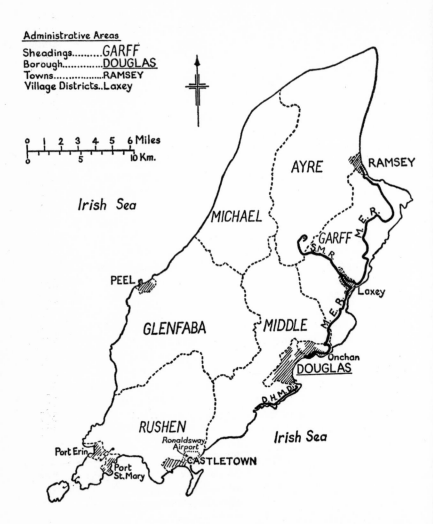

Administrative Areas

Sheadings..........*GARFF*
Borough..............<u>DOUGLAS</u>
Towns.................RAMSEY
Village Districts..Laxey

0 1 2 3 4 5 6 Miles
0   5   10 Km.

Irish Sea

RAMSEY

AYRE

MICHAEL

GARFF

S.M.R.

M.E.R.

PEEL

Laxey

GLENFABA

MIDDLE

M.E.R.

Onchan

<u>DOUGLAS</u>

D.H.M.D.

RUSHEN

Irish Sea

Ronaldsway
Airport

Port Erin

Port
St. Mary

CASTLETOWN

Introduction

In mid-summer of 1945, the writer set sail for what was then, to him, a miniature new world—the Isle of Man. The particular attraction of its transportation was at once felt, and from this, and the friendliness and enthusiasm of operating and administrative staffs, has grown this book. Though primarily an account of the tramway undertakings, it is also to some extent a history of the island's growth as a resort, and of its latter-day difficulties, and the writer hopes that Manx readers will show the same indulgence to a mainlander's examination of their affairs as they did towards his many queries.

The Isle of Man lies a little to the north of centre of the Irish Sea, and is geologically rather similar to England's Lake District, which at one point is only thirty miles away. The island's mountainous slate backbone (rising to 2,034 feet at Snaefell) shelters a rather gentler limestone country in the south-east, whilst the far north consists of a remote plain extending to the Point of Ayre. The island's greatest length is 33¼ miles, the width 12½. The ever-present sea gives vegetation of a greenness only paralleled in the west of Ireland, a scenic resemblance furthered by the structural simplicity of the older Manx cottages. The towns are of moderate size; Douglas with around 18,800 inhabitants (1961) contrasts with Ramsey's 3,700, Peel's 2,500, and the four others all with less than 2,000. The island's total population in 1961 was 48,150.

Its people, and the near-extinct Manx language, are of complex origins. Rich in pre-historic remains, the island also played a major part in the events of Celtic Christianity. From its thirteenth century status as part of the Kingdom of Norway through successive Scottish and English overlordships, its history was continuously unsettled until it passed to the Dukes of Athol in the early eighteenth century. The Athol regime did little to improve the island economically, smuggling being a dominant means of livelihood, but from 1829 the island was once more brought under the English

Crown and a more ordered economy evolved, centred at first around the herring industry and an improved agriculture, and later on the expanding holiday industry. The governorship of Sir Henry Brougham Loch from 1863 marked the start of the most rapid period of evolution, in which the writer's fellow Mancunians (of past generations) played a major part. The island's tramways were at once the product and the means of the tourist industry's growth, and are an essential part of that industry today.

The island has in its Tynwald the oldest unbroken Parliamentary tradition in the world. The lower house, the Keys, dates in its present elected form from 1866, and with its corresponding Legislative Council (the upper house) has exercised a marked influence on the status of the island's tramways. Inspections of new lines were made at the behest of the Governor, originally by island-resident men (as in 1876) but later by borrowing the inspecting engineer-officers of the mainland Board of Trade. The word 'Act' in this book refers in every case to an Act of Tynwald.

No effort has been made to cover the history of the island's steam railways, already well described in works by the late Ian Macnab and more recently by J. I. C. Boyd. The Groudle Glen Miniature Railway has intimate Manx Electric connections, but is covered briefly in Mr Boyd's book, and a fuller description by Mr B. E. Crompton impends.

To my wife for her patient execution of an unimaginable volume of paper work, to my illustrative collaborators, to a host of Manx friends, and perhaps above all to those who run the present-day Isle of Man tramways, my thanks. May this account bring enhanced recognition of their work, and of the intrinsic value of the substantial part of the former network which happily survives.

Poulton-le-Fylde
Lancashire
1969

F. K. PEARSON

Monochrome prepared by K. M. Chapman, ATD, FRSA, from a photograph taken north of the Lifeboat House on the first day of operation, 7 August 1876, showing Douglas Bay Tramway No 2 with the Lightfoots as top-deck passengers. J. W. Lightfoot appears as conductor, and manager Leadbetter is seen leaning against the corner pillar

Douglas in about 1878, showing the course of the horse tramway for almost two-thirds of its length. In the foreground is Castle Mona Road, with the tramway laid hard by the seaward wall; beyond are the Iron Pier, the Lifeboat House and the newly-built Loch Promenade

CHAPTER ONE

The Douglas Horse Tramway, 1876-1900

'. . . tinkling tramcars, like toast racks,
Sweeping the curve of the bay.'

(Hall Caine)

In 1870 Douglas, ranked among the more select of watering places. The beautifully-engraved Ordnance Survey map of 1869 shows the spacious splendour of Castle Mona's gardens contrasting with the rabbit-warren of Old Douglas, whilst villas lined the bay to the north. Except in the old town, the impression is of one huge garden, with winding paths, shrubberies, formal rose-beds, summer houses and conservatories. The Peveril hotel was not yet built, and the visitor leaving the new Victoria pier faced a motley group of buildings around Fort Street, Duke Street, Drumgold Street and Strand Street, all typical of old Douglas.

Strand Street lay nearly parallel to the shore of the bay, and continued as Castle Street to the start of the Colonel's Road, at the site of the future Lifeboat House of 1875. No promenade had yet been formed here, the shops and houses backing on to an irregular sea wall. With the Colonel's Road began what was then called the Esplanade, formed in 1864 by building a 1,000-ft paved stone embankment about seventy-four feet to seaward of the existing sea wall and filling in the intervening space to form a lawn. In later years this took the name Harris promenade, after Samuel Harris, first chairman of the town board (1860) and later High Bailiff, who had borne much of the cost. This esplanade fronted the late Regency Villa Marina, formerly Government House,

B

whose garden wall ran along to Broadway (then only twenty-six feet wide), and here the Esplanade came to an end, at the 1869 Iron Pier.

From this point the shore road, here called Castle Mona Road, continued past an irregular group of buildings to the relative grandeur of Clarence, Esplanade and Derby Terraces. Castle Lawn Terrace had gardens which ran down to the shore road, and to the north the shorter Castle Terrace adjoined the gardens of Castle Mona, built in 1804 as a residence for the Duke of Athol but by now a hotel. The northern gardens now occupied by the casino were protected from the casual eye by a grass embankment opposite the battlemented Falcon Cliff, and the seaward parapet wall was here interrupted by the slope of McCrone's Slip. The road now ran gradually inland to form The Crescent, with gardens, pavilions and a house to seaward and more villas to landward. Approaching the foot of Burnt Mill Hill, the cliff face included quarry workings, whilst a large enclosed 'playground' flanked the narrow entrance to Strathallan Crescent, with a further slip giving access to the shore. The road further east and that up Burnt Mill Hill to Onchan lie outside our immediate interest.

Among those who chose to retire to the Isle of Man at this period was Thomas Lightfoot, the creator of the Douglas Bay Tramway. Born at Carbrook, near Sheffield, on 4 November 1814, Lightfoot became a civil engineering contractor and, according to family tradition, was concerned with the boring of the first Woodhead railway tunnel. He retired early, and in about 1870 came to Douglas with his wife and the younger of his thirteen children, taking up residence at Athol House, a seaside villa near today's Little Switzerland, a site now occupied by Westlake's Sea-Level hotel. Only fifty-six years of age, Lightfoot's instinct for new enterprise at once saw great possibilities in the future expansion of Douglas.

The period from 1870 did indeed prove to be one of rapid development, and much of the present-day promenade architecture of Douglas dates from this time. Visitors rose from 60,000 in 1872 to 182,670 in 1884 and 275,500 (summer only) in 1890. The year 1869 saw the construction of the £6,500 Iron Pier by a syndicate, and a New Street Board was set up to plan and build a new main street (Victoria Street) and a new promenade. On 18 April 1874 the line of the new sea wall was set out, and work began on 19 June. The new Victoria Street was opened on 21 April

1875, and on 9 June the Lieutenant-Governor and Mrs Loch informally opened the new 80-ft Loch promenade, which lay up to 370 ft to seaward of the 1870 shore line. The new promenade, which was handed over to the town commissioners on 26 February 1877, provided a substantial carriageway with a pavement on both sides, terminating in a walled dead-end at the Lifeboat House, to leave the lifeboat's slipway unobstructed.

This work offered the prospect of a continuous sea-level roadway from the Victoria Pier around Douglas Bay to Burnt Mill Hill, and Thomas Lightfoot was not slow to see the possibility of a tramway along its course. His first proposals, deposited in the Rolls Office on 27 November 1875, consisted of a lithograph route plan titled 'Loch Promenade and Douglas Street Tramways, Isle of Man, 1875', together with a written description and an elegantly inscribed but poorly drawn plan and section of the track. The route plan showed the line in the centre of the road, with double-track stub-end terminals and no depot. At the new Peveril hotel, the terminal tracks swung round parallel to the then sea-wall, while the transition from Loch promenade to Colonel's Road involved an acute S-bend across a former enclosed garden; these and the passing place at the Iron Pier were shown much as built in 1876. The line was shown to end at Burnt Mill Hill, at a point where the road was only twenty-one feet wide. The lowest point was north of Clarence Terrace, 16 ft 6 in above sea level, and the highest (the northern terminus) 28 ft 8 in.

By the spring of 1876, with local support obtained, Lightfoot promoted the necessary Act of Tynwald. The Douglas Bay Tramway Act, 1876, was read before Tynwald on 6 June, and received the Royal Assent on 12 August. Meanwhile, Lightfoot's plans were far enough advanced in May to permit of his ordering material; in a letter of 8 May 1876 Lightfoot, at Athol House, The Crescent, Douglas, wrote to Thomas Hill, harness manufacturer of Sheffield, acknowledging quotations for sets of harness and asking about sizes of horse collars. A note of 15 May to Thomas Tyers, 11 Corn Exchange, Leeds, reads : 'Rails and chairs not heard of yet— horses idle—men paid off for want of chairs—serious matter for us'.

The Act quoted the promoters as 'Thos. Lightfoot, his heirs and assigns', and gave the route as extending from the west end of the Queen Victoria Pier by the Loch promenade or 'shore enclosure', thence along the Colonel's Road and the highroad to Conchan (*sic*) as far as the corner of the road turning down to the shore at Strathallan Crescent. The Act defined the relationship between the promoters and the town commissioners, specified the gauge as three feet, limited the width of the carriages to a maximum of twenty-one inches outside the outer face of each wheel, and gave the promoter exclusive use of the tramway by 'trams with flange wheels'. Each horse was to carry a bell (the cars themselves had no warning gongs until 1907-8), and after sunset each car was to display a red light at the front and a green light at the rear. A further clause limited the maximum fare to 3d, and another required six double journeys to be run on each working day, Sundays excepted. Up to 14 lb of luggage were to be allowed free, and other weights were to be charged at appropriate rates, save for items over 56 lb, for which the promoters might charge what they thought fit! As on the mainland, Lightfoot had to maintain about six feet of paving (including eighteen inches on either side of the rails), and could only use animal power, except by permission of the road authority approved by Tynwald Court. Any goods traffic would also require road authority permission. Finally, the road authority could purchase compulsorily the line and ancillaries at a current valuation twenty-one years after six months from the promulgation of the Act (6 December 1876), subject to due notice in the Press and a two-thirds vote in favour.

The Bill was signed in Tynwald on Tuesday 6 June 1876, and Lightfoot, arriving in Douglas the same evening, determined to start work at once. At 11.30 next morning, 7 June, his lawyer, A. W. Adams, applied a pickaxe to the road near Athol House, watched by a small crowd which included Stanley Keig, vice-chairman of the town commissioners. A 'dejeuner' that followed was equally informal. A description of this 'cutting of the first sod' appeared in the *Isle of Man Times* of the following Saturday.

A section of the type of rail used, weighing about 35 lb/yd is preserved by Douglas Corporation transport department. As to its mode of support, Lightfoot's 1875 plan shows what can only be either Kincaid's system with 'side fastening' or that installed by Fowler at Salford and described in Vol 50, Part IV of the *Proceedings of the Institute of Civil Engineers*. This obviously owed much to Kincaid and more closely resembles Lightfoot's sketch. The surviving rail section has been worn down to about 30 lb/yd. Paving was in granite setts beside the rails, with a central tread-way of tar and broken stone, this being confirmed by early photo-

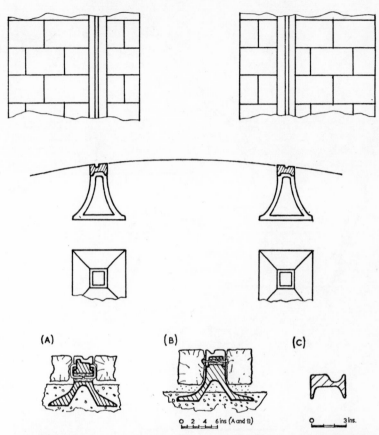

(A)   (B)   (C)

0 2 4 6ins (A and B)   0   3ins.

Douglas horse-tram track construction. Above, Lightfoot's plan and section from the deposited plans of 1875; below, Kincaid's system (A), the Salford variant (B) thought to have been used in Douglas, and the worn 1876 rail (C) preserved today by Douglas Corporation transport department

graphs. In later years, the passing places were stone paved overall.

Work began at The Crescent, near Lightfoot's house, and a surviving plan of part of the line as built, dated 31 January 1877, shows that for much of its course Lightfoot adopted the less usual of two alternative locations offered in his written description of November 1875 (at the side *or* centre of the carriageway). Thus, along The Crescent and Castle Mona Road the single track was

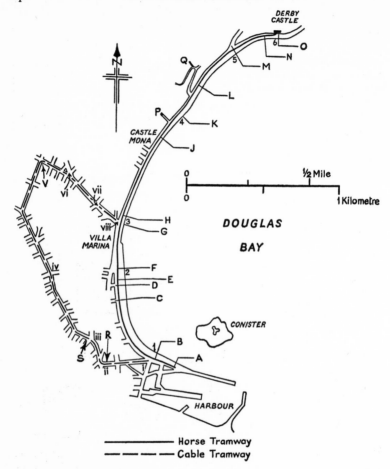

The evolution of the Douglas Bay Tramway, 1876-1968, showing also the former cable tramway. Present and historical locations mentioned in the text are Victoria Pier terminus (A), Walpole Avenue (B), just short of the former Peveril Hotel terminus, Senna Slip (D), the Lifeboat House (F), the Iron Pier opposite Broadway (G), the Palace (J), McCrone's Slip (K), Athol House (L), Burnt Mill Hill (M), Derby Castle terminus (O), the Falcon Cliff Lift (P), and the Little Switzerland Lift (Q). The roads traversed are Loch Promenade from 1 to 2, Harris Promenade (formerly Colonel's Road) from 2 to 3, Central Promenade (formerly Castle Mona Road) from 3 to 4, Queen's Promenade (formerly The Crescent) from 4

laid fairly close to the sea wall. On the Colonel's Road, the line enjoyed an odd reserved track status, with a pronounced ledge (shown on an early photograph) between the paved tramway track (here laid in a 7-ft footpath) and the roadway. On the Loch promenade, however, the track lay centrally, 44 ft 6 in from the seaward parapet.

By the end of July 1876, the line was substantially complete as far as the Iron Pier, and on Tuesday, 1 August, two tramcars arrived from Liverpool on the ss *Tynwald*. On 4 August Thomas Lightfoot's eldest son-in-law, J. Wheeldon, (the line was very much a family affair during these early years) wrote to Governor Loch asking for the line to be inspected as far as the Iron Pier, and next day William Kneale, chairman of the town commissioners, told the governor that the commissioners had no objection to Lightfoot using the portion of the tramway so far completed. They also endorsed his request for an inspection, 'such inspection not to be considered as an inspection under the Act (which had not yet been promulgated) but in the interests and safety of the public'. J. Garrow, highroad surveyor, was at once appointed as inspector and submitted his report on Monday 7 August.

The line was then complete from the foot of Burnt Mill Hill to the first lamp post on the south side of the entrance to the new Iron Pier. Lightfoot had laid down the rails and fixed the granite setts along the sides of the rails very much as his section of the work had shown, and had sent his men to clean up the rails that day, one of the new cars with two horses attached being run backwards and forwards several times. The rails appeared accurately gauged, the car ran easily and freely along the line and the inspector saw no objection to the proprietor being allowed to open the line for public use.

In fact, the line appears to have started to carry the public that same day, 7 August, and without any particular ceremony. *Mona's Herald* for Wednesday 9 August reported the success of the in-

---

to 5, and Strathallan Crescent from 5 to 6. The tramway is now double track throughout, with crossovers at B and E and disconnected crossovers at H, J and L; a crossover also existed until 1935 at N. The cable tramway traversed Victoria Street (i to ii), Prospect Hill (ii to iii), Buck's Road (iii to iv), Woodbourne Road (iv to v), York Road (v to vi), Balla-quayle Road (vi to vii) and Broadway (vii to viii); Thomas Street (R) and Hill Street (S) are also shown. It should be noted that about the turn of the century Burnt Mill Hill was renamed 'Summer Hill'.

spection, while the *Isle of Man Times* of the following Saturday referred to cars having been in operation 'through the week'. Opening day photographs show Lightfoot and his wife, Jane, as top-deck passengers, his young son, J. W. Lightfoot (about fifteen years of age), neatly equipped as conductor, H. Leadbetter, and a standing figure who was probably J. Wheeldon. Leadbetter was the line's first manager, being succeeded after some years by William J. Parker, and the first driver was an Onchan man, Jack Davies.

Fulsome praise was given to the line in *Mona's Herald* of Wednesday, 16 August:

> The opening of the Douglas Tramway is an event of by no means everyday interest. The spirited projector and proprietor, Mr Lightfoot, is deserving of much commendation and encouragement for the venture; which is, whether it obtains it or not, deserving of eminent success. . . . It was no doubt a costly venture to invest £7,000 or £8,000 in a tramway running around Douglas Bay, with but a sparse population . . . Eight and nine hundred persons have been carried over the line daily, which, at 2d each, means a large weekly return. The carriages are really elegant, and, as they roll along, add materially to the interest of the panorama. . . .

In the same issue of the paper there appeared the following advertisement:

DOUGLAS BAY TRAMWAY

THE CARS ARE NOW RUNNING DAILY (Sundays excepted), about every half-hour, from BURNT MILL HILL to the PROMENADE, the first Car leaving Burnt Mill Hill at about 8 am, and the last leaving the Promenade about 10 pm.

The location of the first depot was 'domestic' too. In August 1830, John Cloke, proprietor of the Crescent hotel near the foot of Burnt Mill Hill, bought from John, Duke of Athol, the hotel and a large walled garden that lay to the seaward side of the shore road. This passed by inheritance to S. K. Thorburn of Newcastle upon Tyne, and on 20 December 1875 the entire property was bought by Thomas Lightfoot, who renamed it Athol House. Lightfoot used the garden for his car shed, and stabling for fourteen horses was available at the house. The car-shed building itself has left no more tangible evidence of its existence than the outline of its walls shown on a plan of 1888, and an equally indistinct

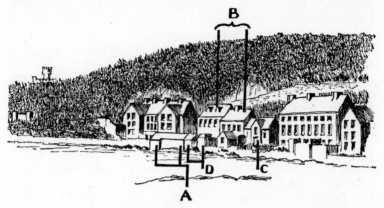

Lightfoot's original 1876 car shed on The Crescent, copied from an indistinct photograph. A is the shed, B the two portions of Athol House, C is Shell Cottage and D the latter's two seaward pavilions

photograph from which the accompanying sketch has been prepared.

By 19 December 1876, following good progress with the remainder of the line, Leadbetter asked Governor Loch for permission to run the cars to the Peveril hotel, 'as next week being Christmas, it would be a great accommodation to the Public'. The governor duly wrote to Captain Richard Penketh, MHK, JP, of Hampton Court, Braddan, on 23 December asking him to proceed with an inspection of the whole line 'as required in Section 5 of the Act'. Penketh (an Englishman) carried out his inspection on 1 January 1877 and reported at length on the 3rd. The line had been built in a 'substantial and workmanlike manner'. Minor problems included levelling up the road to the new datum which the tramway effectively provided, relocating the Iron Pier loop (which conflicted with road traffic as first laid) and easing the severity of the reverse curves at the Lifeboat House, where a diversion had been made to leave room for a pavilion then proposed by the town commissioners. Penketh, however, approved of the line's use pending settlement of the last-mentioned point.

The New Street Board and Lightfoot had already met on 27

December, when the Lifeboat House curve and the Iron Pier loop were discussed. By 1 January, the loop was in course of being relaid to seaward, and by 31 January the inspector's fears of congestion had been met by relaying the S-bend a little to the north. The town commissioners' chief objection to the original curve had been the valuable land it had rendered unsaleable. The Lifeboat House itself had meanwhile acquired a veranda on its north, east and south faces, to serve also as a public shelter.

In a letter from Government House dated 31 January 1877, the governor authorised the opening of the completed tramway as from that date.

What were the costs of the enterprise, which was financed by Lightfoot from among his personal circle? The figure of £7,000 to £8,000 already mentioned is an approximate guide, and contemporary analyses of similar lines elsewhere (in *Tramways, Their Construction and Working*, by D. K. Clark) confirm this figure. The Douglas line, being predominantly single, can be considered as $1\frac{5}{8}$ miles of track.

Turning to operating costs, Lightfoot's practice varied between single and double horsing. There is evidence that public criticism soon obliged Lightfoot to use two horses on a line otherwise remarkable for its level character, though strong headwinds sometimes made two horses necessary with a double-deck car. For the three cars, he probably had a stud of about fourteen horses. On the small tramway at Dewsbury described by D. K. Clark, the horsing allowance was eight per car, worked as three pairs per day. Horsing at Dewsbury accounted for 5.92d/mile compared with 0.73d for drivers' wages, 0.06d for car repairs, 0.18d for track maintenance, 0.91d for management and fare collection, and 0.47d as general charges, a total expense of 8.27d per car mile. On the Douglas Bay line, higher costs due to the short journey might have been offset by family help. With a daily car mileage of about sixty-seven, the Douglas line must, in fact, have cost around 8d to 9d per car mile at this date.

Of the horsing cost, about 64 per cent was for food, 10 per cent for renewals, and the remainder went to farriers, veterinary services, and labour. A tram horse's typical daily diet was 17lb of a mixture of oats, peas, maize and bran, 12lb of chopped hay, sometimes with straw, and $1\frac{1}{2}$lb of steeped linseed. Other periodic treats included carrots, green clover, and spells of grazing. On a hard-paved line, shoe life was only from eight to ten days, and horses worked for

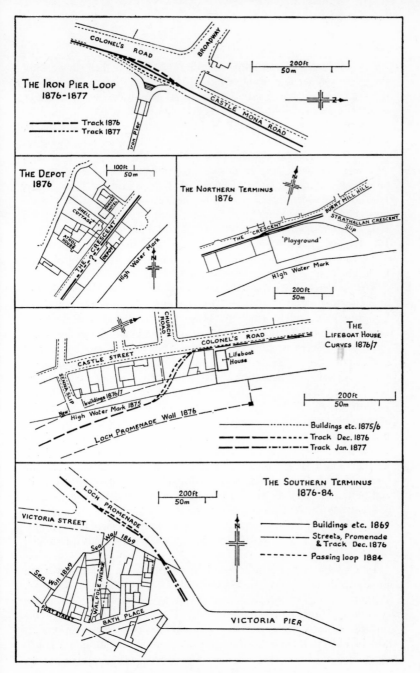

The Bay Tramway: original track layouts

up to six years before being sold off. The Douglas horses, working on softer paving and level track, had an easier time, with little of the rail-groove choking that was the chief cause of excessive draught on other horse-car lines.

The lot of the crews was perhaps harsher. On the mainland, a fifteen-hour day was commonplace, with driver's pay 4s daily; conductors began at thirteen years of age, at a rate of 1s a day. Nor was the work free from risk; the record was marred at the outset by the death on 23 December 1876 of driver John Kelly, who fell between his horse and the car and was killed. Fare collection was by a fare-box system, without tickets. One legend tells of a conductor discovered by Lightfoot sitting on the shore in the shadow of the sea wall, occupied in counting out the contents of his fare box into two dissimilarly-sized heaps to the chant of 'One for Lightfoot, two for me!'

Within three years the Loch promenade had been fully built up, and the first dance hall (the Derby Castle Pavilion of Mr N. A. Laughton) opened in 1877. In May 1877, Lightfoot matched this expansion by buying the houses and land which today form 'Tramway Terrace' and its stabling. The latter, by 1902, had evolved as three distinct units holding eight, eighteen and seven horses respectively, of which the first had separate access; these are still in use today.

Ever enterprising, Lightfoot in 1878 seized the opportunity of buying from the liquidator the Marine Baths and Aquarium premises in Victoria Street, and embarked on the erection of the block now containing the public baths, the Regal Cinema (built as the Grand Theatre), shop and office accommodation, and the Grand Hotel. The building was completed in June 1882, but its completion nearly emptied the Lightfoot coffers, mainly because a disastrous theatre fire at Exeter had focused public attention on the need for adequate emergency exits, and making these major alterations to his new theatre brought Lightfoot into financial difficulty.

In consequence, Lightfoot sold his tramway on 6 January 1882 to a group consisting of Walter Pitt, G. J. Cuddon and F. W. Barnett, who formed a Manx company to work it. The new company, The Isle of Man Tramways Ltd, published its prospectus on 18 February 1882. Its office was at 46 Athol Street, Douglas, and its objects included power to make, equip and maintain tramways in the Isle of Man, to use steam or any other motive power, and to run omnibuses and vans in connection with the tramways. The capital was to be £20,000, and the promoters guaranteed a dividend of 7½ per cent. The amount for which Lightfoot sold the line was not stated, but was probably about £15,000, of which £4,000 is known to have been in shares of the new company; these he promptly sold, reducing his holding by January 1883 to a mere £100. Among stated intentions was an early increase in the number of cars (now four), for which provision was made in the capital.

The directors of the new company were Major J. S. Goldie-Taubman, Speaker of the House of Keys and a director of the Isle of Man Railway, together with William Cottrill, Thomas Popple and Lieut-Col Stratham, all from Manchester; T. Klein, a banker from Staffordshire; and F. W. Barnett, secretary, of 14 St Ann's Square, Manchester. Capital began to flow in, and Isle of Man Tramways Ltd began business, purchasing the line on 21 March 1882.

To facilitate the running of its additional cars, the new company applied to the commissioners for a further four passing places or 'sidings'. The most southerly was to be at Victoria Street, the next a little north of Granville Street, another at the south gate of Castle Mona fronting Castle Terrace, and the fourth at McCrone's Slip, opposite Falcon Cliff. An inspecting committee of the town commissioners, along with clerk Nesbitt and surveyor Cartwright, met on 15 November 1882, concluded that much of the line needed relaying in any case, grumbled at the Lifeboat House curve, and reported back on 6 December. The Granville Street and McCrone's Slip passing places were duly approved, provided that both were on the seaward side, and permission was given to lengthen that already existing at the Iron Pier, but the remaining two were not accepted due to alleged congestion at Victoria Street and the narrow roadway at Castle Terrace. The two loops approved were put in by the following spring, and the company decided to appeal to the governor against the rejection of the other two.

In the same month, on 18 December 1882, an application was made to the town commissioners (apparently by or on behalf of the Isle of Man Railway) for a tramway from the I M R station to the Victoria Pier. This was a re-emergence of a scheme of 1878, and was destined to reappear periodically in subsequent years, each time without result.

With the population of Douglas now approaching the 14,000

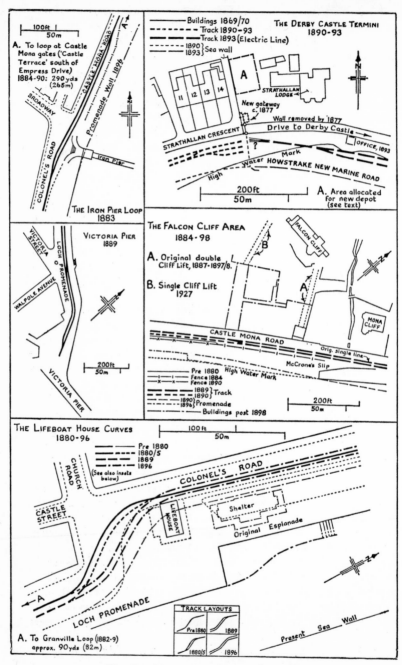

The Bay Tramway: changes after 1880

mark, Isle of Man Tramways also now sought to extend in the other direction, to the Derby Castle pleasure gardens. Application was made to the commissioners on 17 January 1883 by Captain Penketh (who had inspected Lightfoot's line in 1877 and was now with the company), Major J. S. Goldie-Taubman, and another new name, engineer Hunt, for an extension of the tramway to the gates of Derby Castle. This did not materialise for another eight years.

The annual general meeting, with Major Goldie-Taubman in the chair, was held on 25 April 1883, and reviewed the new company's operations for the year from 27 March 1882 to 26 March 1883. Receipts were £977 3s 6d, allowing a dividend of 8 per cent. The meeting voted to create £10,000 new capital in 6 per cent preference shares, as the ordinary shares had raised only £14,000 5s 0d, and Lightfoot was still owed £10,000. Goldie-Taubman underlined the lack of sufficient passing loops, pointing out that this limited service frequency to a maximum of twenty minutes and was causing loss of patronage.

The implied promise of a more frequent service if the loops were sanctioned seems to have had the desired effect. The governor had already appointed one, J. F. Gill, to give judgment in the continued argument over additional passing places, and after hearing the company's evidence on 1 May and making an inspection on 2 May, he reported in favour. However, it was too late to do the work for the 1883 season, and so the loops at Victoria Street and Castle Mona were added early in 1884. The twenty-minute service was adequate for the winter, with two cars in use and forty-one double journeys; the daily mileage was 144, starting at 8.30 am in connection with the 9 o'clock steamer and requiring six men and eight horses.

The next annual general meeting, held on 26 April 1884, was far from calm, for Walter Pitt was accused of paying Lightfoot £10,000 more than the tramway was worth. Only 2 per cent dividend was paid, and the winter service was said to run at a loss of 2½d a mile. To help traffic, books of twenty tickets were being sold to residents at a 10 per cent reduction. Two new cars, bringing the total to eight, had been obtained at a cost of £250 each, but, as later emerged, were not yet paid for. This purchase was attacked in the Press by William J. Parker, Lightfoot's second manager and cashier, who had been replaced in December 1883 by John Davie, and who thereafter became a public critic of the company's conduct of its affairs.

In April 1883 land was bought for a new terminus and depot adjoining the shore at Burnt Mill Hill. Begun in the spring of 1884, in addition to replacing Lightfoot's old car shed, it provided a covered awning to shelter cars and passengers, this being prominently lettered 'Derby Castle Station'. Connection with the original line must have involved an acute reversed curve. By 31 January 1885, Athol House and the old depot were sold (the rails were removed by 12 May), but the company retained possession of a strip of ground parallel to and 36 ft 6 in from the garden wall, presumably with an eye to a future passing place. The former depot survived until 1889-90, and by 1893 six new hotels occupied the Athol House garden and the southern half of the site of Athol House; the remaining half was similarly obliterated later.

During the winter of 1884-5, the passing loop at McCrone's Slip was lengthened, and about this time the track in the Colonel's Road was incorporated into the roadway, with a separate footpath to seaward, and a new fence that reduced the esplanade's grass strip by some six feet. Each new or lengthened passing place north of the iron pier encroached on the shore, protected by a timbered sea wall with a post and rail fence at the seaward edge of the new footpath.

Deputy-chairman P. J. Pittar, whose active part in the company's affairs led to his later being nicknamed 'the tramway king', must have felt himself fully vindicated when addressing the annual general meeting held in April 1885. He referred to the new passing places at Victoria Street and Castle Mona, and went on to announce, to applause, a profit of £2,994. A dividend of a mere 4 per cent, however, caused some caustic comment. Car mileage for the year was 64,122, and passengers totalled 361,553; about 1,800 were carried each week during the winter, but as many as 6,765 on one day (4 August 1884) and 33,284 during one week. The seasonal traffic had accounted for 226,230.

Summarising the rolling stock position, Pittar reminded the meeting that the past year's greatest innovation had been the purchase of two open cars. 'Ladies and families,' he said, 'have been known to travel up and down in them three or four times without getting off, simply for the pleasure of having a ride round the bay, and these were ladies who would not have gone on to the top of the larger cars.' Shareholder George Brown criticised the expensive new terminal buildings at Burnt Mill Hill (still in course of erection), and Lightfoot agreed that Athol House would

Page 35

(above) *No 4 at the north end of the Loch Promenade, about 1882;* (centre) *No 6 at Derby Castle depot, about 1928. Nos 7 and 8 were similar, but with seven windows;* (below) *No 9, almost unaltered after fifty years' service, at Strathallan Crescent crossover in* 1934

(above) *A 'toastrack' heads west-
wards along Strathallan Crescent,
about 1891. Nos 27-29, as yet unvestibuled, and eight more 'toastracks' occupy the terminal sidings
outside Derby Castle gates;* (centre)
*rebuild No 18 at the south end of
the Harris promenade, about 1910;*
(below) *the Derby Castle station in
1896. No 27 and its neighbour are
now vestibuled; beyond are No 5
or 6 and a 'Douglas and Laxey'
train. The tracks had not then been
diverted into the new station*

stable fourteen horses and could have accommodated another seven. It emerged that the old car shed held nine cars. Autumn horse sales reduced the winter stud to between fourteen and twenty animals, new horses being purchased each year in May.

Meanwhile, Douglas grew apace. The Derby Castle Company Ltd (formed October 1884) proceeded to double the size of their dance hall, and drew up plans for extending the promenade to their entrance. A rival establishment, the Falcon Cliff Pavilion, raised its enormous glasshouse bulk on the cliff-top, and at one stage paid a dividend of 20 per cent! Other attractions sprung up on the former southern garden of Castle Mona, which was not permanently built over until the turn of the century.

On 24 April 1886, Isle of Man Tramways applied to the town commissioners to lengthen the Falcon Cliff loop at its northern end and to put in two further passing places, on the Loch promenade at Howard Street, and about midway between Castle Mona (Castle Terrace) and Falcon Cliff, hitherto McCrone's Slip. Whether these two loops were installed is not known, for the track was doubled soon afterwards at both points.

The company's next meeting on 3 May 1886 heard the declaration of a dividend of 5 per cent, in spite of a curtailed season. Operating costs were now 5¾d a mile, against receipts of 11d a mile. Car mileage was 66,942 and passengers totalled 385,960, plus 300 dogs. The highest weekly total was 36,172, that for the visiting season was 281,455. The Burnt Mill Hill terminus was newly completed, but the car fleet still stood at ten; a further open car arrived at some time during the succeeding year. The arrival of six second-hand cars early in 1887 is recounted in Chapter 4, and was the major subject of discussion at the annual general meeting on 28 April 1887.

With the Loch promenade built up, the Villa Marina still in private hands, and few sites still available between Broadway and Castle Mona, building development found the greatest potential on the Crescent, north-east of Falcon Cliff. The town commissioners decided to create a new Queen's promenade incorporating the land between the Crescent road and the sea. A further extension was to front Strathallan Crescent to reach Derby Castle. The tramway company, who owned some of the land concerned, agreed in February 1888 to convey a portion to the commissioners in return for permission to lay double track along the entire Loch promenade and northwards from Falcon Cliff to Burnt Mill Hill, the new track

C

being to seaward of the original. A double-track extension was also sanctioned from Burnt Mill Hill to Derby Castle, all the new lines being brought within the terms of the 1876 Act. All past liabilities by the company to the commissioners for 'facilities' were discharged, but the company was to pay £1,557 17s 9d towards the scheme. The agreement was confirmed by Tynwald in the Douglas Crescent Improvement Act of 1889.

At the same time, February 1888, the commissioners were negotiating with the Derby Castle company, who were to build the new promenade along Strathallan Crescent, receiving in return the commissioners' rights over the foreshore fronting their property as far as 'Purt y Vattey', anglicised to Port e Vada. On taking this over, they had to maintain a public footpath eight feet wide along its seaward edge. The agreement gave the Derby Castle company the provisional right to lay a double line of tramway on their new promenade, and 'to run electric or other tramcars thereon'; eyes had obviously been turned to pioneer developments at Blackpool. This sanction was only applicable if the tramway company failed to extend its own line, and work it at existing fares, as soon as the new promenade was completed.

The Derby Castle company were also to convey to the commissioners some 3,000 sq ft of land (subject to a £10 annual ground rent) for the erection of tramway carriage sheds of ornamental design 'as soon as the present carriage sheds on Crescent are removed'. It may seem odd that two other parties, neither directly concerned, should thus discuss the fate of the tramway company's terminal buildings, but the commissioners were concerned to see the last of the obstructive Burnt Mill Hill premises, and as potential future tramway owners were anxious to see the future depot requirements catered for.

The company's meeting on 26 April 1888, under the chairmanship of P. J. Pittar, heard that passengers had totalled 549,579 and car miles 79,278, with receipts of 13.46d/mile against costs of 7.39d. The next meeting, held on 22 April 1889, was an optimistic one; in spite of a wet summer in 1888 and a drop in visitors, earnings fell by only £239. Car miles stood at 85,005 and passengers at 515,671½; cost per mile had fallen to 7.22d, but receipts were down to 11.66d. £29,508 had been spent on new buildings, cars and facilities, and doubling of the Loch promenade track to a point north of the Granville passing place at Senna Slip would be complete by the summer season. However, a bus service to and from the railway station via Finch Road and Athol Street had not been a financial success. The dividend (6 per cent) was paid in May, and the financial year was changed to end on 31 October, the next meeting falling on 17 December 1889.

Double track had meanwhile been laid both on the Queen's promenade and beyond to the Derby Castle gate, but service had not begun over the latter as the surrounding promenade was incomplete. Agreement was reached on 29 November with the Derby Castle company for a further extension along their intended new promenade to the Castle's pavilion, an enlargement of the footpath provided for in the DTC/DCC agreement of February 1888.

Excitement mounted at the impending opening by the Lieutenant-Governor, Sir Spencer Walpole, of the new Queen's promenade on Tuesday 8 July 1890. Press accounts traced the history of the project from January 1888, mentioning the tramway company's gift of land, plus £1,557; other landowners had followed their example, and in all 5,240 square yards of land had been given up. Only one-third of the authorised special improvement rate had thus had to be levied. The Queen's promenade carriageway was now 52 ft wide, an increase of 30 ft, and Strathallan Crescent had been widened from 16 ft to 72 ft. On the Crescent, a 24-ft promenade adjoining the lawn had been formed from the old enclosures. The total cost had been £6,876.

The opening procession assembled at the 1887 Jubilee Clock at 2 pm on 8 July, and moved off at 2.30 towards the ceremonial arch erected at the southern end of the new promenade; the Villiers coach was followed by the entire fleet of twenty-two loaded tramcars. Opposite the lifeboat house was another (informal) triumphal arch, from which 'hung a few articles which are most used at public bathing grounds', the constructors standing hard by and wearing false noses and other accoutrements. The main triumphal arch was at the southern end of the Queen's promenade, and had a smaller rival at the foot of Broadway. The governor, speaking of the improvements, also mentioned the government's recent construction of the broad triangular approach to the Victoria pier. There ensued 'other events': the launching of the new lifeboat, a practice by all lifeboats and the rocket brigade, a turn-out by the fire brigade, and music by the bands of Castle Mona, Falcon Cliff, the Palace and Derby Castle. Blondin performed in the evening at the Palace, to the music of the town band, and the day was rounded off by the illumination of the steamers and of the whole bay.

Double track from Castle Terrace to the Queen's promenade was added with a further section of timbered sea-wall by December, but became a sea-wrought ruin on the morning of 18 October 1891. Temporarily repaired, it sufficed until T. G. Taylor's new central promenade became a reality in 1896. All this track work of 1888-90 was in orthodox girder rail on transverse wooden sleepers, the rail section being of 48 lb/yd. The syndicate which had bought the Castle Mona estate in October 1888 had built a huge, wood-framed dance pavilion on the site of the north garden (and later sold it to the Palace company of 1890); this, and further development at Falcon Cliff, brought more traffic to the tramway.

The company meeting on 17 December 1890 was an optimistic one. Receipts had attained £6,394, and 6 per cent was distributed in dividends, after paying for all new works and for further work in hand, for which the rails were stacked ready. With two-thirds of

The tramway station at Burnt Mill Hill, *circa* 1891. The wording over the 'arch' had been newly altered following the extension along Strathallan Crescent

the line doubled, the tramway had become a pleasure ride 'the same as taking a carriage'. The obstructive Lifeboat House was said to be 'nearly doomed', though a new home for the boat had yet to be found.

Among the speakers at the meeting was a shareholder, Dr Richard Farrell (1840-1925), an Irishman who came to Douglas from London in about 1881 and had opened a private school, Victoria College. He spoke of a visitor who had ridden twelve times up and down—twenty-four miles of beautiful coast driving for two shillings—and he summarised the year's result as '£6,394 10s 10d in tuppences!' He then criticised the substantial payments for renewals, saying that receipts were double those of 1887 yet there had been an increase of only 1 per cent in dividend. He also contrasted the numerous directors of the small 1882 concern with

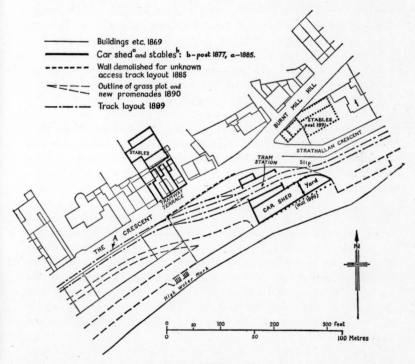

The complex layout at Burnt Mill Hill, with the Strathallan Crescent extension completed

the three of 1890. All ended cordially, with two more directors appointed, one of whom was Dr Farrell!

There is some doubt whether the new Derby Castle extension remained open in winter, for apart from the residents of Strathallan Crescent it would not have generated much traffic. Mr Ramsey B. Moore recalled that the section beyond the Burnt Mill Hill shed was worked in the easterly direction by gravity, the horse trotting alongside the free-running car. In June 1891, the company bought No 1 Strathallan Crescent and its garden and stables, and developed it as offices, stabling, and temporary storage for cars; this yard was known as 'the Brig'. The stabling here was increased by 1902 to thirty-five.

The following year, 1891, saw twenty-six cars in service, but the company meeting on 16 December was overshadowed by the realisation that the town commissioners had the right to acquire the tramway by compulsory purchase in 1897. One major single-track bottleneck, between Loch promenade and Castle Terrace, remained along which cars had to run in convoy. Passengers had totalled 628,842, of whom 259,602½ had travelled in August; a 6 per cent dividend was declared. Contrary to expectations, the old Lifeboat House still fronted the site of the future Sefton hotel. John Davie's competent management of the fast growing traffic was singled out for special mention.

On 13 January 1892, the Derby Castle company resold its 1888 foreshore rights to Frederick Saunderson, a civil engineer, who was negotiating a lease of the Howstrake estate for real estate development, and wished to build an access road along the strip of land concerned, taking in the land to seaward to create a wider promenade than originally envisaged. The agreement included his right 'to lay a double line of tram rails, and run cars thereon by electric, horse or other motive power'. An enabling Act of Tynwald, the Howstrake Estate Act, was passed on 22 March 1892, but a clause gave priority to the November 1889 agreement between the Derby Castle company and Isle of Man Tramways. However, if the tramway company did not extend their line within six months of Saunderson completing the first 150 ft of his new roadway (as far as Derby Castle's own 360-ft iron pier), the right to build it would pass to Saunderson.

The general meeting on 21 December 1892 heard of better gross receipts despite unfavourable weather. Passengers carried totalled 803,144½ (623,625½ of them during the 'season') and 111,213 car-

miles had been run, with costs per mile of 8.12d and receipts of
13.07d. The year's profit was £2,907. The proposed extension on
the Howstrake New Marine Road (Saunderson's promenade) was
generally welcomed.

The prospect of obtaining agreement to double the rest of the
line appeared remote, for argument had continued with the town
commissioners since June 1890 regarding the removal of the
outer shed at Burnt Mill Hill (but not the station part, which it
was intended to keep). The company was insisting that the commissioners should both purchase the site and provide equivalent
accommodation elsewhere ('it is not likely that we are going to flit
till we have other premises of a suitable character'). The directors
had also been studying the possible adoption of electric traction.
The year's surplus was £4,595, but with so much uncertainty, the
directors decided to limit the dividend to 6 per cent.

On 10 January 1893 Thomas Lightfoot died, aged seventy-eight,
at Birkdale, near Southport; he was buried at Onchan four days
later. On 26 April the company was dealt a sad blow by the sudden
death of its manager, John Davie, whose funeral was attended
by directors Curphey, Sutherland, Kelly, Dr Farrell, secretary
Young and twenty-one head drivers. A former driver, Mr Ching,
was appointed as his successor. Press obituaries mentioned Davie's
introduction of several improvements, notably 'a coiled spring
attached for relieving the horse of a great part of the weight of the
car when starting', which could well be the Vereker and Yeatts
ratchet-wound coil spring on the car axle described in *Engineering*
for 16 March 1894. Another source quotes the device used at
Douglas as the invention of one of the Knox family—this may,
however, be a reference to the pair of small coil springs still used
between the traces and the drawbeam.

Meanwhile, on 10 September 1892, Frederick Saunderson had
transferred his rights to a new company, the Douglas Bay Estate
Limited, whose tramway intentions now extended to Groudle, the
then-envisaged northern limit of the estate, but as late as December
1892 the Derby Castle Company still preferred to rely on the 1889
undertaking of Isle of Man Tramways Ltd to extend their horse
tramway to the pavilion. Later, on 7 March 1893, a new Douglas
and Laxey Coast Electric Tramway Company was registered to
build a line onward from the Howstrake estate to Laxey, and on
Thursday 7 September they opened for a short season their new
electric line from Derby Castle to Groudle, with a railhead only

some 40 ft from the 1890 terminal of the horse cars. This effectively put an end to any further thoughts of extending the horse line to Port e Vada.

The new electric tramway brought some extra traffic to the horse cars, and increased revenue had accrued from advertising. Posters were now carried on the dashes of 'toastrack' cars (one on either side of the car number), and the iron arches supporting the candle lamps were fitted with curved boards carrying painted announcements, often for the Falcon Cliff. The open cars also carried advertising flags. For 1893 summer horse-car service began on 8 July, with a ten-minute service until 11 pm, and on 26 August (but not for the first time), the company was fined for permitting overcrowding, sure evidence of a good season!

The Douglas scene was changing; the town had bought the Iron Pier for demolition, and the Douglas Promenade Shelter Act 1892 authorised a new building in place of the Lifeboat House. Surveyor T. G. Taylor's 1889 plan for a proper central promenade was at last taken up : widening the Colonel's Road by 11 ft from the iron pier to McCrone's Slip, at the expense of the grass strip, it enabled the road to be brought to a uniform width of 70 ft, with a 40-ft carriageway and a 23-ft promenade, all behind a new seawall. At last the tramway company could double their remaining portions of single line, and in November 1893 it was revealed that the company had offered £1,100 for permission to widen the road and double the line themselves, though they resisted subsequent suggestions that they should pay for the whole scheme.

Regarding the terminal buildings, the chairman of the improvement committee had been asked to arrange for the erection of suitable tramway sheds on the site in Derby Castle grounds. Meanwhile, from 1 November 1893, the service had been reduced to weekdays only at a fifteen-minute interval and a penny fare, the summer fare being twopence. Whether this was the first year of differential fares is not clear.

Included in the articles of association of the Douglas and Laxey Coast Electric Tramway Company were the significant words 'to purchase, lease or otherwise acquire any tramway or tramways in the Isle of Man.' On 2 December 1893 someone leaked to the Press the fact that the new company intended to start negotiations with Isle of Man Tramways Ltd with a view to purchasing the horse line, and that the town commissioners were considering the matter. The Coast company's tentative offer to the commissioners was to

double the line and electrify it at once, in return for a new lease
from 1897 and the right to build tramways to other parts of the
town. They would pay an annual sum to the town, which would
largely meet the cost of the new central promenade. With current
agitation for a tramway to Upper Douglas, the commissioners were
at first in favour.

At the tramway company's annual meeting on 21 December
1893, with chairman William P. J. Pittar in charge, the offer by
the Coast company was still *sub-judice*, and the matter was not
mentioned. The year had been splendid, with a profit of £3,784,
allowing a 6 per cent dividend; 121,843 car-miles had been run
and 911,410½ passengers carried (728,510½, of them in the 'season'),
with receipts of 13.72d per car mile against costs of 7.73d. Two
more cars were on order, which would bring the fleet to thirty-
one.

After complex negotiations (described in Chapter 5), a firm offer
to purchase was received from the Douglas and Laxey Coast company on 15 February 1894, and an extraordinary general meeting
was called for Friday 2 March. The method of valuation in the
1876 Act's compulsory purchase clause was obscure (English courts
were arguing out a similar case between the London Street Tramways and the LCC), and the offer of £38,000 was about mid-way
between the worst and the best possible valuations. The offer was
for the line as at 31 October 1893, with retrospective adjustment.
Chairman Pittar, questioned as to why there had been no reference to the subject at the December meeting, pointed out that the
intending buyers had also had to negotiate with the town commissioners. In the circumstances, the 20:6 majority in favour of
sale is readily understood.

The Douglas and Laxey Coast Electric Tramway Company Ltd
now changed its title to Isle of Man Tramways and Electric Power
Company Limited, with a trebled capital of £150,000. Its new
board included Pittar and Farrell, and the tramway company's
secretary, W. E. Young, became secretary to the new company.
Share applications were to be lodged between 9 and 14 April. No
2 Strathallan Crescent, now the Manx Electric's managerial residence, was bought by the old company on 27 January, and at 4 pm
on 1 May 1894 the horse tramway was formally handed over and
the old offices at 3 Athol Hall vacated. The new manager of the
combined undertaking was J. Aldworth, with Ching as traffic superintendent.

The working of the horse-car line for the year 1894 and thereafter can only be assessed from annual reports of the Isle of Man Tramways and Electric Power Company. For 1894, the combined undertaking (horse and electric) had earned £10,507 net profit in the eight months to 31 December. The horse section had earned 15.09 pence per mile, running 14,591 miles more than in 1893. The cars earned an average of 4s per journey, but this rose to 5s 3d in July and 6s 7d in August. Fares were lowered to the winter rate of 1d on 30 September, and a ten-minute service maintained up to 31 December, and thereafter twelve-minutes. The division between 1d fare passengers and those who had paid 2d was 13 :87. The winter stock of thirty-nine horses had a stated value of £931.

On 20 February 1894 the demolition of the Iron Pier began. This structure had been 900 ft long and 16 ft wide, with a pier head 90 ft by 40 ft, and it was still in excellent order. In earlier years it had formed the boundary between male and female bathers (gentlemen to the south). The semi-circular embayment to the south was built later in the year.

The Derby Castle tramway extension beyond Burnt Mill Hill 'reopened' by 16 May, and with the reopening of the electric line (and its extension in July to Laxey) this final section of the horse line therafter became a year-round operation. The 1894 report revealed that agreement had now been reached with the Derby Castle company for the erection of a large waiting-room and other accommodation at the terminus. Thus, by 14 June 1895 the company had agreed to remove the outer shed, tramway station, shop, offices and conveniences at Burnt Mill Hill provided the commissioners gave them the already designated plot of land at Derby Castle gates (see earlier plan) and also permitted connecting tracks to the Brig and Tramway Terrace.

By 23 November 1895, work had begun on the Colonel's Road section of the promenade scheme, and a cheque had been received from the Royal National Lifeboat Institution for the new boathouse on the harbour. The land within the original Derby Castle gates, as far as the eastern end of Strathallan Lodge, had been secured from the Derby Castle company for £7,500, and the tramway company could now build a really adequate horse-car shed and proper joint terminal facilities, including an ornamental shed through which Derby Castle retained a right of way. Nos 13 and 14 Strathallan Crescent were also purchased about this time, and the area fronting Strathallan Lodge was cleared by the summer of 1895 to allow work to start on the new car shed and joint terminal, which included waiting-room facilities.

Further growth of Douglas saw the Douglas Corporation Act of 1895, the new corporation taking over from the town commissioners in 1896. Speculation was rife as to who would be the first mayor, and the choice fell on the noted Douglas photographer, Alderman Thomas Keig, JP, FRPS. Earlier suggestions had included Samuel Harris, who had declined.

The new buildings at Derby Castle were brought into use about August 1896. Demolition of the old Burnt Mill Hill terminal, which had started on 3 February, was already complete, and the

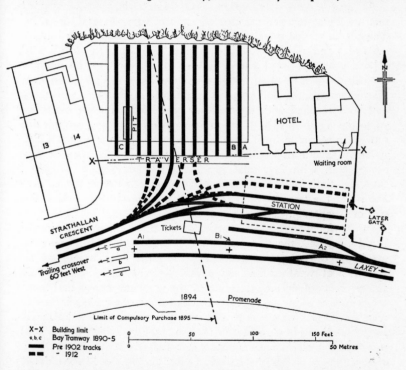

Derby Castle termini (horse and electric) as evolved in 1895-6, with additions up to 1912; no further changes were then made until 1953-4. From 1902-3, horse-car shed track A was used for offices and electric track A1-A2 removed, the centre pole being moved to B1. In 1935 new offices were built over the horse-car shed and tracks B and C were blocked by the entrance and stairs

cars meanwhile stood outdoors. The new car shed had a frontage of 110 ft, a depth of 71 ft and was 13 ft 6 in high, with twelve roads each holding three cars. Entrance was by two traversers, of which the smaller (still in use) carries the 1 o m t title on a W. Knox maker's plate, and a partly obliterated reference to H. Hall; this traverser was originally used at the Burnt Mill Hill sheds. The ornate cast-iron awning over the horse-car sidings measured 82 ft by 35 ft, and was 18 ft high to the eaves. At the other end of the line, a minor extension took the tramway on to the harbour commissioners' land, at a £50 a year rental. By 1899, this had been reduced to a more reasonable £10.

At the company meeting held on 8 March 1897 it was revealed that the horse section had carried 1,521,975 people, and on an increased car mileage of 202,754 had earned 13.24d/mile against costs of 7.32d/mile. Gross receipts had been £10,010 10s 3d, and a horse now cost 9s 3d a week to keep. Track doubling on the new central promenade and Colonel's Road section, now renamed Harris Promenade, had been completed by August and agreement had been reached with the harbour board for a further extension on to the Victoria Pier to a point near the ferry steps, though this did not materialise until 1902. J. R. Cowell, fresh from the USA, spoke in favour of electrification, and when a later speaker supported him with first-hand experience of Dresden it transpired that negotiations were already taking place between the corporation and the tramway company. The outcome is described at the end of Chapter 5.

In the following year, reported on at the company meeting of 10 March 1898, the horse cars carried 1,620,634, with a one-week maximum of 138,342 and a one-day total as high as 30,259, although wet weather had its effect. Receipts were 13.37d/mile against costs of only 6.2d. Some of the tramway horses had spent the winter working on the construction of the new electric line to Ramsey. Deserving of note was the formation of the Palace & Derby Castle Ltd on 29 March 1898, a company which was to hold a virtual entertainment monopoly for sixty-six years. By the turn of the century it ran the Palace, Derby Castle, the Marina dance hall and Falcon Cliff, in later years adding town and out-town theatres and cinemas.

Despite horse-bus competition, the horse cars earned 13.04d/ mile in 1898, and costs were reduced to 5.88d. Miles run were 225,052. The company meeting on 31 March 1899 also recorded

their high regard for their late chairman, P. J. Pittar. J. Aldworth
had left for a new appointment in Nottingham, and former veterinary surgeon T. S. Atkinson was given charge of the horse tramway.
The traffic manager, Mr Kerrigan, had left in October 1898 to
become manager of the Colombo tramways, of which Alexander
Bruce of the I O M T & E P was a director. Before the summer of 1899
the Loch Promenade track was relaid in the now standard 48 lb/yd
rail : track raising on the Loch Promenade and Queen's Promenade
cost £1,443.

The 1899 season was equally as good as the previous year's;
the horse cars carried 1,725,155 passengers with 233,295 car miles,
earning 13.23d/mile against expenses of 6.81d, of which 2.68d was
for horsing. The highest day's total had been 32,952 passengers.
This was the last full year of operation under The Isle of Man
Tramways and Electric Power Co Ltd, and is a convenient point
at which to pause and take up the story of the next tramway in
Douglas, the Upper Douglas Cable Tramway.

CHAPTER TWO

The Douglas Cable Tramway

'No pushee—no pullee—allee samee go like hell'
(unknown Chinaman, apropos San Francisco cable cars, 1873)

By the end of 1893, the bay tramway had caused a definite shift in the pattern of local trade, affecting the business of boarding-house and shop owners in the inland upper town, the late Regency part of Douglas that slopes up steeply to some 160 ft above the bay. It was suggested that the commissioners should lay a tramway to Upper Douglas, serving the older district, and lease it to the new consolidated tramway company. At the first of several public meetings on 19 January 1894, the ratepayers of Ward 3, the worst affected area, pressed for a resolution 'that facilities be given for a tramway right round Peel Road and all the intermediate streets off Buck's Road, which had not facilities compared to the front'. A Mr T. Kelly pointed out that two bus companies serving the upper part of the town had failed, but despite this a deputation was appointed to demand from the commissioners a proper tram service to Upper Douglas. In view of the gradients, any such tramway would clearly have to use some form of mechanical power.

In January 1894, the Press revealed that the town commissioners had received two offers to lease the bay tramway from 6 December 1897, when their right to purchase it took effect. One was from Alexander Bruce, chairman of the electric tramway company, the other from H. H. Crippen, later associated with Falcon Cliff. Crippen's offer included penny fares throughout the year, and he announced a public meeting for 5 February. He proposed to convert the bay line to Dick, Kerr & Co's cable tramway system, for which he held a local concession. His penny fares bombshell upset the negotiations with the electric company, by then advanced to such details as the rail section to be used on the promenade after electrification. Bruce withdrew his offer (by 27 January), and Crippen then did likewise. It later emerged that Crippen was a Derby Castle shareholder, and had tried to get a penny fare promise from Bruce in return for withdrawing his rival bid, his chief object being more grist for his own mill.

Crippen's meeting of 5 February was taken over half-way by two of the three town commissioners present, and ended with yet another plea for a tramway to Upper Douglas, Crippen's original resolution being amended accordingly. Its chief advocate was baker R. D. Cowin, a popular and thoughtful town commissioner, and its opponent was commissioner Edmund Chadwick, a determined conservative in the most negative sense. The next few months saw the issue twisted at times into 'upper versus lower town'.

An Upper Douglas Tramway Committee was formed, and met on 9 April 1894, to good effect; the Improvement Committee of the town commissioners recommended on 18 April 'that it is desirable in the general interests of the town that a system of tramway communication should be laid down between the lower and upper levels of Douglas'. They recommended that the data on hand should be properly tabulated and a report prepared by the town surveyor.

Surveyor Taylor reported in July 1894 to the effect that while the line would be a burden on the rates, it would also be an immense boon. A route via Victoria Street, Prospect Hill, Buck's Road and Woodbourne Road to Murray's Road, thence by Glen Falcon Road to Broadway was suggested. From the various alternative forms of traction, Taylor put forward two proposals; one was for an electric conduit line with single track and loops, costing £18,790, the other for a cable line estimated to cost £25,000. Either would be likely to lose some £1,500 a year. Electrification of the horse line on the conduit system and its joint operation with the Upper Douglas line was envisaged. The report was pigeon-holed, and by December a newspaper was criticising the commissioners for having set aside this subsidised tramway scheme until the town was safely through other undertakings already in hand.

Meanwhile, Bruce had sensed better things ahead, and reopened his discussions with Isle of Man Tramways for the purchase of the horse line, achieving this by May 1894. He now renewed his negotiations with the commissioners for the continued ownership and future electrification of the horse line, whilst several of the commissioners, for their part, realised that this could be the means of securing a tramway for Upper Douglas.

Early in 1895, Bruce, Farrell, Callow and Aldworth of the Isle of Man Tramways & Electric Power Co and town commissioners R. D. Cowin and J. A. Brown travelled to London to visit the Streatham Hill cable tramway and were sufficiently impressed for Bruce to accept Dick, Kerr & Co as the builder of any future Upper Douglas tramway. They had already had considerable experience of cable traction, having taken over from the original Patent Cable Tramways Syndicate that stemmed from the San Francisco lines. Their initial surveys and drawings were to be prepared by June 1895 and bargaining with the town commissioners continued.

Meanwhile, a public meeting in Tynwald Street school on 21 January 1895 reviewed the lack of progress over the past year. In Upper Douglas annual rents of £40 had been reduced to £25, but still people were being brought to court for non-payment. Ward 3 and parts of Wards 4, 5 and 6 were equally affected. R. D. Cowin's speech placed the whole matter in a larger perspective, making the point that the lucrative bay line should help to carry the cost of the cable line instead of imposing a betterment rate on those served. Opponents, led by Chadwick, still resisted any action, but public opinion forced their hand, and by February the committee appointed to look into the issue recommended that the commissioners should lay down the proposed line and lease it for twenty-one years to any company that would undertake to work it, the first four years to be free of any rental. They disliked Bruce's continuing wish to link the construction of the cable line with a lease of the bay line. By 19 February, the commissioners had agreed to meet a further deputation from Upper Douglas, and the clerk was instructed to approach the directors of the tramway company and arrange a meeting.

Four weeks later, Bruce made a definite move. On 27 March, an I O M T & E P meeting at Mather & Platt's Manchester office passed a resolution which offered both the construction of a tramway to Upper Douglas and free electric lighting of the entire promenade and Victoria Street, in return for a new lease of the bay tramway

Page 53

(above) *Cable tramway construction in Victoria Street, May* 1896; (below) *Saloon cable car No* 79 *waits, half in shadow, at the Victoria Street terminus, about* 1897. *No* 36 *horse car is in the background*

Page 54

Tracklaying on Prospect Hill, May 1896

Buck's Road about 1904, showing kerb side running

Cable car No 78 in York Road after its 1903 Corporation rebuilding

for twenty-one years from 1897, authority to electrify and double the line throughout, to supply electric power for general use, and to extend their tramway to the railway station. Dr Hopkinson had reported on the technical aspects. The commissioners were offered 10 per cent of the bay line's receipts, as rental. Although the recent Upper Douglas Tramway petition had received the signatures of over half the relevant ratepayers, the commissioners side-stepped most of the issues and in reply suggested merely a new lease of the bay line at a minimum of £3,000 a year.

Still determined, Bruce offered to meet the town commissioners. Bruce, Callow and Farrell were invited to meet the improvement committee on 30 May 1895, and in return for a new twenty-one-year lease of the bay line and power to double the remaining portions of single track, offered to build an Upper Douglas cable tramway, provide an interim bus service to Upper Douglas, pay the commissioners 15 per cent of the receipts of the bay line, remove the horse-car sheds (but not the station) at Burnt Mill Hill, and to build the replacing shed at Derby Castle themselves. The bus service would run every ten minutes from Whitsun to October and every twenty minutes in winter. On 10 June the company (now really anxious) wrote again to the commissioners to say that even if the cable tramway were not built, they would run a guaranteed horse-bus service in Upper Douglas for 1895, 1896 and 1897 in return for permission to double the horse-car track, and on 14 June they offered to remove the rest of the horse-tramway buildings at Burnt Mill Hill.

By the end of June, the commissioners had decided to accept the company's offer of 30 May and join with them in promoting a Bill in Tynwald, later to become the Upper Douglas Tramway Act, 1895. Since all parties were now anxious to have a cable tramway working by Whitsun 1896, Tynwald on 10 July suspended its standing orders to allow a special committee to examine the application at once. The committee comprised Deemster Gill (as chairman), the Attorney-General, J. R. Cowell, J. T. Cowell and J. T. Goldsmith. Messrs G. A. Ring, Kneen and Brown appeared for the company.

At the hearing on 16 July a joint petition by commissioners and company was read, after which plans were produced and witnesses heard. The consulting engineer, James More, Assoc Inst C E, who had had thirteen years' experience of tramway construction, revealed that he had drawn out his plans in a mere three weeks, by

D

dint of spending two 'on the ground' from 5 am to dusk. He proposed three-rail double track with shared centre rail on 130 ft of Prospect Hill (from Dumbell's Bank to Athol Street) and for 240 ft to seaward of Glen Falcon Road on Broadway, with double track elsewhere. The cars were to be 5 ft 6 in wide, and the maximum gradient 1 in 10.6. Other witnesses were William Mackenzie of Toronto, and W. H. Andrews of the London Tramways Company, whose Streatham cable line had by then carried 9-10 millions a year on 2¾ route miles against 75 millions on 21 miles of horse-car line. The London cable cars had a much lower accident rate than the horse cars, and could stop in less than their own length. George Flett, director and joint manager of Dick, Kerr & Co, was able to point to 120 miles of tramway then built by his firm, and stated that Newcastle also proposed to have a cable line.

For the commissioners, clerk Nesbitt revealed that they looked on the bus service (introduced on 20 July) as a separate reciprocal bargain for the double horse line from the Iron Pier to Castle Terrace. Commissioners J. A. Brown and S. R. Keig added favourable comment : Keig lived on Prospect Hill, whose widening would overcome an earlier objection by Edmund Chadwick that on the double track only 4 ft 6 in would separate a car from the kerb. Witnesses R. D. Cowin and Robert Archer described their losses in running buses in Upper Douglas, attributing them to the public's refusal to ride up the steep Prospect Hill on seeing the equestrian effort involved.

The opposition now spoke. Chadwick's recapitulation of past offers and negotiations was brought to an end by the Attorney General, and his financial doubts were countered by Keig quoting several instances of lines built as a social necessity in the full knowledge that they would be unprofitable. Alexander Gill, a builder, fared even worse, and seems to have been associated with the drivers of other conveyances who would lose business to the tramway. The findings of the committee were to be presented to Tynwald on 23 July if no further objections were received, and on that date they duly gained acceptance.

The report restated the agreement, adding a new clause to the effect that after seven years the cable line should pay 5 per cent of its gross receipts to the town. The committee agreed that it was mechanically practical, that Prospect Hill needed widening in any case, that the line was needed, and that the agreement was a fair one. The resulting indenture between the commissioners and the company on 15 October 1895, specified a minimum £1,500 annual payment for the bay tramway and required the bus service to run daily (except Sunday) from 8 am to 11 pm between 1 May and 30 September, and from 8.30 am to 10.30 pm in winter. All this was subject to the Act being obtained within twelve months.

The Bill was read a first time in the Legislative Council by 3 August, and the Act was passed on 8 November as the Upper Douglas Tramway Act, 1895. After dealing with the bay tramway, it specified that the new tramway was to be worked by wires, ropes, cables or chains, and fixed engines, and stated that :

> . . . the tramway shall commence at a point forming a junction with the Douglas Bay tramway at or near the Peveril hotel . . . . thence pass the Jubilee Clock up Victoria Street, to a point opposite the offices of Dumbell's Banking Company Limited, thence up Prospect Hill, Buck's Road, Woodbourne Road, past the top of Murray's Road to the next road beyond (ie, York Road of today—AUTHOR), down the last-mentioned road into Ballaquayle Road and down the same and through Broadway to a junction with the Douglas Bay tramway at a point thereon about fifty feet south of the south building line of Broadway, and such tramway so far as the same is a double line—that is to say, from the junction near the Peveril hotel to the road above Murray's Road—shall as far as possible be laid so that the outer rail of each line shall be at a distance of two feet three inches from the nearest curb thereto; and as to the remainder of the tramway and crossing places, the same shall be so laid as the commissioners shall determine.

The gauge was specified as three feet, and the promoters were required to maintain the road surface within eighteen inches of the outside of the rails, and reinstate the road within six weeks of any abandonment. The promoters had the right to alter their lines, subject to approval by the commissioners and the governor, but repairs that involved opening up the roadway were subject to seven days' notice and not more than 100 yards in every 440 were to be opened at any one time.

The Act incorporated a complex list of penalties for delay in completing repairs, including a fine of £20 a day for interrupting gas or water mains. The governor (upon application by the road authority) could require the promoters to adopt improvements in

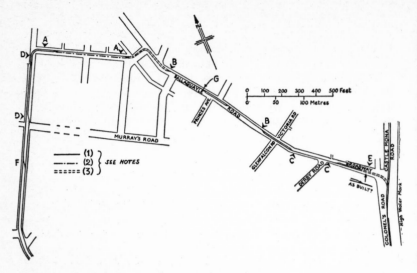

The most complex section of the Douglas cable tramway, from Woodbourne
Road to Broadway, showing (1) track as laid in 1896, (2) track doubled
in 1905, and (3) proposed tracks not built. For track layout between A-A
and B-B as actually constructed, see depot plan. Tracks A-A and B-B were
laid 4 ft from the northern kerb, C-C 2 ft 3 in from the southern kerb,
D-D 2 ft 3 in from the western kerb with 5 ft clearway. From Murray's
Road to Hill Street the tracks were laid at opposite sides of the road. The
line from G to E was closed in 1902 and cars then terminated at Stanley
View (G); a crossover was added at F about 1927. The Avondale (Salisbury
Terrace) crossover lies immediately below the upper 'D' and was re-used
in building 'F', (see p 85). A gradient profile appears in Appendix 7

the tramway, and the road authority (with Tynwald approval)
could require portions of the tramway to be lifted and relaid at
the promoter's expense where inconveniently placed. The Prospect
Hill section was subject to the commissioners widening the road
at this point, and an inspector appointed by the governor was to
approve the line before opening. The line was to be built within
one year of the Act's promulgation (11 January 1896) and the
works were to be substantially commenced within three months.

The road authority could specify the speed limits, the distance
between following cars, and the amount of traffic on the route, and
the 1876 Act's red front and green rear lights were pepetuated.
Hinting at trailer operation, the Act stated that '. . . at all times a

bell shall be attached to the front carriage on such tramway which, by its ringing, will give notice that the carriages are in motion'. The promoters could make and exhibit byelaws concerning time-tables, interference with the line, passenger behaviour, etc. A person guilty of contravening them could be detained, and if unknown as to name and place of residence could be taken before a High Bailiff or JP. Penalties were mostly the classic £5 fine, but for non-payment of fare only forty shillings. Removal of offending pas-sengers was permitted, and those who could not pay a subsequent fine might find themselves sojourning for up to three months in gaol.

Passengers, luggage and parcels were to be carried, and fares were fixed in the Act. Those on the bay line were to remain at 2d in summer and 1d in winter, whilst those on the cable line encouraged 'assisting' downhill loads by offering differential fares: from the Jubilee Clock to Woodbourne Road via Buck's Road in summer was to cost 2d uphill and 1d down, but the winter fare would be 1d each way. Through fares of 2d uphill and 1d down* were also offered from Jubilee Clock and Derby Castle to Wood-bourne Road via Ballaquayle Road, by changing from horse- to cable-car at Broadway, this fare also becoming 1d each way in winter. Children under thirteen years of age were to travel at half fare, and the summer fares were to apply from Whit-Saturday to the end of September. Charges for luggage ranged from 3d to 9d for weights between 7 lb and 56 lb, and parcels exceeding 56 lb in weight could be charged as the promoters might think fit, though they were not obliged to carry parcels exceeding 28 lb.

As the roadway was marked out, Victoria Street tradesmen realised that cable cars would run only 2 ft 3 in from the kerb, and at once went to the improvement committee. Experimental tracks in Victoria Street from Duke Street to the Villiers hotel were used for a demonstration run by horse cars on 21 January 1896, in-cluding cars standing opposite each other while traffic passed between, watched by the improvement committee, the directors of the tramway company and the town surveyor, along with many traders. Later, at the commissioners' office, the traders urged that a double line be laid in the centre of the road instead of a single line along each side. After discussion with engineers Flett and More, Bruce agreed to do what was asked.

* But 2d for Woodbourne Road to Jubilee Clock via Ballaquayle Road downhill in summer, exceptionally, doubtless to prevent overloading of the bay line's busiest section.

The *Isle of Man Times* warned Bruce that he was putting himself into the hands of his enemies by thus departing from the letter of the Act, and early in February this proved to be true; centrally placed track in Woodbourne Road, on a section specifically legalised for track at the side of the road, was found to be on top of the water main. By 15 February the entire work had stopped and between 200 and 300 men were laid off, the Press commenting that if the track were laid at the side it would be 'on the gas' and if in the centre, 'on the water'. Despite the formation of the new town council in March, only recourse to the Legislature could put things right and sort out the mess into which affairs had meanwhile drifted. An amending Act was finally signed on the morning of 13 May 1896, permitting the Victoria Street—Prospect Hill line to be

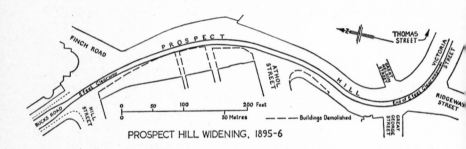

PROSPECT HILL WIDENING, 1895-6

laid as a centre-of-road double track with a four-foot clearway, increased to five feet on the Prospect Hill bend. Elsewhere, the line's original position was substantially maintained.

By 2 May cable track was being completed down from Woodbourne Road to Broadway, but only 1,000 yards had been laid by the end of the month; the rest was finished by August. The junction with the horse tramway at Broadway (mentioned in the Act) was apparently not built. Its probable purpose would have been to allow the through working of horse cars, as on the Streatham cable line in London, but this did not materialise. There had also been protests over the intended operating speed of eight mph, and despite the company's protest the Clerk of the Rolls insisted on six mph from Hill Street to Thomas Street and from Clifton Terrace to the foot of Broadway. Any such local speed limit on a cable tramway has a universal effect over the entire system.

On a site at the foot of the future York Road, the company built a power station and car shed, a pleasing structure in red brick. A corner of the land originally purchased was relinquished to form a public road, so as to give the tramway a straight run into Ballaquayle Road. They also bought two houses in Laureston

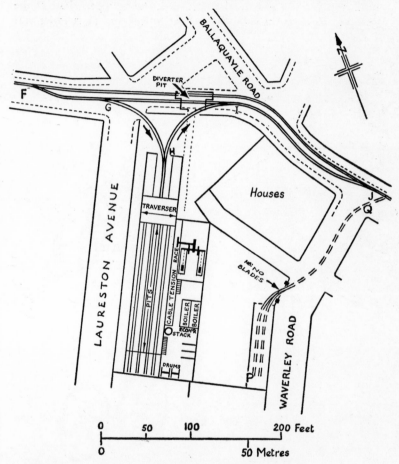

POINTS: F & J sprung open to left; **G, H & I** moveable at will.

The cable tramway depot and winding house. The track beyond F was doubled after 1905 (the points F being removed) and the track P-Q was laid after 1902 for access to horse-car storage

Avenue which might be affected by the vibration, and let them to their workmen! On a sloping site, the buildings were on two levels. The upper part comprised a car shed 235 ft long, 37 ft wide and 15 ft 9 in high, with four tracks and access by a traverser. Each track held five cars, and each had a pit save at the far end, where, until the pits were extended in 1902, the grippers had to be detached to clear the solid floor. Next to this and 11 ft lower was

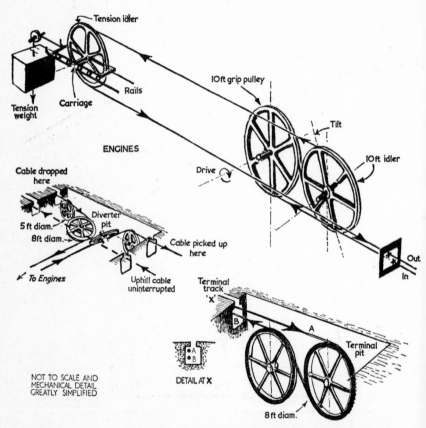

(i) The internal cable circuit in the Douglas winding house. Note the ingenious use of a tilted idler (above)
(ii) The diverter pit outside the winding house. Downhill cars dropped the cable and coasted across; the uphill cable was uninterrupted (below left)
(iii) Terminal pit layout (Broadway and Walpole Avenue) (below right)

the boiler room, 62 ft long, 27 ft wide and 13 ft 6 in high, and beyond this was the engine house, 65 ft long, 37 ft 6 in wide and 18 ft 6 in high, with a floor level 2 ft 9 in below that of the car shed. On the seaward side was an open yard, with bunkers for the coal.

The boiler house contained two hand-fired Galloway boilers, 30 ft long and 7 ft in diameter, working at 100 lb/in². The boiler flues led to an 80-ft brick chimney. Auxiliaries included feed pumps and a Green's economiser that raised the feed water temperature from 60° to 250-300°F. The original water supply was by an underground tank below the firing floor, fed by a spring, but by 1902 this had been augmented by a 6,000-gallon elevated tank using town water at 2s per 1,000 gallons.

There were two high-pressure non-condensing engines of 250 hp, supplied by Dick, Kerr & Co, with 20 in bore and 42 in stroke, and with live-steam-jacketed cylinders externally cased in polished mahogany. Each engine was fitted with Dr Proel's governor and expansion gear, Corliss exhaust valves, and a 13 ft 4 in-diameter flywheel. Either engine could be connected by its flanged coupling to a centre shaft from which the winding pulley was driven by shrouded double helical gearing. The original drive included a Weston friction clutch, so that the engine might be loaded while running, but in later years direct drive was substituted and the engine had to be started against the dead load of the stationary cable.

Here the cable was to start and finish its run. The incoming cable was passed round the grip pulley for nearly 75 per cent of its circumference, then round an adjacent idler to the ensuing idler pulley of the tension race. This, by its half-ton counterweight, kept the cable taut enough to ensure an adequate grip in the white-metal-lined groove of the driving pulley. Going out from here through a tunnel to the diverter pit, the cable next passed over pulleys arranged to turn it through 90 degrees and parallel to the surface of the road, and so continued eastward to Broadway, where the large pulleys of the terminal pit reversed its direction. Coming back along the opposite track, it passed over the cables leading to and from the power station and continued to Victoria Street's terminal pit, returning to the re-entry tunnel outside the depot. In this way, uphill cars had a continuous cable past the depot and only descending cars had to release and coast past the entrance.

Trackwork consisted of 76 lb/yd Belgian rails laid on concrete, connected by tie-bars to cast-iron yokes laid 3 ft 6 in apart. The concrete-walled centre conduit had upper edges formed by 38 lb/yd slot rails bolted to the cast-iron yokes, and spaced to give a slot $\frac{11}{16}$ in wide on straight track and $\frac{3}{4}$ in wide on curves. The cable ran in this conduit, passing over an appropriate succession of 12-in diameter grease-lubricated pulleys. Pulleys used on straight track had bushes in lignum vitae, a naturally greasy wood. On straight track, the pulleys were vertical and generally 49 ft apart, but on curves they lay horizontally and came as close as 3 ft. The cable's direction of travel was reversed by two large pulleys in the terminal pit at Broadway and a similar pair at Victoria Street.

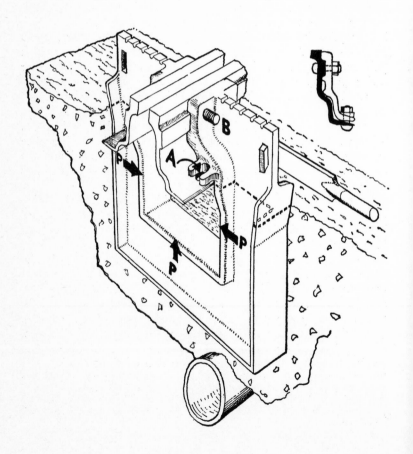

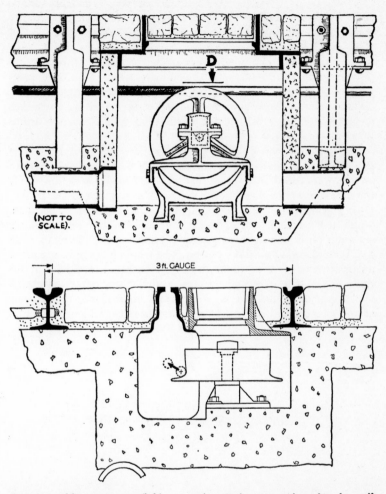

Douglas cable tramway: (left) a cast-iron yoke supporting the slot rails of the cable conduit, which were secured by bolts A and B; the profile of the concrete-walled conduit is shown by arrows P. The separate end view is of a twelve-bolt fishplate. (Above top) section through a pulley pit on straight track; arrow D shows the maximum depth of the car gripper, when fully lowered. (Below) a transverse section on curved track; this drawing also shows the twin centre rail intended for use on Prospect Hill, before widening was agreed. A passing car displaced the cable as shown by the arrow

A one-piece cable by Geo Craddock of Wakefield arrived early in July 1896. More than three miles long and weighing twenty tons, it came on two drums because of a fifteen-ton crane limit at Douglas. A later spare cable came from T. & W. Smith of Newcastle; both were hemp-cored, six-strand cables of $3\frac{1}{2}$ in circumference, each strand having thirteen wires. Two traction engines were used to haul the first cable up the hill to the engine house, but they slipped to a standstill and had to be helped by a windlass and ropes before reaching one of the two special storage drums in a rear extension of the boiler room.

'Threading' began at 3 am on Wednesday, 5 August 1896. The two traction engines picked up the cable end from the diverter pit and proceeded down to Broadway and back along the whole route as far as the Salisbury hotel, in Victoria Street, by 10 am. Here a sewer excavation meant that a pilot cable had to be taken on to the terminal pit, opposite the flank of the Peveril hotel. By 1 am on 6 August this was ready, and by 5 am the main cable had been passed around the pulleys. The winding house was reached again after another $2\frac{1}{2}$ hours, and the exhausted men laid off for three hours. The eighty-foot splice needed to complete the circuit was begun at 11 am the same day, and on Friday 7 August one of the engines was started to remove the slack, which was found

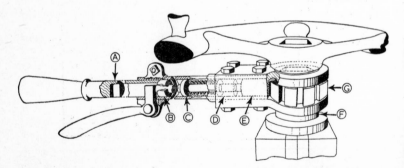

The gripper controls as used at Douglas, drawn from the surviving specimen. The gripper was applied and released by the hand wheel, and a ratchet handle served for the final tightening and initial release. Handle A could slide out for greater leverage. Sprung collar C kept the ratchet E disengaged during handwheel operation; to engage the handle, the trigger was lifted, moving the ratchet spindle through the collars B and D, engaging ratchet dog E with wheel G. F is a cylindrical collar on the gripper screw which spigots into the lower part of the handle assembly

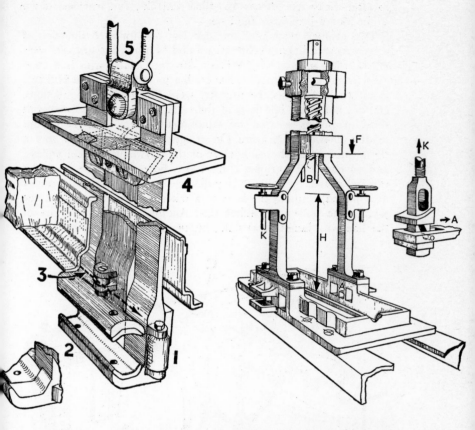

Lower and upper parts of Colam's gripper. The twin stanchions supported on the gripper foundation plate act as guides for the nut whose lowest position is shown by F. The handwheels K operate securing bolts A (see detail) which retain a loose plate to which the gripper's fixed jaw is attached. The nut when raised from position F normally closes the gripper jaws, but if the cable is removed and bolts A withdrawn the entire gripper unit may be drawn up through height H, lifting the gripper clear of the conduit through an access hatch. The rods B (numbered 5 on view of lower portion) allow the pull of the nut to be transmitted to the top frame of the moving jaw. 4 is the loose plate carrying the fixed jaw, 3 is one of the two side rollers (shown in relation to its bearing on the inside of the slot rails), and rollers 1 serve to align the cable with the centre of the gripper jaws (2), whose renewable soft metal jaws are also shown. The ratchet handle operates the gripper screw through its squared upper end

to total thirty feet. A car was then sent out, and travelled down to the foot of Broadway and back.

Two grippers were used on each car, one for each direction of travel. As at Edinburgh, Streatham and Matlock, the grippers were of the type patented by William Newby Colam, who had been assistant to E. S. Eppelsheimer on the pioneer Highgate Hill line in 1884. At Douglas the grippers were single-sided, as junctions, etc, did not exist. The jaws of the Colam gripper were fitted with soft-iron inserts secured by white-metal rivets, and were thus readily renewed when worn. On straight track, the vice-like jaws of the gripper lifted the cable clear of the adjoining vertical pulleys, and on curves the gripper's side rollers bore against the inner slot rail and caused the cable to be pulled clear of each horizontal pulley as it passed, forming the apex of a triangle whose base was a line joining the pulleys on either side. Another important feature of the line was James More's slot brake, which consisted of vertical

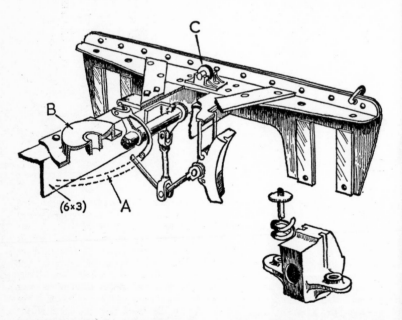

Bogie frame detail of Douglas cable car, with axlebox and spring detail shown separately. A is the link for the brake pull rod, B is the centre pivot, and C is the side bearing roller, later replaced by a block with a felt pad insert

calliper jaws that gripped the slot rails from above and below when applied by a cross-handle.

On the afternoon of 8 August 1896, a car fitted with slot brakes was sent out to test the line but experienced difficulty on the Avondale curve. Next day James Walker, engineer to the Harbour Board, carried out the official inspection and reported on the 10th, specifying the length as about 1 mile 4 furlongs, 5.76 chains. The tramway consisted of a single line with four passing places for about 700 yards and the rest of the line was double. The sharpest gradient was 1 in 10.6.

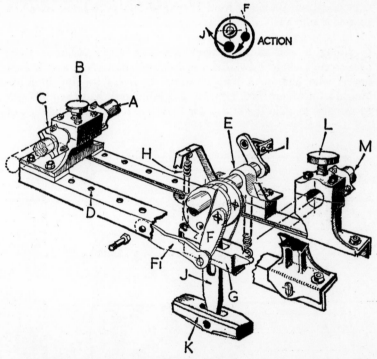

Axle-hung gripper plank, showing slot brake detail. A and M are the outer and inner axles, B and L are the suspension bearing greasers, C the locating collars which limit side travel to maximum slot displacement and D the holes to which the gripper assembly is bolted. The slot brake was applied by a pull on rod I turning discs on shaft E whose links F force upper shoe G down against springs H, while centre link J pulls shoe K against the underside of the slot rail. Links F1 absorb the resulting drag

Walker had carefully inspected the whole line, including travelling over it in a car and making some severe tests of both the ordinary and emergency brakes. He found that the latter required attention in order to take the curve at Avondale House more easily and then wanted a trial made of the emergency brakes at Prospect Hill and Broadway. Finally, he wanted an alarum bell fitted to each end of every car. He deputed his assistant, Mr Nevill, to report to the governor's secretary, Mr Storey, when these requirements had been met as the line would then be safe to operate.

Four days later, on Thursday, 13 August, Nevill was able to report that the inspector's requirements had been met. The warning bells had been obtained from Liverpool and were hung from the roof-edge to the left of the driving position.

On Saturday, 15 August 1896, three cable cars entered service, providing a ten minutes frequency. The crews included three Manxmen, George Edward Lace, Edmund Butterfield and Robert Leary, who had spent the preceding six weeks training in Edinburgh, whilst men from London and Edinburgh had been brought to Douglas to train the others. Dr Farrell also gave an exhibition of

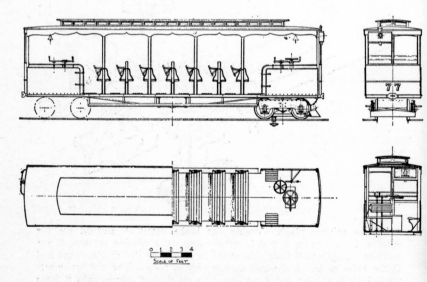

Open Douglas cable car of 1896, series 71-78—a conjectural restoration from photographs, prior to the preservation of an actual car

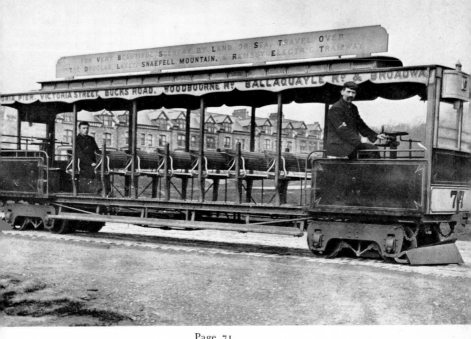

(above) *Cable car No 77 in York Road just before its rebuilding to saloon form in 1903. The roof gutters, lifeguard, and absence of sanding gear are the only changes from original condition. Driver John Thompson in command;* (below) *staff in the cable winding house at York Road, about 1908. Manager Stephen Robinson in bowler hat, senior gripman George Lace to his right, with child. Engineer Arthur Tyson in centre, with dog*

Page 72
*Horse-car
No 1 in the
first post-
war livery,
1951*

DOUGLAS CORPORATION TRANSPORT.

*Bus haulage im
mediately befor
the 80th birthda
parade, 7 Augus
1956. No 36 near
est the camer
beyond a* UEC *ca
and two ten-benc
rebuilds*

*No 46 in
action on the
Loch Pro-
menade sum-
mer 1964*

the art! George Lace, who died early in 1968, once told the writer that he believed that only four cars were on hand at the opening, and that the remaining eight (four open and four closed) arrived after the start of public service. The Press reported four cars in service on 17 August, and five by the following Saturday, 22 August; the full service (eight cars?) only awaited the training of further crews. The journey time was given as twelve minutes from the Jubilee Clock to Avondale, which would be fast even today.

These initial cars were numbered from 71 to 78, leaving 1-70 for the bay tramway. They were roofed, 32-seat, cross-bench cars with bulkhead ends, four single seats, and seven full-width benches for four. Alternate side pillars extended to the roof. From photographs, the overall dimensions appear to have been: length 29

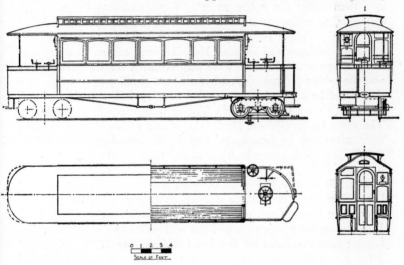

Closed Douglas cable car of 1896, series 79-82. The dotted lines show the roof and platform as actually built, the solid lines as shown by Milnes' drawing of 1896

ft, width 5 ft 6 in and height 8 ft 6 in. The two bogies were of 3 ft 6-in wheelbase, and at about 21 ft $4\frac{1}{2}$ in centres. Sanding gear was fitted but later removed. The later arrivals, closed cars Nos 79 to 82, differed from the builder's drawing, suggesting that they were altered during construction. The overall length of these cars was 28 ft $10\frac{1}{2}$ in, width 5 ft 6 in and height 9 ft $10\frac{1}{2}$ in; other dimensions are apparent from the drawing. Interior lighting was

E

by Colza oil lamps.

On both open and closed cars, the complete route was displayed above the windows, the inscription reading 'VICTORIA PIER, VICTORIA STREET, BUCKS RD, WOODBOURNE ROAD, BALLAQUAYLE RD & BROADWAY.' On the open cars, a shaped, hinged flap, was soon added to obscure 'BROADWAY' when lowered, and thus cater for short workings to Ballaquayle Road. In later years gutters were fitted to these cars and the flaps removed. Notes on the livery of the cable cars will be found in Chapter 4.

To celebrate the year's innovations—the new promenades (completed by June) and the cable tramway—a lavish two-hour procession was arranged for Wednesday 26 August. It was to start from the foot of Broadway, proceed round the cable tramway route and then along the entire series of promenades to Derby Castle terminus, returning to a public gathering on the new promenade fronting the Palace grounds, where there would be speeches from a dais by Lieutenant-Governor Henniker and others. The day was fine; horse- and cable-cars were all decorated for the occasion, as was the whole promenade, and ran where conflict with the procession could be avoided. The speeches were typical of their day, and the I O M T & E P Co and T. G. Taylor were specially commended. The three bands (Palace, Derby Castle and Foxdale) then resumed their afternoon performances, and in the evening Pain's W. E. Jolliffe provided fireworks from Derby Castle's pier and from the Tower of Refuge.

The following evening, 27 August, the tramway company and Dick, Kerr & Co provided a sumptuous dinner at the Douglas Bay hotel. The proceedings had begun at 3 pm with a visit to the York Road premises, where George Flett and colleagues acted as guides. Dining notables included the Lord Bishop, Mr W. B. Dick, and John Kerr; the guest list was widely drawn and included a full complement from both Dick, Kerr's and the I O M T & E P Co. Bruce was chairman, and claimed that as a result of the new service, property values in Upper Douglas had risen by 20 per cent. Dr Farrell said that he could address himself to his toast ('The Contractors') for a fortnight, and wandered into philosophy, including the gem :

> Man wants but little here below
> As someone said before
> But when he gets it don't you know
> He wants a little more.

Over the first month, several stoppages occurred, none of which was serious. The curved sections of Prospect Hill required daily greasing of the horizontal pulleys, and the maintainance gang had to start at 6.30 am. A soft cast-iron pulley at the Avondale corner was found to have a life of as little as seven hours, and a chilled iron replacement was soon put in. The Avondale curve had in the end to be eased, and while this was done a horse was used to haul short-working cars across the adjacent crossover, and at times around the corner itself.

What was the tramway really like? Imagine an early morning in the winter of 1896; in the relative darkness of the car shed, lit by a thin scattering of batswing burners, the shadowy forms of the cars sit over the deeper blackness of the pits. The duty car's oil headlight gleams yellow within its polished brass rim, with the obligatory red lantern panel lamp hovering above, whilst below the

Frontage of the cable winding house and car shed

gripper hangs down from its axle-borne supporting plank, both having already been subjected to careful scrutiny by the lamp of the shed fitter. Nearby, the steady pulsation of the engines is partly masked by the more strident note of the main shaft gearing.

One of the duty men climbs aboard, and almost at once the harsh metallic sound of a released handbrake is replaced by the faint hiss of journals as the strong shoulders of his colleagues roll the car forward towards the waiting traverser, to the accompaniment of an increasing rumble from the treads. Once halted on the traverser, the deeper sound of the traverse is followed by a metallic click as the rails are locked in line, and with a touch of the warning bell hung on his left, the driver stands ready as the car is pushed out on to the descending curved track leading east into Broadway. He applies his wheel brakes and the car comes to a halt on the townward track, within earshot of a continuous humming sound, which becomes a faint but insistent vibration as a long hooked steel bar is passed through the slot and used to push the running cable into the lowered jaw of the leading grip, the headlamp, meanwhile, being brought to the leading end of the car.

With time for departure on hand, the driver takes up his stance, the slot brake screw column's handle on his left, the gripper to his right front, and the hand-wheel of the chain-operated wheel brake a little behind him to the left. Simultaneously he winds on his gripper and releases the wheel brakes, and the car moves forward, the rate of acceleration depending on the speed with which the gripper takes hold. A pull on the ratchet handle serves for the final tightening.

The ensuing ride is smooth and quiet, for although the hard paving and plate frame bogies would reflect any sound, the light cars in these early years leave the joints unhammered. Only a periodic flange squeal on the curves marks progress, with a concurrent rumble as the gripper's side rollers bear hard against the inner slot rail, and the occasional rhythmic traverse of pointwork. Beneath the street, the passage of the tramway cable produces odd sounds from individual pulleys, which in some cases tend to ring with low, bell-like notes, and in summer cause visiting dogs from the mainland to stand in the road looking down the slot and barking at the noise. It also tempts local children to drop lengths of paper and string down the slot, to be caught by the moving cable and swept visibly along the road.

At a stop, the grip is released by spinning the wheel and the wheel brakes are applied. The fierce-acting slot brake is only used in emergency or on the steepest grades, where normal service stops are avoided; even with sanding gear, wheelslip would be almost inevitable. On downhill sections, gravity gives the car a start, but in professional gripper operation the cable has always to pull the car, and never vice versa, a forbidden practice known as 'slipping the cable'. Approaching the terminal pit, the gripper-on-brakes-off sequence is repeated, and here the cable runs to one side so that it leaves the opening jaws of the grip as the car rolls to a halt, whilst the returning cable comes within reach of insertion. A flat bar could be used to knock out a reluctant cable if need be.

So much for the driving technique; what of the route? The line as built comprised 1.38 miles of double track, and 0.633 miles of single track. Victoria Street's terminal spur was linked to the horse-car line, thereafter the cars ran directly on either hand of the centre line of the street, with a 4-ft clearway, as far as the curve at Ridgeway Street leading to the foot of Prospect Hill. There, the 40-ft radius curve required a wider clearway of five feet, and the track climbed the sinuous curves of the hill with this wider spacing until the junction of Finch Road where, at Government Office, the tracks diverged to the kerbside position originally intended for the whole line, each track being 2 ft 3 in from the kerb. An earlier plan showed this divergence planned instead at Demesne Road. Thus far, and onward to Avondale, the architectural surroundings on either hand are little changed today.

Just beyond Murray's Road, the seaward track swung across to join the other before negotiating the acute Avondale corner, again with a 5-ft clearway. A crossover joined the two tracks, and the ensuing sharp curves brought the tracks into what was later to be called York Road, the outer one being four feet from the northern kerb. The track now became single, and continued to the promenade as a succession of loops and single track, with two curves leading into the depot. In 1896, the vacant sites on each side outnumbered those built upon, but on reaching Ballaquayle Road the older properties on either side again survive little altered. Only below Glen Falcon Road, where the walled gardens of Villa Marina and smaller properties occupied the southern side of the still narrow 'Broadway', did the architectural scene differ greatly from today's. The double junction shown at the promenade is unconfirmed, and the section intended as interlaced track between Glen Falcon and Derby Roads was instead built as shown on our plan.

The line carried no less than 193,645 passengers from its August 15 opening to the end of December, against 91,776 for the previous bus operation. Dick, Kerr's Mr Windsor stayed on until January 1897. At the company meeting held on 8 March 1897, Bruce described the cable line as a 'one time much maligned, but now highly appreciated, convenience . . .' More than the statutory minimum service was still provided. The line was the largest single item in the £133,954 17s 10d spent during 1896 on new works and equipment, but this also covered the doubling of the track on the Central and Harris promenades.

During 1897, the cable line experienced a stoppage on Whit Monday and twice in August, with ensuing chaos while workmen searched for the cause. As a result the year's passengers only reached 489,682 : staff had spent days and nights in rectifying the faults. Bruce later hinted that the failures originated in drivers' errors, which had since been reduced thanks to one, Moar, who had been recruited from Edinburgh. The cable line's working costs had become painfully apparent, with costs of 13.64d/mile against earnings of 8.93d; mileage run had been 72,995.

In 1899, 91,682 car miles were run and 633,624 passengers carried; the one-day maximum was 7,979, the cost per mile 14.45d, and earnings per mile 9.4d. The average earning per journey was only 1s 4d. To reduce power costs, in the spring of 1899 I O M T & E P announced a plan to draw hydro-electric power from the Sulby River and install electric winding gear, shutting down the steam plant except in mid-summer.

On Saturday 3 February 1900, Dumbell's Bank collapsed, and with it the Isle of Man Tramways & Electric Power Company; Alexander Bruce had been the bank's general manager. The events that followed are described elsewhere. A delayed annual meeting held on 24 May 1900 was followed by others in an effort to keep the concern afloat, but liquidation came on 11 July and the whole enormous concern was put up for sale. W. H. Walker was appointed liquidator on 25 July, and invited offers for the purchase of the various lines.

Douglas Corporation saw their opportunity and on 22 October 1900 wrote to tramway valuation expert, Sir Frederick Bramwell, of Bramwell & Harris, asking for an assessment. They asked that he take into account 'the onerous conditions imposed upon the company for its concession'—truly an admission this, coming from the corporation! The cable line, they stated, was losing between £1,500 and £2,000 a year.

Bramwell offered the services of his partner, H. G. Harris, at a fee of 150 guineas and, this being accepted, Harris went to Douglas and completed his examination in one day. On 15 December he wrote to the company secretary for further information, and in July 1901 he submitted his report, a clear and concise summary of the lines, their physical state and their finances, quoting figures for both 1899 and 1900, since 1900 was under the cautious managerial policy of the liquidator. Those for 1900 were as follows:

Expenditure, Bay Tramway and Cable Tramway, 1900

	Pence per car mile	
	Bay Tramway	Cable Tramway
Maintenance of way and works	0.75	0.58
Power and horsing	3.43	11.10*
Car repairs	0.27	1.55
Traffic expenses	2.07	3.99
General charges (office etc)	0.68	1.80
Sundries	2.84	1.25
Aggregated pence per car mile:	10.87	20.27

Totals for the year 1900:   £8,813 8s 1d   £6,184 17s 5d

*—4.35d on the cable and its repair, excluding steam plant.

He recommended a price of £50,000, and thought that conversion of both routes to electric traction would cost £105,000. In a later letter, he allowed that 'the cable tramways are a dead loss' and thought that the corporation need not be in any hurry to puchase, but could await the course of events. Nevertheless, by 12 August 1901 the corporation had tendered £40,000 and had been refused.

On 25 September their new offer of £50,000 was accepted. The Tramways Purchase Sub-Committee's report of 7 October explained at length the reason for the council's increased offer; the value of the two lines on the I O M T & E P books had been £110,000, and any company buying them for £50,000 might well earn 5 per cent on its capital and also benefit from the enhanced value at the end of their concession. Up to £1,300 a year might be saved under corporation management. The last paragraph began: 'all municipalities aim at possessing the tramways within their boundaries . . .'

The corporation then applied to Tynwald for a loan of £52,000, repayable over thirty-five years. A special committee comprising

Messrs Ring, Moore, Goldsmith, Kerruish, Kitto and Clucas, and presided over by Deemster Kneen, heard evidence on 13 November and 4 December 1901. H. G. Harris came to Douglas again, and emerged as a MICE, MIEE, council member of the Institute of Mechanical Engineers and vice-president of the Society of Arts. His valuations were based on the naturally poor year of 1900, and he contrasted superior 1899 results from an earlier company report. The £50,000 did not include the horse stud; the horse-car track was worth about £14,000, and the land and buildings amounted to £15,559.

Cruikshank, counsel for the corporation, summarised the passenger receipts for the cable and horse lines as respectively £1,586 and £11,191 in 1896, £2,717 and £11,953 in 1897, £3,041 and £12,232 in 1898, £3,577 and £12,861 in 1899, and £3,271 and £11,015 in 1900, ignoring cartage earnings and sales of manure. No cars had been run down to Broadway from York Road car shed since the beginning of 1901, though the cable still ran there in its conduit; the pit at Broadway had suffered from silting up. A replacement cable then cost £600 and was expected to last for fifteen months, though annual replacement had been allowed for. Contractor Mark Carine appeared as valuer of the real estate, and the next witness was Frederick Saunderson, who gave his opinion of the present day value as £65,125, and quoted current values for the materials, the cost of construction, rails, yokes, etc., which latter alone had totalled over 850 tons. Finally, Harris re-appeared to give details of relaying of horse-car track carried out since the spring of 1900 and the town clerk showed that the town was well able to afford the intended purchase. The committee's report was favourable, and the purchase went ahead.

To close the present chapter there follows an account of changes to the plant and working of the cable line carried out under corporation auspices. The purchase sub-committee had already obtained a report from Joshua Shaw of the I O M T & E P on the possible physical curtailment of the Broadway cable line, and on 20 December 1901 recommended that Shaw's scheme for a new terminus at Stanley View be accepted. On 24 December Shaw joined the new undertaking and took charge of the cable line at a salary of £10 monthly. He carried out the change between 21 and 28 February 1902, shortly before leaving the island to become electrical engineer to the Mersey Railway Company; his successor as cable-line supervisor was Arthur Tyson. On 25 March Shaw reported that the shortening of the cable had brought a fall in coal consumption of 8 cwt in a fourteen-hour day, the previous daily figure being 3 tons 15 cwt. The Depot—Broadway section had been described in 1898 by an I M R officer as 'almost unworkable', owing to the gradients and the narrowness of the streets; it is said that only two specified drivers had been allowed to take cars down to Broadway from the shed. The governor questioned the legality of the curtailment.

By 14 May track between Victoria Road and Derby Road was being lifted and re-used in extending the horse tramway on to the Victoria Pier. The rest of the abandoned track as far as Stanley View was removed later, and a low-roofed, two-road, horse-car shed was built in the yard adjoining Waverley Road. The access track abutted at about 75 degrees on to the cable track just above Stanley View, and the cars reached it by halting just opposite and being lifted bodily round, stern first, on to the access track. The corporation subsequently erected substantial stop signs around the route, and built a stone shelter at the Avondale corner. Horse-car overhauls, previously carried out at Derby Castle, were now done at York Road, the car being shunted over the connecting line at Victoria Street and towed from there by a cable car.

The four closed cars were insufficient for the winter traffic, and on 10 November 1902 the council agreed that open car No 78 should be enclosed. Its trial run took place on 14 January, and Mr J. Faragher received a (part ?) payment of £20 for the work. The result was rather fine, Mr Faragher's elegant panelling being well set off by the varnished finish; the 28-seat saloon was 13 ft 6 in long, and the four platform seats were retained. This de luxe conversion may have proved a little expensive, for the next conversion was done on simpler lines.

On 9 December 1903, a sub-committee accepted a quotation from Messrs Faragher & Quiggin of £31 13s od to enclose cable car No 77. The result is shown in the drawing overleaf (prepared from a poor photograph). The seating capacity was the same (32). During November, the corporation had been in touch with Dick, Kerr & Co about speeding up the cable from its sedate six mph and providing a condenser for the engines, but nothing was done. In September 1904 spare parts were unsuccessfully sought from the L C C Streatham Hill cable line.

In 1905, the open cable cars were modified to allow easier carriage of luggage, by hingeing the four small single seats on the

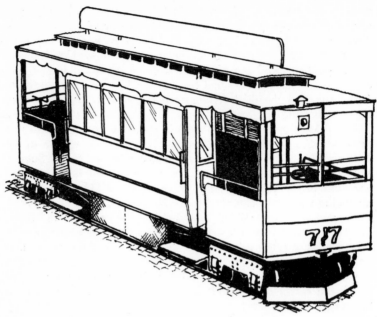

Cable car 77, as rebuilt early in 1904

end platforms. The saloon cars had similar seats added in later years. Electrification of the line on the conduit system was considered in 1905, but rejected, and attempts to extend the cable cars to the Victoria Pier were rejected by the Harbour Commissioners. In June 1905 in an effort to combat competition and secure steamer passengers for the cable line, new tracks were laid to allow connecting horse cars to run from the steamers to the cable terminus in Victoria Street.

On 13 December 1905, the corporation decided to double the cable track between Avondale corner and the depot, and this was carried out in 1906. As a result, cars could no longer run downhill direct into the depot; instead, cars arriving at Palatine Road (just above the depot) dropped the cable there and continued by gravity down to Stanley View. To enter the shed, they picked up the uphill cable to reach their run-in position above the depot and then, with the cable dropped, coasted round the curve and with a skilled driver just rolled on to the traverser. Leaving the shed, a water can was always kept handy to wet the downhill curve, making the task of pushing the cars out easier. The 'wye' system of depot working ensured that the cars changed ends each day and evened the wear. When next repainted, the wording on the car letterboards ended in 'WOODBOURNE RD, BALLAQUAYLE, STANLEY VIEW, BROADWAY.'

In February 1907, the corporation ordered two 32-seat cable cars from the United Electric Car Company of Preston; these arrived in June, and cost £348 each. They took the numbers 69 and 70. Their design owed much to Nos 71-78, but they shared with the new horse cars, Nos 43 and 44, the useful adjunct of sprung proofed canvas roller blinds, and had full height pillars throughout. In February 1908, side screens for winter use were fitted to the platforms of converted cable cars Nos 77 and 78.

The year 1908 was marred by two fatalities, one of which occurred at the top of Victoria Street on 21 April. The victim was a man of poor mobility and eyesight—the cars could stop 'in two or three yards'—but the corporation thereafter provided a safety flagman at this curve in winter as well as in summer. The other (very rare) case was the death from heat stroke of cable tramway boilerman, William Kelly, on 3 July.

Another new cable car, No 68, came from G. C. Milnes, Voss & Co of Birkenhead in May 1909. It had the usual seven cross benches and four single seats, and resembled Nos 69 and 70 in being fitted with canvas blinds. Two-window end bulkheads were retained, with a lamp-box at the near side and a clerestory roof. In March 1911, Milnes, Voss supplied another similar car, No 67, which had wooden roller shutters instead of the blinds. No 67 cost £327, and brought the fleet to forty-five horse cars and fourteen cable cars. In the same year (1911) Sunday cable-car service was at last begun; Sunday operation had been an election issue in November 1906, and defeat had rewarded its proponents. The boilers' economiser was replaced during 1913. The tramway committee's accounts for the ten months to 31 January 1914 showed the usual disparity between the two corporation lines: the cable cars had cost £5,633 and earned only £5,163, whereas the horse cars had earned £21,547 against outgoings of only £10,327. Estimated cable-car earnings for the next two months were only £279 11s 10d, against expenditure of £969 16s 1d.

The cable cars continued to run throughout the 1914-18 war, with a reduced service, but their mechanical condition deteriorated. Evening cars would stop on the way down at Duke Street, where the driver would remove the splendid oil headlight and replace it at the rear, thus avoiding the danger of providing free illumination for German submarines!

By 1919, wear and tear on the cable line was causing concern and arrangements for its short-term repair were put in hand. The estimates for 1921-22 provided £945 18s 2d for temporary cable track repairs and £1,260 for a new cable (against £649 in 1913). If the track was to be properly relaid this was estimated to cost £33,500. In the year to March 1920, the cable cars cost £9,740 and earned £7,156, the winter losses being even greater than before; during February and March 1920, the cable line cost the corporation £2,252 to run and earned only £645!

Until 1920, the cable cars had bulkhead oil lamps as on the horse cars, though acetylene lighting had been tried in 1908. The year 1920 saw a general change to acetylene lighting, the large and obstructive bulkhead oil-lamp box being replaced by a long and narrow acetylene-lamp box hung externally on the narrow panel above the heightened end window, with a hinged metal flap inside the bulkhead for access; thus considerably altering the end aspect of the open cars.

In 1920, the corporation bought five 26-seat Tilling-Stevens petrol-electric buses, and for the winter of 1921-22, these took over the cable route; thus shelving the renewal problem. An earlier closure, from 9 April 1921, was probably due to the mainland coal strike; cars ran again from 24 June to 19 October, but thereafter complete winter closure occurred, and the season of cable-car operation grew shorter each year—for 1922, 16 May to 30 September, for 1923, 16 May to 17 September, and for 1924, 3 June to 17 September. For 1925, the period was 26 May to 16 September, and for 1926, 20 July to 28 August only. Meanwhile, the bus fleet grew apace.

There were secret daredevils among the cable line crews. Early one morning two policemen sheltering in the porch of St Mary's Church (opposite Finch Road) saw a car hurtle down Prospect Hill, the driver slipping his cable. After a moment's thought, they followed it to investigate the anticipated pile-up—and met it at Duke Street, intact, on its way back! Wear and tear had by now made operation so noisy that the seasonal Sunday service was always withdrawn during the hours of church service. During these intervals two cars normally stood opposite the former Grand Theatre in Victoria Street, ready to resume operations.

Whence the noise? On straight track, the vertical pulleys had worn unevenly, producing as they revolved substantial thumps whose vibration reached adjoining properties. Corrugation by now affected the inside rail of many curves, and the closed cars (nicknamed 'Devils') suffered from window rattle and acted as an amplifying box. Chilled-iron disc wheels were not of the quietest, especially when associated with plate-frame bogies. The points had a fixed mate on the inside, and these had worn considerably. The worn cable varied in thickness, and at stops the gripper had to be left well loosened, but even so it vibrated and rattled as the cable slid over the lowered bottom jaw.

On the sections with kerbside track, other difficulties arose. At least one dray horse, habitually seen waiting outside premises on the Buck's Road section, had fully conditioned its thinking to cable tramway peculiarities. When an approaching car pulled up and sounded its gong, the horse would take itself and vehicle to the centre of the road, look round to check the clearance, wait for the car to pass, and then return to its roadside stance athwart the tracks!

The cable-car line was destined to survive for three more years as a seasonal transport ghost. Indeed, it became moderately profitable, typical earnings being £3,336 19s 2½d in 1928 against an expenditure of £2,468 9s 9d. In that year (from 24 July to 1 September) it ran 22,327¼ car miles and carried 216,639 passengers, against 35,538¼ miles and 336,970 passengers in the slightly longer season for 1927, from 1 July to 4 September.

In 1927, the Salisbury Terrace crossover was moved to Woodside, south of Murray's Road, where cars could coast through it downhill and so provide economical short workings. With the running lines on opposite sides of the road, the new installation looked decidedly odd. No special destination was now shown on these short workings, for the preceding car to Stanley View waited for that following and any through passengers were allowed to transfer. At about this time, road widening between Hilary and Derby Roads left the townward track remote from the kerb.

However, the end had to come, for the thirty-three-year-old trackwork and pulleys were worn out and the bus fleet was now of adequate size. The 1929 season was the shortest yet, from 23 July to 19 August, with only 11,968 car miles and 78,981 passengers, the effect of the slump being apparent. The last day's traffic returns, for Monday, 19 August 1929, were receipts of £27 17s 4d, made up of 1,978 3d fares, 216 2d fares, 138 1½d fares and 115 1d fares, with 2,447 passengers carried on 192 car journeys and 528 car miles; there were also 219 journeys by contract holders. The end had come, and the *Isle of Man Times* wrote 'What a strange quiet place Douglas was on Tuesday, the clanking noise had gone—the cable trams had stopped. Monday was their last day—perhaps for ever'. In their last season, the cable cars had cost £1,482 15s 10d, and had earned only £1,010 10s 3d.

The cable was soon drawn out of its slot, and the considerable task of filling the conduit and lifting the track was put in hand. The job took at least three years, Buck's Road being left until 1932. The last trams to use the line may have been horse cars hauled by motor vehicle on their way to York Road for winter storage and overhaul; thereafter these transfers were carried out by using a special low trailer consisting of two rails set to 3-ft gauge. The depot was altered to serve as the corporation's omnibus depot, with the engine house and boiler room serving as workshops and paint-shops, and the former open yard converted to become, partly, addi-

Cable tramway fleet at maximum, 1911 to 1929

Fleet Numbers	Type	Builder	Date	Seats (as built)
67	Cross-bench car with wooden roller shutters	G. C. Milnes, Voss & Co	1911	32
68	Cross-bench car with canvas roller blinds	G. C. Milnes, Voss & Co	1909	32
69, 70	Cross-bench car with canvas roller blinds	United Electric Car Co	1907	32
71-76	Cross-bench cars without side blinds	G. F. Milnes & Co	1896	32
77	Originally as 71-76, rebuilt 1904 as a combination car	G. F. Milnes & Co	1896	32
78	Originally as 71-76, rebuilt 1903 as a combination car	G. F. Milnes & Co	1896	32
79-81	Unvestibuled saloon cars with corner entrances	G. F. Milnes & Co	1896	32

Nos 79-81 seated twenty-eight passengers on longitudinal seats in the saloons and four on hinged double seats on the platforms. The open cars had seven benches seating four each, and four single seats on the plat-forms. Nos 72 and 73, when dismantled at Jurby in 1968, revealed other bulkhead seats for four at each end; these must have been usable only at the non-driving end, and would thus give a capacity of thirty-six.

tional depot accommodation. Specimens of the tramway cables used in different years have been preserved by the transport department, together with a gripper handle and car headlight, and one of the large tilted diverter pulleys and its access tunnel are still there beneath the roadway, though invisible to a passer-by.

The winding engines were broken up on site, and the sixteen cars were all sold to Charles McArten of Spring Valley. His intention was to convert them to holiday bungalows, and two of the original open cars of 1896 (Nos 72 and 73) survived until July 1968, heavily disguised but still on bogies, as part of a dwelling near Jurby. One car (and parts of the other) were then rescued for eventual restoration as museum exhibits, and have returned to the York Road premises which they had left almost forty years previously. The rest of the cars have now been broken up.

CHAPTER THREE

Still in Harness

'I trust . . . you will not discard certain features which may seem out of date, but which are in fact of great attraction to visitors. There are, for instance, the horse trams . . .'— Sir Peter Hyla Gawne Stallard, KCMG, CVO, MBE, Lieutenant-Governor, 13 October 1966

It is necessary now to return to February 1900, when the failure of Dumbell's Bank put the Isle of Man Tramways and Electric Power Co into liquidation. W. H. Walker was appointed liquidator, to manage the tramways pending sale and, as already mentioned, Douglas Corporation became the owner of the cable and horse tramways. A tramways committee was set up to manage the undertaking, succeeding the sub-committee responsible for the takeover arrangements, and on 24 October 1901 they appointed T. S. Atkinson to take charge of the horsing at £10 monthly, and Stephen Robinson as cashier and accountant at £150 a year. Other appointments (working engineer, traffic superintendent, and plate-layer) were made on December 30.

At take-over on Thursday, 2 January 1902, special inaugural cars left their respective depots at 10 am. These were cable car No 79 driven by the committee chairman, and three horse cars, the leading one of which was driven by the mayor, Mr S. Webb. The cars met at the Jubilee Clock at 10.40 am, and a photograph shows a good civic turnout in spite of earlier rain. Travel was free until noon, and some young hopefuls remaining on cars as the hour struck were dismayed to learn that the deadline affected uncompleted journeys.

Page 89
Inside No 1 horse car some young passengers enjoy a new experience. Summer, 1964

Mare 'Polly', earlier bought from Ireland, presented the Tramways Department with a foal, 'Ramsey', in 1966. Both are seen here with Tramways Committee chairman R. L. Quayle and stables' foreman J. Moughtin

Page 90
(above left) *Thomas Lightfoot, circa* 1890; (above right) *John Davie, circa* 1890; (below left) *Alexander Bruce, circa* 1897; (below right) *George Noble Fell, circa* 1923

The full fleet comprised thirty-six horse cars, Nos 2 to 37, and the twelve cable cars, Nos 71 to 82; the fate of thirteen road vehicles listed by the liquidator is unknown. The thirty-six horse cars filled the 1896 shed at Derby Castle, but one track was partly replaced by an office for Mr Stephen Robinson, and this, together with an order for three more open cars (February 1902), meant that cars would again have to be kept in winter at the Brig stables and at York Road. Stabling was available at Tramway Terrace and the Brig for sixty-eight horses; nine horses were bought in March for the 1902 season, bringing the stud to forty-eight. The corporation's title was painted on the cars, and advertising had been let to Mr Schenk of the new Manx Electric Railway, the bargain including the free supply of tickets.

Derby Castle horse-car depot of 1895. In 1902, after the corporation took over, the furthermost bay was turned into offices. An upper storey was added in 1935

In a new agreement with the harbour commissioners the 1896 terminal tracks in Peveril Square were to be replaced by a new line on the Victoria Pier itself. This was to be double to a point 110 ft beyond the pier buildings, and single for the 30 ft beyond, and, as mentioned earlier, was laid in May, 1902. An extension to the I M R station was again proposed in January 1904, but without result.

F

The corporation's financial year ended each year on 31 March, and in 1902 the profit to the end of March was £2,650, including retrospective adjustment. Stephen Robinson had now been appointed manager, and reported on wages and hours of work in Douglas and other towns. He proposed a winter week of sixty hours, instead of seventy. The rota would include long days of 12 hr 40 min, short days of 9 hrs 25 min, and relief days of 6 hr 25 min. Cable drivers now received 24s a week, horse-car drivers 20s, and conductors 18s. In the year ended March 1904, £500 was paid towards the relief of rates, and by 31 March 1905 the total had reached £2,350. During 1905, Robinson prepared a report on motor buses, comparing the different makes available.

The cable line's winter deficit was such as to absorb much of the profit on the horse cars. Electrification might turn the loss into a profit, and 1906-8 saw several proposals for electric trams in Douglas. In January 1906, the Manx Electric Railway Co offered to lease and electrify the bay tramway in return for royalty payments equal to the average net profit for the preceding three years, the aim (as in Bruce's time) being through-running from Ramsey and Laxey to the Victoria Pier. This the corporation unanimously rejected and instead they instructed Stephen Robinson to report on the electrification of both the horse and cable lines. There was also discussion of a new corporation electric line up to Peel Road and Circular Road via the North Quay.

Mr Robinson reported on 10 October 1906. The two tramways could be electrified for £77,820, the net expenditure after selling surplus property being £67,889. York Road would become the tramway power station, retaining the existing boilers and adding new generating equipment (£15,750). New track and foundations on the bay tramway would cost £21,000, plus £2,100 for the overhead (with centre poles). New rails and filling in the conduit on the cable line would cost £11,000, plus £2,200 for the overhead. Alterations to the winding house would cost £3,500, and a traction battery £4,000. Ten new, 44-seat, single-deck bogie cars would be required at £710 each, and ten, 30-seat, four-wheel cars at £650 each. In addition, electrical equipment would be fitted to the twelve cable cars (£4,620) and some of the horse cars would be kept as trailers.

Meanwhile, the tramway superintendent was already pressing for ten more covered horse cars, five 'toastracks', and three cable cars, but only two horse and two cable cars were ordered in February

1907. In July, the corporation obtained powers to run buses, and after an offer from Joshua Shaw of Mersey Railway motor buses was considered and declined, a contractor was engaged to run what proved to be a markedly unprofitable wagonette service along Peel Road. The conductors, who still had neither uniforms nor overcoats, agitated for a fifty-six-hour week in place of sixty.

Also in 1907 the corporation set up a special committee to report on municipal electricity supply, which would have involved a new generating station capable also of supplying the tramways. The combined undertaking was estimated to cost not less than £100,000, which put it out of court. Manx Electric Railway now repeated their 1906 offer, but after some months of discussions they were finally and firmly rebuffed (in August 1908) and told that 'the question of the electrification of the tramways was not now being considered by the council, and in any case they would not be prepared to consider any scheme involving the leasing of the lines to a company'. This was the last serious attempt to provide Douglas with electric tramways, and most of the town retained gas lighting until the 1920s.

In August 1906, a boy was killed by horse car No 12 on the Harris promenade, his attention having been distracted by a brass band. After two similar fatalities, a coroner's jury in July 1908 urged that the bandstand should be moved and that the cars should be fitted with lifeguards. These had been considered in 1902, without result, but now some Hudson Bowring guards were obtained and tried. These were unsuccessful, and the final choice of lifeguard was influenced by the use of traversers at Derby Castle; the type used, when raised, stays well clear of the ground even when the car is on the traverser ramp.

The maximum turn of duty for a tram horse in 1909-11 was eight journeys, but there was no similar limitation for the men. All horse-car men in 1911 received 28s 6d a week for unlimited hours, and in summer the working week sometimes amounted to as much as 114 hours. Cable drivers now earned 32s a week and conductors 24s 6d, but when Sunday cable cars were instituted in 1911 the crews were at first expected to work them without extra pay. The committee then offered a 73-hour seven-day week instead of the previous 78-hour six-day week, but the men wanted a six-day week of 72 hours, with Sunday paid separately, or another day off in lieu. The horse-car men were now demanding 32s 6d for a specific week of 84 hours.

A strike was planned for 13 July 1911, but on Monday, 10 July, an altercation between Stephen Robinson and three cable men ended in what the manager stated to be their voluntary departure, but what the men claimed was their dismissal. Both tramway sections promptly ceased work. The cable men returned to work the same evening, having secured a settlement giving them 30s and 27s for a six-day week of 72 hours, with separate Sunday pay. The horse-car men stayed out until 11.30 on Tuesday, and gained a 72-hour six-day week at 27s, with overtime payment and an extra 4s 6d for Sundays. No overtime was worked on the cable line. To recoup their outlay, the corporation could now charge higher fares, an amending Act to that of 1895 having been obtained on 14 May to allow fares of 2d downhill during the summer from Stanley View.

Between 1910 and 1913 new 65-lb rail was laid from Tramway Terrace to the Derby Castle terminus and from the Villiers hotel to the northern end of the Loch promenade. The shelter, bandstand and gardens on the Harris promenade were removed, and the tram tracks, on leaving the Loch promenade, now continued by more gradual curves to regain their older alignment. The year 1913 also saw the opening of the Villa Marina as a public park, and in 1914 the track was relaid from Greensill's Corner (the former Lifeboat House) to the Palace gates, at a cost of £2,510 5s 6d. Modern surfacing of the promenade resulted in regular gradients; from the northern termnius a car climbed at 1 in 216 and then 1 in 108 to a summit at Summer Hill, then down again at 1 in 216 for most of Queen's promenade and again to the Palace. Thereafter the line was mainly level, except for a short climb of 1 in 108 near the southern terminus.

In the year ended 31 March 1914, the tramways paid £1,700 to the relief of rates. The horse cars had made their usual profit, earning £21,547 in the first nine months against costs of £10,327, and the cable line had earned £5,163 against costs of £5,633. A bus service newly instituted along the Peel Road with the first corporation motor buses had cost the department £177 and only earned £82, and the fleet stood at forty-five horse cars, sixteen cable cars and three buses.

With the outbreak of the 1914-18 war Douglas became something of a ghost town, with Cunningham's camp and other suitable areas converted to floodlit internment camps. The holiday industry rapidly became a mere shadow of its normal self, and transport

STILL IN HARNESS

services were reduced accordingly, the previous winter level of service now continuing throughout the year. There is no record of the employment of women staff.

Labour relations in the island changed. Until 1917, the Isle of Man had no effective non-craft unions, but Alfred J. Teare and his associates realised that advancement for working people could best be obtained by forming a Workers Union; its first secretary was Charles Duncan, MP for Barrow-in-Furness. This catered for all the semi-skilled, such as transport platform staffs, and about fifty men attended the inaugural meeting on St Patrick's Day of 1917. Social legislation was almost non-existent in the island, for in the absence of taxation such things as old age pensions were not regarded as feasible.

In July of 1918, the wartime flour subsidy was withdrawn in the island, and the 9d loaf became 1s. A 'bread strike' took place on 4 and 5 July on this issue, and the horse, cable and electric cars (and outgoing steamers) stopped until mid-day on 5 July when, amidst rejoicing, the 9d loaf was restored. Underlying this was pressure for an island-controlled income or similar tax that would make possible the introduction of old age pensions and similar social benefits, first sought by Teare and his colleagues in 1909-10. In 1935, the Isle of Man 'Workers Union' became part of the Transport and General Workers Union, and after another half-day transport strike in June 1935 compatibility was generally achieved with mainland north-west area rates. Since then, employer/labour relations have been friendly and service has not been interrupted by such troubles.

In the first postwar season, 1919, 343,332 visitors came to the island, against 615,726 in 1913; the Steam Packet Company's fleet was at only half its 1914 capacity. Costs had risen considerably, and for the year to March 1920 the cable cars cost £9,740 against earnings of £7,156, whilst the horse cars had cost £17,453 and earned £29,804. By 1921 the horse and uphill cable car fares had risen to 3d, with 2d downhill. A cargo of coal now cost 54s 6d/ton.

During 1920, with visitors totalling 554,350, the department's total expenditure, including sinking fund, reached £50,422 against earnings of £62,067. The renewals fund at £7,273 was faced in 1921 with relaying the Queen's promenade section and the ex-cable rails on the Victoria pier, at an estimated cost of £6,768. Maintenance of the fifteen cable cars had cost £724, against £826 for the forty-four horse cars. Mr Robinson was granted a rise in salary to £350 a year, plus his house.

In 1926 motor buses ran on the promenade for the first time, and proposals were made to replace the horse cars by buses. However, the five-car 7½-minute winter service continued until 1927, when on the evening of 2 November a half-century of virtually unbroken service (since 1876) ended and the horse-car service thereafter became seasonal.

Winter closure facilitated track renewals. The mid-twenties had seen the new layout (with scissors crossover) installed on the Victoria pier, and November 1928 saw the commencement of the widening of Loch and Harris promenades from the Victoria pier to the war memorial, which took until 1934. This was mainly a 'winter work scheme', a form of unemployment relief peculiar to the island. Relocation of horse-car tracks did not begin until 1932, partly because of doubts about the horse tramway's future.

On 9 May 1932, Mr Stephen Robinson retired and the corporation selected as their new manager Mr C. F. Wolsey, M Inst T, whose previous post had been at Lowestoft. Mr Wolsey saw the horse tramway's future as promising and the tramways committee embarked on a comprehensive scheme of track renewals, linked with the promenade improvements already begun. In December 1933 appeared the first estimates for reconstruction, and since horse-car tracks of the substantial variety now used at Douglas have a life of some forty years, the corporation in authorising the new track had firmly indicated their intention of keeping the horse trams. The new track consisted of 65 lb/yd 'wineglass' rail by Dorman Long of Middlesbrough, laid on a five-inch concrete bed. The Loch promenade widening and the final realignment from Greensill's Corner to the war memorial was completed by June 1934, and the track relaying was largely completed through to Summer Hill (formerly Burnt Mill Hill) in 1935.

The horse car surplus for 1933 was £8,000, giving a departmental profit of some £3,720 after allowing for a loss on the buses, a pattern repeated in subsequent years. Early in 1935, new offices were superimposed on the old depot at Derby Castle, including an entrance hall which blocked off two of the twelve original depot roads, and a new staircase which partly eliminated a third; more cars now had to spend their winters in the Brig stable yard or at York Road. The bus fleet was modernised with new A E C vehicles, and the old Tilling Stevens petrol-electrics were sold off; one of these dating from 1923 was retrieved from a private owner in 1955 after negotiations initiated by the writer, and became a chassis exhibit in the Museum of British Transport at Clapham.

In 1935 the Municipal Tramways and Transport Association held its annual conference at Douglas, and Mr Wolsey's article in *Transport World* for 20 June 1935 gives an excellent picture of the undertakings. Passengers in 1934 had totalled 2,471,542, and the resident Douglas population of 20,000 was swollen by 550,000 summer arrivals. The stud of 135 tram horses now involved stabling at the Queen's hotel and at St Barnabas' church in Fort Street, in addition to that at Tramway Terrace and the Brig.

The year 1938 saw a gross profit of £9,650, and by this time a special pattern of shoe had been evolved for the horses which included a rubber pad. In conjunction with this, a special rubber/asphalt paving compound was laid between the rails, making an excellent foothold.

The outbreak of war in September 1939 brought about an abrupt visitor exodus. Horse-tram operation continued until 30 September, but in the spring of 1940 the tramway horses were sold off and the cars remained tucked away in their respective depots for the next six years. This left unused the forty-nine acres which had served for winter grazing and for five years the corporation's transport department took to farming. Many seafront hotels were requisitioned for internees and (later) for prisoners-of-war, and barbed wire fences were erected half-way across the tram tracks.

By early 1946, derequisitioning made possible the seasonal resumption of tramway service, and in April the inhabitants of Buck's Road were awakened one day at 12.30 am by a veritable cavalry detachment of Irish horses, forty-two in all, newly off ship. Staff recruitment followed, and early May saw Sir Geoffrey Bromet, the then lieutenant-governor, learning to drive a horse car in readiness for the official opening of the service at 10 am on 22 May 1946. At this time the undertaking still possessed eight double-deck cars, and several saw service in 1946-8. Tynwald sanctioned a new 2½d fare, and all might have been thought well, but in fact the line was under fire from several directions. The profit for 1946 was only £226, though this was with only about half the cars on the road.

In February 1947 it was agreed to give the line the chance of another season, at a new fare of 3d. A public meeting in March produced a 5 : 1 majority for retention, and the chairman of the I O M S P C A gave a favourable verdict on the working conditions of

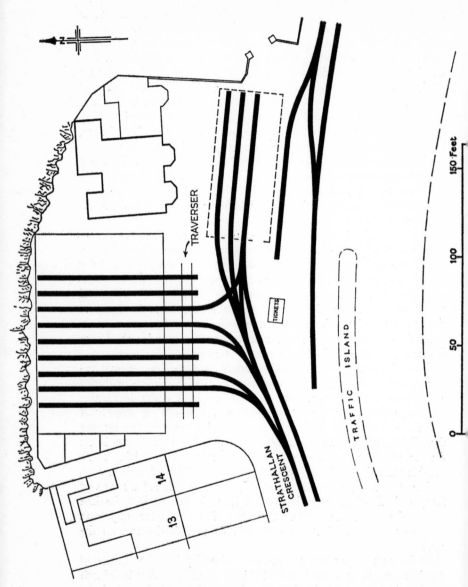

The simplified layout adopted at Derby Castle in 1953, showing also the
Promenade widening of 1939/47

the horses. The 1947 season was an immediate success, and a ticket-back referendum was overwhelmingly in favour of retaining the horse cars. On 11 November the council themselves voted 21 : 1 in favour of retention, whereas only twenty months before there had been a tie of 5 : 5.

These were the years of Manxland's postwar boom, and by January 1948 ample justification emerged in the previous year's profit of £4,000; the undertaking as a whole contributed £7,000 to the relief of rates. The widening of Strathallan Crescent's promenade, interrupted by the war, was completed in 1947 and the track relaying programme was here resumed, being completed in 1953. No action was taken on a 1949 report by Messrs Arnold, Robinson and Wright of the Tilling group, which had included the suggestion that open-top double-deck buses should replace or augment the horse-car services.

A further report was however commissioned in 1950 from W. G. Marks and R. C. Moore, both mainland transport managers, probably as a result of losses incurred by the buses. Their 1952 report sought to rearrange the department's affairs completely, including the substitution of twelve 44-seat single-deck buses for the horse cars. Only their wish to see integration with the out-of-town routes, of the Road Services seems to have seen fulfilment.

In 1951, the department was for the first time host to the Light Railway Transport League, and reports of Douglas tramway events thereafter became a regular feature in their magazine. The profit for 1952 was £5,454, and £7,500 was subsequently spent on relaying the terminal and depot approach tracks at Derby Castle, the former still beneath the ornamental station awning erected by the I O M T & E P Co. Only one double-deck car (No 14) now remained, no longer in use, and on 3 March 1955 it left Douglas for a temporary home at Norwood tram depot in London prior to inclusion in the new Museum of British Transport at Clapham. Bad weather prevented an intended ceremonial run along the promenade with the mayor and deputy mayor aboard, and the car slipped away almost unnoticed.

The eightieth season (1956) began with an opening by Dame Regina Evans, OBE, on 10 May (other celebrities had performed this function each year since 1946, and continue to do so), and a competition was arranged in which children were to choose names for the thirteen new horses. The department commissioned an anniversary brochure from the present writer, and this is an

appropriate place to thank the corporation for their permission
to re-use information acquired whilst employed in this connection;
however, the present account is in no way an official publication.
The following operational description is taken from the 1956
brochure and most is equally applicable to the present day :

> The tram service . . . reaching a maximum of 26 cars and 30,000
> passengers per day in early August. The journey round the bay
> takes 20 minutes, at a speed of 7-9 miles per hour, and the service
> varies from a minimum of 10 minutes to a car every minute and
> a half . . . the remaining intermediate crossover at Church Road
> (Falcon hotel) being only used at peak hours. . . .
>
> Interest centres, of course, on the horses, of which there are at
> present 80 . . . so that the department can claim to be a model
> equine employer! Whereas in 1893 only 50 horses were used for an
> all-day, all the year round service, today's stud numbers 80 and
> spends eight months of the year out at grass. . . . The heavy
> double-deck cars no longer exist, and although a horse can still
> pull as many as 42 people (including the driver and conductor) . . .
> The roller bearings now fitted to all cars offer very little rolling
> resistance; this can be seen at the depot, where the cars are generally
> shunted by hand! . . . each horse is named and has its own stall. In
> addition to the veterinary surgeon and stable hands, a saddler is
> employed making and repairing saddlery and a shoesmith and
> assistant make 700 pairs of shoes. . . . The horses are mainly
> purchased in Ireland . . . the older hands among them know
> precisely when their turn of duty ends, and will stop of their own
> accord opposite the stable and wait to be relieved, then making their
> own way indoors when unhitched . . . the consumption of provender,
> which is mostly bought during the winter months for use in the
> succeeding summer, amounts each year to about 100 tons of hay,
> 4,500 bushels of oats and 30 tons of straw.

The main celebrations took place on 7 August 1956, the eightieth
anniversary of the opening, and were certainly all that might be
wished. The horses were paraded at the Victoria pier, watched by
a distinguished gathering that included the Lieutenant-Governor
and Lady Dundas, international horsewoman Miss Pat Smythe,
and Mrs d'Echevarria, of Southport, a granddaughter of Thomas
Lightfoot. The official party then proceeded aboard car No 40,
driven by Pat Smythe, to Derby Castle, the depot and stables, and

then back to the Villa Marina, along promenades lined with people seldom less than three to four deep who cheered and applauded. Prior to the procession of tramless horses to the parade at Victoria Pier, three convoys of six horse cars were drawn down the promenade by corporation buses. An excellent view of the parade appears in Dennis Gill's book *Tramcar Treasury*.

The year 1956 was a moderately good one by postwar standards, but soon the decline in Manxland's holiday patronage began to show in the corporation transport returns. The Marks-Moore report of 1952 had admitted the difficult task of the undertaking, with the odd layout of the town and the great disparity between summer and winter traffic, and the year-round earnings of the department had already fallen, leading to a horse-car fare increase in 1956. Parked cars in Douglas are evidence enough of where the resident traffic has gone! Co-ordination of corporation and Road Services routes was advocated, and became a reality on 1 July 1957. During the Suez fuel crisis, the committee had considered starting the 1957 horse-car season early to save petrol and fuel oil, and in August 1957 an anonymous donor presented the department with a set of sunbonnets for the horses, in five different colours and with ribbons attached!

A sad loss to the department, in the Winter Hill air crash of 27 February 1958, was the death of Mr J. D. Craine, whose thirty years with the undertaking had led to his appointment as engineer. Without his reminiscences, much of the cable tramway section of this book could not have been writen.

For 1958, twenty new horses were obtained and were seen being broken in, rodeo-style, by pulling empty cars. Mr G. B. Stubbs, MRCVS, was appointed veterinary surgeon vice the late Mr J. C. Naylor, MRCVS. The summer was a wet one, with the net horse car profit £1,645 against expectations of £5,500. The passenger figure was 1,250,000: previous profits were quoted as £3,779 in 1953, £4,303 in 1954, £6,377 in 1955, £4,556 in 1956 and £5,905 in 1957. Abandonment was rumoured, but was promptly and officially denied.

The year 1959 was a better one, with an opening by Lady Dundas. In October, the *Examiner* reported that horse-tram operation now cost 6s a mile as against 4s 2d in 1954, but that earnings were now 6s 6d as against 5s in 1954. That autumn, the council decided to reduce the stud of horses slightly in future.

The new lieutenant-governor, Sir Ronald Garvey, KCMG, KCVO,

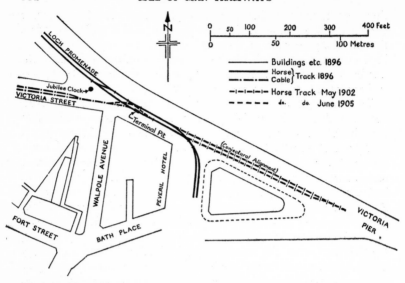

Victoria Pier terminus, 1896 to 1961. The upper plan shows the 1896
horse and cable termini, the pier extension of 1902 and the double track
junction of 1905; the lower plan shows the 1961 diversion which preceded
the building of the new Sea Terminal

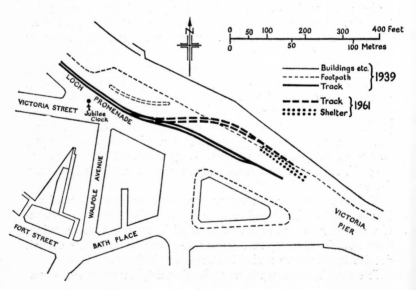

MBE, opened the 1960 service. By late summer, plans were published for the new bus and tramway terminal associated with the new Sea Terminal buildings at Victoria Pier, replacing the triangular building of 1890. In September, the Municipal Passenger Transport Association visited Douglas, and the season's profit duly emerged as £2,785, with earnings of 82.233d/mile against costs of 74.06d.

In February 1961, Tynwald was asked to approve new fares of 8d and 4d to replace the previous 5d and 3d; the line was now regarded by some as a speciality ride. The opening for the year on Saturday 20 May was by Mr J. W. Fowler, chairman of the Light Railway Transport League, and included the new terminus, a subject of much favourable comment. Since then it has only been used at steamer times, which seems wrong to the outsider, for the other terminus at the Peveril crossover in a wide expanse of road is hardly suited to present-day road conditions; the explanation is a heavy toll levied by the Harbour Board.

Mr C. F. Wolsey, by now Britain's longest serving transport manager, retired in October 1961, after twenty-nine years' service. The corporation, recognising the unique experience of its own staff, appointed the two senior employees, Mr D. Halsall and Mr A. Hampton, as joint controllers, an unusual step adopted provisionally for one year but extended for five. Mr Halsall retired in 1966, leaving Mr Hampton in sole charge as controller, and now (1969) as manager.

Manx complacency in the face of the Fleetwood steamer closure (September 1961) was shattered when the drop in day excursionists came to be measured in 1962, with yet another wet summer as an additional burden. The year's passengers fell to 1,047,749, but higher fares of 9d and 6d gave a working profit of £3,000, though this was criticised as unduly rapacious. The year 1963 was somewhat happier, for the undertaking was graced by a visit from Her Majesty Queen Elizabeth, the Queen Mother, on Friday, 5 July, when car No 44 (beautifully turned out) served as royal car from Summer Hill to the Villa Marina, with senior driver Sam Caley and conductor Paul Gregson. A senior horse, Winston, hauled the car, and showed some reluctance to pass the normal stops!

During 1964, with the stud down to fifty-six, there was further local pressure to scrap the trams, rebuffed by a public opinion poll in August with results overwhelmingly in the horse cars' favour. Congestion occurs on the narrower parts of the promenade, especially north of Broadway, where parking on both sides of the road

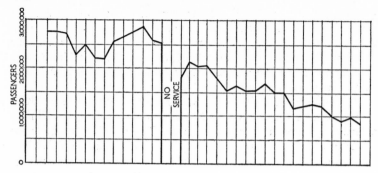

For 1966-9 the following were attained: 789,000, 924,000, 949,000 956,000

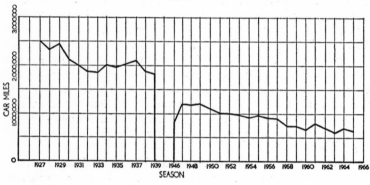

Douglas horse tramway traffic, 1927 to 1965

is common, and coach and taxi proprietors have feared the imposition of parking restrictions. In August and September hopes were raised of widening the central promenade's worst stretch, but were rejected by the finance committee and council in mid-October. Tra dy liooar . . .?

The good results in 1964 (when Bank holiday Monday saw twenty cars in service and takings of £654) led to new horse purchases early in 1965, bringing the stud from a winter forty-three up to fifty-eight The fifteen new horses were chosen by Councillor E. G. Griffin, a riding enthusiast, and arrived on Wednesday 14 April. Twenty-four more horses came early in 1966. Older tramway horses have a long retirement to look forward to, for the Home of Rest for old horses (started in 1950) received in 1955 a considerable bequest by Mrs E. M. Cubbon that allowed the purchase of a forty-four acre farm, Bulrhenny, and most tram horses go there.

On Tuesday, 6 July 1965, the line again enjoyed royal patronage, this time from Princess Margaret and Lord Snowdon. In September, the Press reported schemes for the redevelopment of Derby Castle, bought by the corporation for demolition in 1964. The project envisaged the removal of the cast-iron station awning, and although this was still intact in late 1969 new landscaped terminal arrangements are now planned. In June 1965 the corporation presented a Bill in Tynwald giving them control over fares; this was duly enacted, and the 1966 fares became 9d adult and 4d child for any distance.

To end with, an impression of the Derby Castle terminal is offered. Having been a departmental employee for a time in 1956, the scene from the open door of the adjoining conductors' paying-in room (occasionally invaded by a particularly sociable horse named after a senior fellow-employee), became a familiar one to the writer. Especially at night, the dimly-lit shed still affords the sights and sounds of the Victorian era, experiences of eye and ear now nowhere else to be enjoyed. Between turns, horses stand tethered to the roof pillars while crewmen sit on adjacent cars, as the sound of chilled iron wheels rolling in from the clanking traverser accompanies the clicking of released ratchet brakes. In the pay-in office, the traditional Bell Punch tickets stand in their cubicles while the duty clerks make up boxed sets with waybill, punch and leather bag for the crews. To an outsider, the exchange of native wit between the older hands on both sides of the counter was a never-to-be-forgotten experience, especially when heard after 11 pm . . .

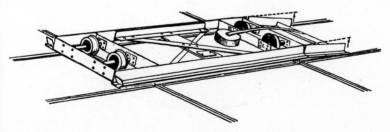

The smaller traverser at Derby Castle shed. The ramps are normally kept raised by the counterweight; this drawing shows the position as a horse car enters or leaves

The department's rule book, originally issued in 1912, still includes many unusual items—for instance the departmental telephone number of the veterinary surgeon—and particularly pleasing is the injunction to see that 'the lamps on the cars are lighted when darkness sets in'. The existence of passenger seats on the driver's platform calls for a rule ensuring that such riders do not come between the driver and his view ahead. The onus is on the driver to provide a whip and whistle of approved pattern, and fast driving on the last car home is forbidden. Among conductors' duties is the use of chamois for drying outside seats in wet and stormy weather, and traffic inspectors are required to see that wheel guards are lifted before the cars go on the traverser, which they would otherwise foul.

The byelaws incorporated in the rule book are basically familiar, passengers being forbidden to distribute handbills or other printed matter, play or perform on any musical instrument, beg or collect money, or sell or offer for sale any goods or merchandise. It would need an equestrian expert to describe the niceties of driving, in which the horse and driver work as an intuitive team, or to do justice to the splendidly-managed stables, and these subjects have been left aside. The stables are gladly shown to the interested student, but a prior appointment is a necessary courtesy.

I would like to take the opportunity here of acknowledging the friendship of the corporation staff, and their ready acceptance of the writer as a colleague when employed by the department in 1956. It is the writer's earnest hope to be able to pay equal tribute on the Tramway's centenary.

(above) *Electric line construction in hand at Porte e Vada, 1893. The horse-car shed at Burnt Mill Hill is visible beyond Strathallan Crescent;* (below) *No 3 on trial near the present Braeside, August 1893. Joshua Shaw stands, elbow on handwheel, while Frederick Saunderson occupies the front seat of the trailer*

Page 108

(above) *The 1893 terminus with car No 3. Note original sea wall in background. A wooden ticket office stands behind the car; (below) Derby Castle terminus early in 1895 with the theatre nearing completion in the background. The illustration on page 36 is a slightly later view taken after the demolition of the original Derby Castle gate and the erection of the horse-car terminus awning*

CHAPTER FOUR

The Horse-Tram Fleet

Fifty-one cars have been operated for varying periods on the Douglas horse tramway, and thirty-one of these remain to-day. The narrow gauge and consequent disparity between the width of the car body and the inset position of the wheel trunnions was successfully overcome by incorporating an inner sill with underseat cantilevers. In most other respects, the cars were typical of their period, and modifications over the year have not been such as to impair their historical value.

At the outset in 1876, Thomas Lightfoot ordered three tramcars from the firm which supplied horse cars to his native Sheffield. This was the Starbuck Car & Wagon Co Ltd of 227 Cleveland Street, Birkenhead, and this order marked the start of a long association between the Birkenhead works and the various tramways in the Isle of Man. George Starbuck, an American, had the honour of being the first tramcar builder in Britain (from 1860) and his venture became a limited company in 1872. In 1886 Starbuck was bought out by his secretary, George F. Milnes, who carried on the business at Birkenhead until 1902, latterly in association with German interests who opened a second and much larger works at Hadley, Shropshire, in 1900. G. F. Milnes & Co Ltd failed in 1904, but meanwhile Milnes' son, George Comer Milnes, established in 1902 a separate business at the other end of Cleveland Street, Birkenhead, in partnership with Thomas Voss to supply tramcar accessories and top covers. This concern, G. C. Milnes, Voss & Co, later built complete cars for Douglas tramways, until closure occurred in 1913.

By 1876, when the first cars were built for Douglas, horse-car

G

design combined constructional strength with lightness to a remarkable degree. Oak or ash was used for framing, with panelling in ⅜-in mahogany. George Starbuck at this time allowed a little over seventeen inches of seat per passenger, an inch more than in contemporary omnibuses, and structural refinements had brought body weight down to about 1.7 cwt per passenger. The wheelbase was usually 5 ft 6 in, with chilled iron wheels of 30-in diameter on 3-in axles. The cast trunnions contained plain-brassed axleboxes borne on egg-shaped rubber springs, two per box. Simple strap-hung brake beams were operated through a lever system, giving a theoretical mechanical advantage of about 72 : 1. The car body used its roof clerestory as a functional support for the outside knifeboard seat, but the less functional eye-window in the clerestory end was a survival from the period when fares were passed up to a driver who sat at roof level like a coachman.

No 1 *Starbuck Car & Wagon Co Ltd* 1876

Thomas Lightfoot's original order to Starbuck appears to have comprised two double-deck cars for summer use, and one single-deck saloon (No 1) to work the line in winter. It may well have been similar to the Starbuck one-horse single-deck cars built for Sheffield and other towns from 1874, of which one survives at Crich museum. These cars seated fourteen or sixteen, and cost about £190.

In the winter of 1884-5 one Douglas car was sent back to the maker 'to have outside seats and a staircase put to it', at a cost of £96. This can only have been No 1, since all the other cars are fully accounted for. It was still in stock in 1894, but had disappeared by the time the liquidator of the I O M T & E P compiled his full catalogue of the undertaking in 1901. The number remained vacant until 1913, and was then used for a new single-deck car described later.

Nos 2 *and* 3 *Starbuck Car & Wagon Co Ltd* 1876

The first cars to arrive in Douglas, on 1 August 1876, were the two double-deckers Nos 2 and 3. These were six-window double-deck cars with a top-deck knifeboard seat for sixteen persons, reached by a spiral stair of a primitive rung form that gave access to the centre of the canopy. Large advertisement boards served as screens for female feet and ankles; that ladies did ride on top is confirmed by the opening-day photographs. Platform access was possible from both sides, with the dash cut low on the off-side to allow for the overhang of the stair spiral. Internally, the slatted wood longitudinal seats, again for sixteen, had a patent leather curtain below their front edge and may also have had a carpet strip by way of upholstery. The delicately curving roof was of bent-wood sticks and matchboarding, still perpetuated in surviving later cars.

Later double-deck cars had a more convenient quarter-turn stair, and in 1884 Nos 2 and 3 were so altered to match cars bought new in 1883. One was in the corporation takeover ceremony on 2 January 1902, along with Nos 5 and 6. Under the corporation the capacity was re-rated as thirty-four, and by 1906 No 2 had been given an extra single seat on each platform, bringing the capacity to thirty-six. Associated with this was the addition of leathercloth screens (with a window panel) between the stairs and the bulkhead.

In 1934 the double-deck cars, including Nos 2 and 3, were among the first to be fitted with Hoffman roller bearings, as part of Mr Wolsey's reconstruction programme. The new trunnions by Maley & Taunton Ltd incorporated rubber and metallic springing. Both cars were used again in 1947 and 1948, but in the following winter both were tipped on their sides outside the shed and cut up : this (seen retrospectively) was one of the most unfortunate events in the line's history.

No 4 Starbuck Car & Wagon Co Ltd 1882

This car was the last to be ordered by Thomas Lightfoot. It was a double-decker, again seating thirty-two, but with more orthodox 90 degree closed-tread stairs giving corner access to the upper deck. The canopy was shorter, since the centre pillar of the archaic open spiral stair was no longer available to support it. The two-sided platform access facility was retained, and arch tops again lent elegance to the saloon windows. As new, the car lacked advertisement boards, but these were fitted later, probably in 1884. The seating capacity was later re-rated to thirty-four.

No 4's later career was similar to that of Nos 2 and 3; roller bearings were fitted in 1934, and the car survived until the winter of 1948-9, when it was withdrawn and broken up.

Nos 5 and 6 Starbuck Car & Wagon Co Ltd 1883

These two cars were ordered by Isle of Man Tramways Ltd and

entered service in March 1883. They were six-window double-deckers similar to No 4, with orthodox canopies and stairs, but had more box-like bodies with square-headed instead of arch-top windows. Two-sided access was provided on each platform, but by the nineteen-twenties the front nearside entrances under the stairs had been closed off by a small grille. Seating was for thirty-two, as before, but by 1906 this had been re-rated to eighteen outside and sixteen in, total thirty-four. Both cars were given roller bearings in 1934, and were broken up in 1949.

Nos 7 and 8 Starbuck Car & Wagon Co Ltd 1884

These were the last two new double-deckers bought for the bay tramway. The chairman described them as 'large cars for winter service' and it seems that for some years they maintained unaided the half-hourly winter operation. Much like their predecessors Nos 5 and 6, they had seven side windows and were thus slightly longer, seating thirty-six instead of thirty-two. They appear to have cost £260 each.

As built, Nos 7 and 8 had double-access platforms as on earlier cars, but between 1906 and 1912 the corporation closed off the front nearside entrances and fitted leathercloth screens with window panels between the stairs and bulkhead, and extended the dashes right up to the saloon corner pillar. Two seats were added on each platform in the enclosed space thus formed, and the upper deck seating was probably re-rated to twenty, bringing the total to forty-two. No 7 was withdrawn and broken up in 1924, but No 8 continued in service, being fitted with roller bearings in 1934. It was finally scrapped in 1949.

Nos 9 and 10 Starbuck Car & Wagon Co Ltd 1884

These two cars were the first of the open 'toastracks' to which the tramway owes much of its popularity. They seated thirty-two on eight cross-benches, very nearly equal to the capacity of the double-deckers but with a most useful saving in the tare weight.

Nos 9 and 10 were 22 ft 9 in over drawhooks, with a floor width of 5 ft 4 in and a total width over footboards of 6 ft 8 in. The seat spacing was generous, and the seats themselves had three centre slats within framed edges. A central iron leg supported each bench, and the pillars to each side carried the reversible backrest. Each dash was supported by eight tapered iron pillars, and curved iron arms connected the pillars of the end benches and supported iron lamp-boxes containing sprung carriage candles.

No 9 remained substantially unaltered until 1952, when it was withdrawn and broken up, but No 10 was lengthened in 1935 to 24 ft and fitted with ten narrower seats, bringing the capacity to forty, with Hoffman roller bearings, narrower platforms, and no

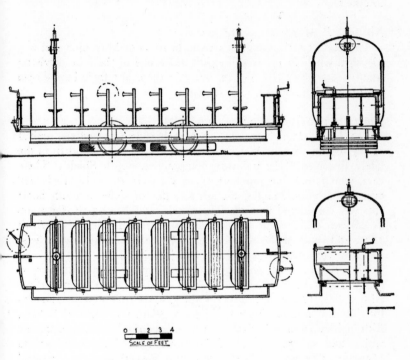

Douglas horse car of series 9-12 as in 1935

lamp arches. In 1963-4 it was given new end-posts for advertise-ment boards, and is now the oldest surviving car in the fleet, though much rebuilt.

No 11 Starbuck Car & Wagon Co Ltd/G. F. Milnes 1886

This was a further eight-bench open car, identical to Nos 9 and 10, and arrived in the latter part of 1886. It was ordered from the Starbuck company, then in liquidation, but in the absence of an arrival date and of maker's plates it is not possible to say whether the builder should correctly be quoted as Starbuck or his successor, G. F. Milnes. No 11 still exists as a thirty-two seat small 'toastrack', and is the oldest surviving car in generally original condition, the main alterations being roller bearings and (in 1963-4) new tall end-posts for advertisement boards, replacing the shortened originals.

No 12 G. F. Milnes & Co Ltd 1888

This eight-bench open car arrived in April or May 1888 and was identical with No 11. It still exists and is one of the four surviving small 'toastracks' (Nos 11, 12, 26, 31); these lost their lamp-boxes and supporting arches by about 1949.

Nos 13 to 18 Second-hand purchases 1887

The *Isle of Man Times* for 19 March 1887 reported the arrival of the first of six double-deck cars bought at second hand from the lately dissolved horse-tramway company at South Shields. These cars, which took the numbers 13 to 18, were the only 'used cars' ever bought for Douglas, though an offer of some ex-Leith horse cars was considered in 1906. The purchase of Nos 13-18 (for £500 4s 4d) was criticised at the company's general meeting of 28 April 1887, and some of the shareholders felt that the two directors who had inspected them were guilty of bad judgment.

The original South Shields tramway company opened its narrow-gauge line from the Pier Parade to Tyne Dock on 1 August 1883, with a fleet of six cars. Five of these were built new in 1883 by the Metropolitan Railway Carriage & Wagon Co Ltd of Saltley, Birmingham, and the sixth had been acquired from a company which had started to build a horse tramway from Ramsgate to Margate. The South Shields line also proved to be a financial failure, and was abandoned on 1 May 1886. Horse tramways were reintroduced in South Shields under other auspices in 1887, with new cars from the Ashbury Co, and ran until electrification in 1906.

Nos 13 to 18 were larger than the previous double-deckers, and were stated in 1887 to seat forty-two, presumably twenty in the saloon and twenty-two on the knifeboard. They were not necessarily identical, but photographic evidence of their years in Douglas is sparse. They differed from the Starbuck cars by having an extremely narrow floor, permitting the main sills to bear directly on to the wheel trunnions, seat width being gained by an acutely curved rocker panel. The bulkhead doors on some or all cars were slightly offset towards the entrance, and the roof sticks incorporated iron bracing. The ceiling between these was latterly lined with a Lincrusta type paper, and the perforated plywood seating in one survivor may also have been a later addition.

The later history of these cars is as complex as their origin. The corporation found a need for two additional single-deck saloons for winter use, and in 1903 decided to convert South Shields double-deck cars Nos 17 and 18 to single deck. No 17 was evidently dealt with first, and was rebuilt by 'removing the top deck and installing drop windows.' It cannot have been very satisfactory, as it was withdrawn by 1914 and replaced by a new car. A photograph of this vehicle as rebuilt has been rediscovered as this book goes to press—it now had five drop windows with arched tops, and platform seats for eight give a total seating capacity of twenty-eight.

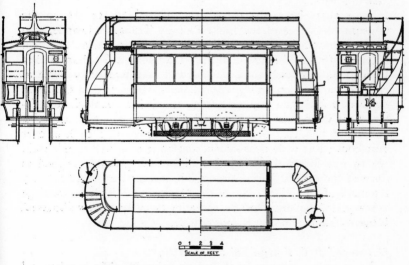

Douglas horse car 14 as now preserved

No 18 was rebuilt in a much more extensive way, which suggests that it may have originally have been the odd car of the six. It was described in 1906 as 'the first tram built (save for wheels and roof) in the island.' It now became an eight-window single-deck saloon, 23 ft 1 in over drawhooks, with a longer body and clerestory, square-headed windows, and centrally positioned bulkhead doors. Seating was now for twenty-eight, twenty in the saloon and four behind a half screen on each platform. Body width was 6 ft 4 in, underframe width 6 ft 1 in, and height 9 ft 5 in. Roller bearings were fitted in 1935, and the car still exists today.

In 1908, No 14 was wrecked by a fall of rock at the depot and was scrapped, No 13 being renumbered to take its place. No 16 was withdrawn and scrapped, for reasons unknown, in 1915. This left two identical South Shields double-deckers, Nos 14 (II) and 15, both of which were given Maley & Taunton running gear with Hoffman roller bearings in 1935. They were used for the last time in 1939, and No 15 was broken up at the depot in 1949. No 14, which had evidently spent the war stored at York Road and had never returned to Derby Castle, remained intact and thus became the last double-decker, being henceforth considered as a potential museum-piece.

Some years later, the corporation offered No 14 (II) to the museum committee of the Light Railway Transport League, who in turn persuaded the then British Transport Commission to accept it for the future Museum of British Transport at Clapham. It left Douglas on 3 March 1955, and arrived at a temporary home at Norwood in London on 19 April. Later it was stored at Charlton, but is now (1969) on display at Clapham. It is a double-deck knife-board car with seven elliptical-headed windows, quarter-turn stairs, and offset bulkhead doors; dimensions are 22 ft 6 in long over drawhooks, 6 ft wide over saloon, and 10 ft 8 in high to side rails. No 15 was identical, and similar dimensions probably applied to some of the others. During restoration, the car was found to carry remnants of a builder's plate of the Metropolitan Railway Carriage & Waggon Company. The official seating capacity, as now displayed, is twenty inside and twenty-four outside.

Nos 19 and 20 G. F Milnes & Co Ltd 1889

These were two more small 'toastracks', with eight benches and thirty-two seats, essentially the same as Nos 9 to 12. They were not rebuilt, and retained their arch lamps to the end, as did Nos 9, 25 and 30. Withdrawn from service in 1949, both were broken up in 1952.

Nos 21 and 22 G. F. Milnes & Co Ltd 1890

These eight-bench 'toastracks' were delivered in May or June 1890, and were used in the Queen's promenade opening procession of 8 July. In May 1908, No 22 was fitted with an unusual form of ridged canvas roof, with gear that allowed the canvas to be rolled back on fine days. It retains the same roof form today, but the roof canvases are now fixed, on light metal frames. Dimensions today are 22 ft 5 in long over drawhooks, 5 ft 5 in wide at floor level, 6 ft 10 in wide over footboards, and 9 ft 9 in high, and it has roller bearings.

No 21 remained in its original form until 1936, when it was rebuilt as a ten-bench 'long toastrack' seating forty, with roller bearings and a reduced seat spacing. The new dimensions were 24 ft 8 in long over footboards, with a floor width of 5 ft 4 in and an overall width of 6 ft 10½ in. It is still in use, and was given lengthened end-posts and advertisement boards in 1963-4.

Nos 23 to 26 G. F. Milnes & Co Ltd 1891

These four cars were again of the established eight-bench open 'toastrack' design, with minor detail variation in the design of the dashes and lamphouses. Nos 23 and 24 were converted to the same umbrella form of sunshade roof as No 22 (No 23 was done in 1908, No 24 a year or two later), but these two cars were broken up in 1952. Nos 25 and 26 remained unaltered, as thirty-two seat open 'toastracks'; No 25 was broken up in 1952, but No 26 still exists today, though not regularly used. It is 22 ft 8 in long over drawhooks, 5 ft 5 in wide at floor level, and 6 ft 11 in wide over footboards, and has roller bearings.

Nos 27 to 29 G. F. Milnes & Co Ltd 1892

In 1892 there arrived perhaps the most elegant of 'bay tramway' vehicles, Nos 27 to 29. These winter saloons, with a well-lit eight-window body, at once acquired the title Pullmans. Platform vestibules were added by 1895, which conveniently sheltered extra seats for six in all and brought the total (with the twenty-four inside) to thirty. As built, they had short dashes and a gap between dash and saloon on the non-boarding side, no doubt closed with a grille. Their saloon doors were offset as on the South Shields cars.

As with earlier cars, the sills of Nos 27-29 lie inboard of the side panels, with under-seat cantilevers. They have the traditional turtle-back roof of the typical horse tram, though in a special form. The portion outside the clerestory was no longer externally concave, since no superimposed walkway was involved as on knifeboard cars;

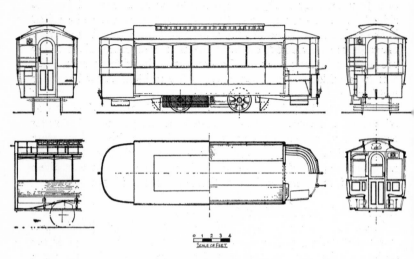

Douglas horse car of series 27-29 after addition of vestibules

instead, it is virtually straight, and steeply sloped to throw off water. Electric tramcars supplied to the island by the same builder in 1893 and 1894 have the same profile, with plain-arched vestibule roofs.

Nos 27-29 still exist today, and are used when the weather is unsuitable for the more open types of car; roller bearings were fitted in 1935-6. They are 24 ft 5 in long over drawhooks, 5 ft 10 in wide at floor level, 6 ft 6 in wide over the body, and 9 ft 2 in high. To the student of coachbuilding, they are much the most valuable cars in the fleet and much sought after by photographers.

Nos 30 and 31 G. F. Milnes & Co Ltd 1894

These were two more standard eight-bench open 'toastracks', and arrived in the spring of 1894. No 30 remained unaltered throughout its life, and was withdrawn about 1950 and broken up in 1952. No 31 still exists as a small 'toastrack', and was fitted with new end-posts for advertisement boards in 1963/4. It is 22 ft

6 in long over drawhooks, 5 ft 5 in wide at floor level, and 6 ft 10 in wide over footboards, and has roller bearings.

Nos 32 to 37 G. F. Milnes & Co Ltd 1896
These six cars were of a new type for Douglas, sunshade-type roofed 'toastracks' with delicately curved roof edge-boards. They seated thirty-two on eight cross-benches, and had broad slatted seat backs and elegant wooden seat-end panels, which latter had disappeared by the nineteen-twenties. Brass grab rails at the seat ends were another refinement, and they had lamphouses hung from

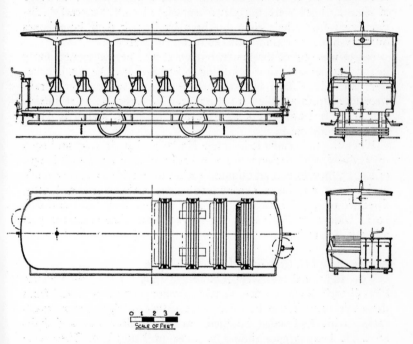

SCALE OF FEET

Douglas horse car of series 32-37 as built

the roof. Nos 32, 33, 34, and 37 still exist, less lamphouses, in this form, modified only as to roller bearings (1935-6) and simple bar seat backs (about 1950); they are 21 ft 8 in long over drawhooks, 5 ft 4 in wide at floor level, 6 ft 10 in wide over footboards, and 8 ft 7 in high to the crown of the roof.

In 1908 No 36 was rebuilt with glazed end bulkheads, extended platforms, and back-to-back seating at the ends, the capacity now becoming forty. It is 24 ft 11 in long, the other dimensions being as for 32-34 and 37. No 35 was given glazed bulkheads in 1966-7, but still seats thirty-two, as seats are only provided inside the bulkheads.

Nos 38 to 40 G. F. Milnes & Co Ltd 1902

These three cars were ordered by the corporation in March 1902, at £65 each (wheels and axles extra), and were among the last trams built at the original Birkenhead works, then on the verge of closure. They were thirty-two seat eight-bench 'toastracks', distinguished from their elder brethren by having their lamp-boxes hung from higher round-cornered rectangular arches.

No 39 was one of the first two open cars to be lengthened, early in 1934, at the same time acquiring roller bearings. The end benches were altered to fixed back-to-back seats, and seat-end grab rails were fitted from a cable car : it now carried forty. No 39 still exists and is 23 ft long, 5 ft 5 in wide at floor level, and 6 ft 11 in wide over footboards.

When the time came to lengthen Nos 38 and 40, in 1937 and 1939 respectively, the platforms were extended to give an overall length of 24 ft 5 in, and two additional benches were added with reversible backs. No 40 now has advertisement boards carried by tall end-posts, fitted in 1963-4. This car is 5 ft 4 in wide at floor level and 6 ft 10 in wide over footboards, for No 39 these dimensions are 5 ft 5 in and 6 ft 11 in.

Nos 41 and 42 G. C. Milnes, Voss & Co. 1905

Two additional cars were required in 1905 for the new Victoria Pier-Victoria Street service, to take steamer passengers to and from the cable cars. These two cars were orthodox eight-bench 'toastracks', with knife-edge boarded seats for thirty-two, and half-rectangle lamp arches similar to those of Nos 38-40. They were ordered on 12 July 1905 at a cost of £63 each, and arrived only four weeks later, on 9 August. No 41 was lengthened to 23 ft 3 in early in 1934, with back-to-back end benches and grab rails, but retained its original knife-edge seats elsewhere; the width is 5 ft 6 in at floor level and 7 ft 1 in over footboards. No 42 was lengthened in 1938, with completely new slatted benches and modified dashes, and now has extended end-pillars for advertisement boards; it is

24 ft 8 in long over drawhooks, 5 ft 5 in wide at floor level, and 7 ft 0 in wide over footboards. Both cars have roller bearings. These two cars are the highest-numbered of today's forty-seat 'long toast-racks', all later open cars being built with roofs.

Nos 43 and 44 United Electric Car Co Ltd 1907

These came from what is now the Preston works of the English Electric Co, and cost £174 each. They were of a new design for Douglas, with back-to-back seats at the two-window bulkheads and six reversible benches intermediately, seating forty in all. As built, they had sprung canvas roller blinds; these and the lamp-boxes have since been removed, but the cars are otherwise as built, including the knife-edge seats, though they now run on roller bearings. They are 24 ft 6 in long, 5 ft 5 in wide at floor level, 6 ft 11 in wide overall, and 8 ft 10 in high. All the seats have grab rails, and No 44 served as the royal car in July 1963, from which it retains the roof boards and insignia. A plate on the car commemorates the occasion.

No 45 G. C. Milnes, Voss & Co Ltd 1908

This roofed 'toastrack' car arrived on 14 June 1908 and was a virtual replica of Nos 43 and 44, save for a square-ended roof canopy and different eaves-board styling. It seats forty on broad-slatted seats and is 25 ft 0 in long, 5 ft 6 in wide at floor level, 7 ft 0 in wide overall, and 8 ft 6 in high.

No 46 G. C. Milnes, Voss & Co Ltd 1909

No 46 arrived from Birkenhead on 14 May 1909, and displays many detail differences from No 45, although both were obviously modelled on the U E C cars of 1907. Seating is for forty, distributed as for No 45, with the same roof styling but with three-window bulkheads. Grab rails are fitted to the end benches only. The car is 24 ft 11 in long, 5 ft 5in wide at floor level, 6 ft 11 in wide overall, and 8 ft 11 in high. It retains its original knife-edge boarded seating.

No 47 G. C. Milnes, Voss & Co Ltd 1911

This car arrived in March 1911, accompanied by the last new cable car, No 67. It was outwardly akin to Nos 45 and 46, but had a steel underframe and canvas roller blinds, and cost £185. No 47 seats forty passengers on knife-edge boarded seating, with grab rails to all seats, and has a three-window bulkhead and a different form of eaves-board scalloping. The blinds and lamp-boxes have been removed over the years. Dimensions are : length 25 ft 1 in over drawhooks, width 5 ft 5 in at floor level and 7 ft 0 in overall, and height 8 ft 9 in.

No 1 (II) G. C. Milnes, Voss & Co Ltd 1913

This single-deck saloon car was obtained in 1913 at a cost of £252 3s 6d to replace the ex-South Shields single-decker No 17 (the minutes say No 11, but this is an obvious misprint). Like No 47, it has a steel underframe. The general styling was that of a contemporary electric car, with centrally placed bulkhead doors, but with slender window pillars : it seats eighteen, plus six on the platforms. It is unaltered save for the Maley & Taunton running gear with roller bearings, fitted about 1934. It is 24 ft 8 in long, 6 ft 4½ in wide at floor level, 6 ft 7 in wide overall, and 9 ft 11 in high, and was one of the last tramcars built by Milnes, Voss before they closed later in the same year.

Nos 48 to 50 Vulcan Motor and Engineering Co Ltd 1935

These cars are of a special convertible all-weather design devised by Mr C. F. Wolsey, and cost £505 each. They are covered 'toastracks' with thirty-four seats (three at each end and four each on seven benches), but in bad weather could be altered to twenty-seven-seat saloons by drawing folding screens along each side and folding away the end seat of each bench to form a side gangway. Two similar motor-bus bodies were obtained at the same time but these were withdrawn some years ago.

Nos 48 and 50 are on steel underframes, and have had roller bearings throughout their lives. They are 25 ft 6 in long, 5 ft 7 in wide at floor level, 6 ft 11 in wide over footboards, and 8 ft 6 in high. The capacity originally quoted was forty, but this included outward end seats which are no longer in use. The only structural modification was the fitting of larger diameter wheels early in their career, which required the cutting of wheel arches in the otherwise level floor. They now (1969) rank as closed cars as the side screens are kept closed.

Certain general features of the horse-car fleet remain to be mentioned. Ratchet brakes were fitted to only two cars before 1914 (probably those built by UEC) but the remainder received them after 1918. Foot gongs were fitted to all cars in 1908, and lifeguards and side wheelguards were fitted by 1910, after trials with different

Horse-car fleet summary, 1969

Type	Fleet numbers	Seats	Total
Small 'toastracks'	11, 12, 26, 31	32	4
Large 'toastracks'	10, 21, 38, 39, 40, 41, 42	40	7
Sunshades	22, 32, 33, 34, 37	32	5
Bulkheads	35, 36, 43, 44, 45, 46, 47	40*	7
Winter saloons	1, 18, 27, 28, 29	30	5
All-weather cars	48, 49, 50	27/34	3
			31

* Car No 35 seats only 32

types, including torpedo and cowcatcher varieties tried on a double-decker. All cars had acquired Maley & Taunton roller-bearings axleboxes by 1956, but most dates of conversion are not known; the trunnions from the withdrawn double-deckers were probably used after 1950 to equip the remaining cars not yet fitted. The single-deck saloons had seat cushions, as did certain double-deckers, but the others had carpet strips.

The first four cars did not have built-in lamphouses, and internal lighting was probably by portable boxes containing oil lamps. From 1883, new double-deck cars, saloons and roofed 'toastracks' had built-in bulkhead lamp-boxes with oil lamps, and all the open cars had carriage candle 'lamps' in lamp-boxes carried on a curved iron arch connecting the pillars of the end benches. As elsewhere, acetylene lighting was tried early in 1908 on the open cable cars, and was adopted generally on these cars from 1920, but was not used for the horse cars.

Low-intensity electric lighting, from batteries, was first tried in 1927, and was adopted generally from 1933. Side lights of commercial vehicle type were fitted to the roofs of some roofed 'toast-rack' cars, and were carried by tall end-posts on many of the 'toast-racks', which now lost their arches, though some acquired ornamental ironwork substitutes carrying destination notices. Since 1960 these have been replaced by low-level sidelights carried at the height of the sills to conform with new vehicle lighting regulations. There are no other electrical fittings such as bells, communication between conductor and driver (or horse) being by whistle.

The original livery of the 1876 horse cars is not recorded, but it was very likely the same as that of Lightfoot's successor company of 1882. This featured dark blue stage-coach style waist panels, lined in lemon chrome, above cream rocker panels lined in red. The dashes were red, as were the corner pillars, and bore heavily shaded numerals. The first cars carried the words 'Douglas Bay Tramway' above the saloon windows, and transfer crest (details unknown) occupied the centre of the waist panel. The new company relettered the cars with the company title (Isle of Man Tramways Limited) above the windows, the words 'Douglas Bay Tramways' now appearing in larger letters on the rocker panel.

The first open cars were finished mainly in brown, but had red dashes as on the other cars. After takeover by Isle of Man Tramways & Electric Power Co in 1894, the livery of the cable cars resembled that of some present-day Manx Electric vehicles with red or teak waist panels above ivory or white rocker panels, but the closed horse cars were in a lighter paint-style, with white rocker panels below what appear to be cream or yellow waist panels. The 'toast-racks' had brown posts and cream or white seat-end panels (on Nos 31-37), and all cars had red dashes.

After 1902, the corporation's title replaced that of the company, being displayed on the rocker panels of the closed horse cars and on the underframes of the cable cars and open horse cars. By 1914, the saloon horse cars had become cream overall, save for the red dashes, with elaborate lining out. The open horse cars acquired white posts instead of brown. After 1960, simpler repaints with Gill Sans lettering began to appear. In 1951, cars Nos 45 and 46 were given a special Festival of Britain repaint with geometric patterns in red, white and blue and a full-width Union Jack on the roof, flanked by the Three Legs of Man. Some open cars later received fairground-style patterns along the footboards.

Car roofs are normally grey, and a dark maroon/brown is used for floor edges, seats, etc. On the open cars, if space permits, the corporation title is carried in red-brown on a yellow ochre ground, and this same yellow colour is used for the eaves-boards. Only within the past ten years has the title on the cars been changed from Douglas Corporation Tramways to Douglas Corporation Transport.

Advertising has been carried in various forms on the Douglas horse cars from the start in 1876. The open 'toastracks' were immune at first, but from about 1893 they carried posters on the two

Page 125

(above) *The inaugural Douglas—Laxey train at Groudle, 28 July 1894; (below) Laxey station, 1894. To the left is the site of the future depot; beyond the tracks lay the Rencell Road cutting, bridged in 1895-6*

Page 126

*Derby Castle depot,
the 1893 power st
and car shed and an
trailer on new sidir
the right; (b
Groudle, summer
with a 10-13 serie*

portions of the dashes on either side of the car number, and the iron arches supporting the lamps were fitted with curved boards carrying painted advertisements, often for Falcon Cliff. Advertising flags were also carried on the open cars at this period.

By the end of the century, the double-deck cars boasted a remarkable 'advertising' livery. The side panel carried an extensive multi-coloured description of the beauties along the electric tramway and the Snaefell line, introduced by the words 'The Douglas, Laxey, Snaefell Mountain and Ramsey Electric Tramway —places to visit' on a narrow panel above the windows. The corresponding end-panels announced 'Reckitts Blue' and 'Zebra Grate Polish', and the stair kick-plates 'Sunlight' and 'Lifebuoy' soaps, whilst the upper-deck decency panels were used for paste-on announcements. The covered 'toastrack' cars on the horse and cable lines carried a roof-top board with a similar lengthy announcement about the electric lines. Advertising, usually for the electric line, also occupied the wooden boards that filled the space between the footboard and the car floor on the 'toastracks'.

Under corporation ownership, advertising continued and gradually increased, especially for 'Jacobs Biscuits', a familiar client for some fifty years. The trend diminished again after about 1950, but since 1964 the spaces have been re-let and the open cars have acquired shaped wooden advertisement boards carried between end-posts. Small clip-on boards on the dashes, which had latterly been used mainly for fare and destination boards, were discontinued from 1960 to 1965, but were revived in 1966, the wording being 'Promenades and Derby Castle'. In 1965, a 'toastrack' car was fitted with hoardings and ran as the 'Daily Mirror' tram but its intended 1966 reappearance was cancelled because of the seamen's strike, and it ran with Tourist Board announcements instead.

Finally, the details of horse cars 43, 44, 46 and 47 may be taken as representative of the styling of their cable contemporaries 69, 70, 68 and 67, otherwise unrecorded.

H

CHAPTER FIVE

The Coast Electric Tramway

'. . . the Isle of Man has been seized by the epidemic of progress, and its people have gotten an electric railway . . .' *Street Railway Journal*, May 1894

An obituary of Frederick Saunderson, published in 1911, included the words: 'Then came the great boom year of 1887, on the strength of which Mr Alexander Bruce, manager of Dumbell's Bank, and other men of more or less standing, including several Keys, launched several big ventures. Mr Saunderson was swept into the vortex, and again came out as Civil Engineer'.

Saunderson was born in 1841 in the city of Armagh, and his early adult life was spent in railway construction engineering in Ireland. About 1865 he arrived in the Isle of Man, where he had family ties with the Rowe family, closely connected with the Castletown lead mines. Later he worked as assistant to Alured Dumbell, then High Bailiff of Ramsey, and by the late 'eighties was engaged in real estate promotion, ie, the South Ramsey Estate of circa 1886. He also designed some waterworks schemes, but his enduring monument is the electric tramway running north from Douglas.

The contorted geology of the clay slates of the northern part of the island had led to the formation of a jagged coastline from which deep ravine-like valleys run inland, chiefly east-west. This difficult terrain had deterred earlier promoters, but by the early 1890s fairly practical surveys had been made, though still involving heavy gradients for a steam line (see Appendix 7). Now, however,

Alexander Bruce evolved his own similar project and, unlike the others, had access to both the technical expertise—with electric traction—and the finance to give it reality.

In Onchan parish, just north of Douglas, lay the considerable estate of Howstrake, mostly rough grazing, with a summit level on Banks Howe of 427 ft. Bruce and his associates saw in this rolling landscape a field for estate development on the grand scale, and resolved to lay out part as pleasure grounds and other parts for housing. In September 1889, Bruce and Saunderson made a provisional agreement to buy part of the Howstrake estate from the trustee, John Travis, and the three members of the Callow family concerned. This was found initially to infringe the trust deed, and an Act of Tynwald had to be obtained (in 1892) to authorise it.

The plan filed with the 1889 agreement shows that the intention was to give access to the new property by building a road along the coast. The first scheme included a severe gradient cut through the steep brow beyond Port e Vada, but a later section shows an incline with successive gradients of 1 in 50, 1 in 30 and 1 in 25, beginning 655 ft from the end of the Strathallan Crescent promenade, obtained by building a level sea wall across Port e Vada creek and superimposing an embankment with stone-faced slopes, thus forming a reclaimed site of which part was used in 1895 by the Derby Castle company for a variety theatre. The road next passed over the edge of the Hague estate before passing on to Howstrake lands. The first part of the road took in the strip of land which the town commissioners had given to the Derby Castle company in 1888.

The scheme for the area beyond Port Jack is shown in a plan of 4 August 1891 for a 'Proposed New Road from Derby Castle Gate to Onchan Harbour'. It bears the name of Alfred Jones Lusty, a London merchant of immense wealth who was a financial backer for Saunderson and others, and who resided for a time at the old Howstrake mansion, a house of Tudor date. A significant later amendment to the scheme altered the gradient to a continuous 1 in 24.

The powers required were granted in the Howstrake Estate Act of 22 March 1892. This not only legalised all the above features of the Howstrake project, but also included tramway provisions. On the entire Howstrake estate, along any roads (new or existing) over thirty-six feet wide, the grantee (Saunderson) could construct a single or double line of tramway and work it by means of animal, steam, electric or other power. The free conditional use of parts of the Hague estate was permitted, and one such plot was made over to Saunderson '. . . for the erection of electric plant and machinery, such electric plant and machinery to be worked with approved smoke consumers'. The original depot and power station also occupied some former sea bed; later, car sheds were built partly on land leased from the Hague estate, which added to the complications of Derby Castle depot's land titles. There was also the protective clause in favour of Isle of Man Tramways Limited described in Chapter 1, and all the work was to be completed within three years of the Act's promulgation on 5 July 1892.

The gauge of the tramways was specified as three feet. An overhang of twenty-one inches outside the wheel faces was permitted and, perhaps with street tramway construction in mind, the track was to be laid so that the upper surface was level with the road. A public road crossing was permitted at Onchan harbour. Clauses like those of the bay tramway Act granted exclusive use of the track and perpetuated the anomaly of red leading and green rear lights. From 30 September to the Saturday before Whit week the grantee was to run not less than six cars daily, and from Saturday before Whit week to 30 September the grantee was to run not less than one car every hour. This clause was inserted at the insistence of the Derby Castle company.

Reading the Act suggests that Saunderson alone was concerned, but the real entrepreneurs were Bruce and Lusty and their associates. Alexander Bruce, born in Banff, Scotland, on 21 March 1843, had served an apprenticeship with the City of Glasgow bank, and then came to a Douglas subsidiary, the Bank of Mona. When the Glasgow bank failed in 1878, he became general manager of Dumbell's Banking Company, an insular concern already secretly on the brink of insolvency. Bruce, a man of powerful character with a particularly captivating magic of personality all his own, took all this in his stride; he kept Dumbell's under full sail, hopefully seeing in expansion a cure for its ills, and almost succeeded. The schemes we are describing were only a part of his endeavours, and by 1892-3 he was also town treasurer of Douglas and a JP.

Bruce had already sought advice on electric tramways, and had been referred to Dr Edward Hopkinson. Born in May 1859, Hopkinson in 1882 became assistant to Sir William Siemens. In 1884 he joined Mather & Platt, of the Salford Ironworks, became a partner in 1887, then managing director and by 1899 was vice-chairman. He was also vice-chairman of the Chloride Electrical Storage Syndicate. Sir William Mather had obtained in 1883 the British rights for the Edison dynamo, and Edward's brother, Dr John Hopkinson, had evolved from this the Edison-Hopkinson dynamo, predecessor of the Manchester dynamo which Mather & Platt began to manufacture. Meanwhile, Edward gained traction experience first with Siemens at Portrush, then, after joining Mather & Platt, at Bessbrook and on the City and South London Railway.

With the Act passed, the promoters formed themselves into the Douglas Bay Estate Limited, registered on 10 September 1892 with a capital of £50,000. The stated objects included the acquisition of Saunderson's rights and the Howstrake estate, the construction of tramways and public roads, and the erection of electric plant. Construction began at once of the stone embankment across Port e Vada creek, and beyond this a roadway was built corresponding to the section reproduced but with only a single tram track.

Beyond Onchan harbour, the new road ran roughly parallel to the coast to the northern boundary of the estate at Groudle Lane. Beyond here was another potential attraction, the Groudle river's glen, and with the co-operation of the lessee, R. M. Broadbent, further land was added to the Douglas Bay estate to extend the road and tramway to a point opposite Broadbent's intended new Groudle hotel. Broadbent also owned Bibaloe farm to the north of this, and during the next four years other land purchases widened the boundaries of the property owned by the 1896 'Douglas Bay Estate & Groudle Glen Limited' to those shown on our map.

By 1892, Bruce had privately resolved that the Howstrake tramway should be the testing ground for a more ambitious project, an electric tramway northward to Laxey. By early 1893 Saunderson had prepared a survey carrying a single line and loop tramway beyond Groudle to a point at Baldromma-Beg, the intended new limit of the Howstrake lands, and this location east of the Liverpool Arms hotel on the main Lonan-Laxey road was the start of the intended future continuation to Laxey. The plan was then made public by the creation of another new company, the Douglas & Laxey Coast Electric Tramway Company, registered on 7 March 1893 with an authorised capital of £50,000, to acquire and construct tramways between Douglas and Laxey and subsequently to operate them.

The capital for the tramway to Laxey actually came from the Howstrake company, and the subscribers were thus largely the

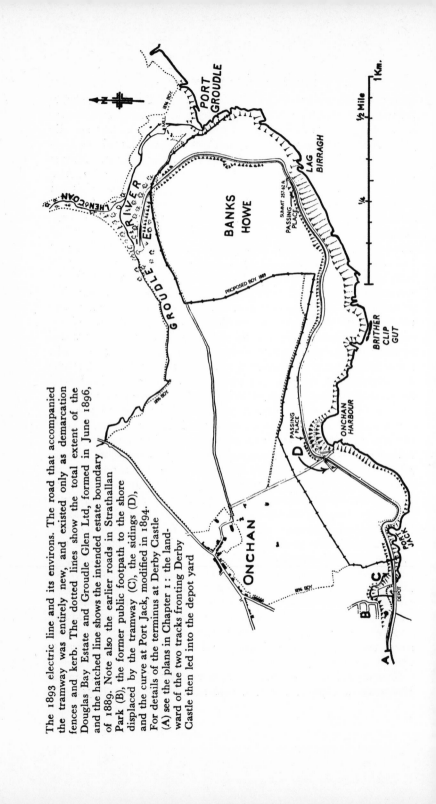

The 1893 electric line and its environs. The road that accompanied the tramway was entirely new, and existed only as demarcation fences and kerb. The dotted lines show the total extent of the Douglas Bay Estate and Groudle Glen Ltd, formed in June 1896, and the hatched line shows the intended estate boundary of 1889. Note also the earlier roads in Strathallan Park (B), the former public footpath to the shore displaced by the tramway (C), the sidings (D), and the curve at Port Jack, modified in 1894. For details of the terminus at Derby Castle (A) see the plans in Chapter 11: the landward of the two tracks fronting Derby Castle then led into the depot yard

same. The signatories were Alfred Jones Lusty, Alexander Bruce, Frederick Saunderson, F. G. Callow (advocate, of Douglas), Richard Evans of Barry, Glamorgan (general manager of the Barry Railway), Frederick Vaughan (a solicitor, of Cardiff) and Edward Franklin, a colliery proprietor of Radyr, Glamorgan. The three Welshmen were evidently brought in by Lusty, who himself hailed from South Wales. To build beyond Baldromma-Beg required a further Act of Tynwald with powers of compulsory purchase, and as a first step Saunderson prepared a plan and section for the complete Douglas-Laxey tramway, now intended as a double line on reserved track throughout. This plan survives in the Manx museum.

At this time, March 1893, the interim single-line tramway to Groudle Glen was already being built. On 15 May the Press reported the arrival of rails, concurrent with the erection of the power station and car sheds and the formation of the new roadway. The single line was laid on the alignment of the outer (seaward) of the future twin tracks, with most of the poles in their intended central position but with single bracket arms. The roadway was not given much attention at this stage, apart from a line of stones dividing it from the reserved track of the tramway. The layout is shown on the accompanying plan, based on a minutely exact section survey by Saunderson dated 16 August 1893. The sidings at Onchan are known only in terms of site area and position. The 1892 scheme had also intended a rather extraordinary layout for Derby Castle's depot, complete with a row of terraced houses, but the only actual deviation from 1894's future alignment was around the site of the Douglas Bay hotel at Port Jack.

Mr G. A. Ring, the new Bill's petitioner, appeared before Tynwald Court on 14 April 1893. Some members of the court thought that the Howstrake line was only being built to Groudle, and wished to stipulate that the line must be a continuous one from Douglas to Laxey. After personal assurances by Saunderson, the court carried the necessary motion and the Bill was then taken up in the Keys, after £600 had been deposited with Dumbell's Banking Company. Saunderson's evidence in the Keys revealed that he originally wanted permission for gradients as steep as 1 in 12. James Walker, engineer to the Harbour Commissioners, had walked over the ground and agreed professionally with the line as proposed. The company sought exemption from any obligation to carry goods, but members saw that the new line would mean the end of any steam railway proposals, and after necessary concessions by the company the Bill was passed by the Keys on Friday, 21 April.

In the Legislative Council, the Bill passed its first reading, and a petition by the rival Manx East Coast Railway Company was not granted a hearing. The council wanted compulsory obligation to carry goods, a lower maximum fare, a minimum year-round service, and official inspection. Saunderson now offered fares over the whole distance of 1s single and 1s 6d return, with one daily journey in each direction and up to ten tons of goods per day. Whilst being questioned about fares, Saunderson stated 'We have no third-class carriages. All our carriages will be first class' (laughter). 'They will be exceedingly well got up'. A further question elicited the fact that the Douglas Bay estate was to build the line and hand it over to the Douglas and Laxey Coast company in exchange for £50,000 in shares and debentures.

The council met again on 28 April, and passed the Bill, having first ensured that the fare was lowered to 2d a mile (with a 3d minimum), that luggage was to be charged at a lower rate than first proposed and that reasonable provision should be made for goods. Two weekday journeys had to be operated throughout the year. The wish for steeper gradients had arisen from plans for a branch to Onchan, where 1 in 15 might be encountered. The governor thought this risky— '. . . I do not want to kill my neighbours'—but had agreed to a form allowing of future consultation. Post Office clauses were inserted in May after the Bill had left the council, and the Keys' acceptance on 10 May was followed by its being sent off for the Royal Assent. On 15 May the *Isle of Man Times* described the work as 'the greatest local improvement'.

The resulting Douglas & Laxey Electric Tramway Act 1893 was promulgated on 17 November. Where necessary, it supplanted the Howstrake Act, and once the Howstrake tramway was completed and acquired, the new company could purchase land compulsorily from Baldromma-Beg northwards to Laxey; two years were allowed for completion. The maximum gradient was fixed at 1 in 20, and curvature at a minimum radius of 90 ft. Speed adjoining highroads was to be limited to 8 mph, and roadside sections did not need to be fenced unless lower than the adjoining road, though a stone kerb could be laid if desired. Crossings of public roads were to be laid level with their surface, and were subject to a speed restriction of 6 mph. Motive power was to be animal or electric only, though steam or other forms could be used if the Highway Board gave permission in writing. The Act specified a compulsory government inspection of the tramway prior to its public use. The company could charge up to 2d a mile with a first minimum of 3d, the tolls to be shown in the car, and each passenger was allowed 28 lb of luggage free. Goods and mails were to be carried, the freight charges were 3d a mile for each 28 lb or part thereof.

By the end of May 1893, work was well advanced on the new generating station and car shed. The site selected by Saunderson was the erstwhile floor of Port e Vada creek. As Dr Farrell later put it, 'There is no such creek. There was two years ago. In yonder cave, boys undressed to bathe in this charming little creek; there is no trace of it now. The creek was in the way of modern progress, and modern progress, like necessity, knew no law . . .'

The floor of the creek was filled to form a level site behind the new seaward embankment, on which three buildings were erected in a common block. To house the cars, a three-track, corrugated-iron depot was erected, 112 ft long, 30 ft 3 in wide and 17 ft 6 in high, with space for nine cars and pits for six. Next to this was an overhaul workshop, measuring 62 ft by 13 ft. Beyond this was a stone-built engine house, 60 ft by 37 ft, with an iron roof (height 23 ft), and next to it there was a boiler house of similar construction, 49 ft by 42 ft with a height of 19 ft 6 in; one wall was of wood to allow for extensions. Water for the boilers came from two streams which fed an underground storage tank. A 60 ft 5 ft diameter chimney completed the building.

Steam was supplied by a pair of Galloway's boilers (a variant of the Lancashire type), each 20 ft long and 6 ft in diameter, with a pressure of 120 lb/in^2, and with a dual installation of feed pump and injectors. All steam piping was of cast iron and in duplicate. The boilers supplied two 90-hp Galloway vertical compound engines of marine design, with 10 in high pressure and 20 in low pressure cylinders, 18 in stroke, running at 150 rpm. From the 9-ft diameter engine flywheels, link leather belts drove two Mather & Platt 'Manchester' type dynamos at 700 rpm, giving an output of 100 amps at 500 volts. Each dynamo had a Kelvin electrostatic voltmeter and amperemeter, and the wiring was such that either the switchboard or the actual overhead line could be connected. A subsidiary switchboard was interposed between the rails and the earth plates to measure the 'earth currents'. The switchgear was also by Mather & Platt, and was of an archaic type with lead fuses instead of circuit breakers; this was destined to be replaced in 1898 by a new installation. For the two miles between Douglas and Groudle, the overhead itself was sufficient to distribute the traction current.

Track consisted of 56 lb/yd rails spiked by 4½-in dog spikes to uncreosoted scotch fir and larch sleepers measuring only 6 ft by 7 in by 3½ in, with earth ballast. Fang bolts were inserted at the joints and at the middle of each rail, but these were later replaced by hardwood chairs screwed down to the sleepers; on the curves these were on the outside of the rails. The tapered poles had ornamental collars (long since removed) and were 20 ft high from the ground, the depth below ground being 5 ft. Normal poles were

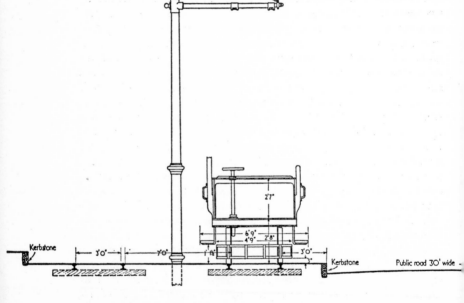

Cross-section of road and tramway by Saunderson (right-hand footpath omitted)

6 in in diameter at ground level and 3 in at the finial, but a heavier type was used where necessary, 7 in at ground level and 4 in at the finial.

On 4 July 1893 the new hotel at Groudle received its licence, and was opened the following day, although the metalling of the new roadway was incomplete. Groudle Glen and the Lhen Coan, with Broadbent's addition of rustic paths and bridges, became just the kind of primaeval public park in which the contemporary visitor delighted. The 5 August advertisement of Groudle's opening hopefully included 'approached by and at the terminus of the New Electric Tramway', though the trams were not yet running. On 8 August the Press reported that the cars had now arrived and that the 2½-mile track was in every way complete, but by the 15th current collection troubles were still holding back the opening.

The difficulty lay in the method of current collection. The wiring was direct suspended at the cross arms, and drooped between them. At each end of the car was one of Dr John Hopkinson's fixed collector bows, intended to leave the wire at each supporting pole while that at the opposite end of the car was in contact with the sagging conductor wire. Difficulties continued until as late as 26 August; how the engineers' efforts were viewed by the hundreds of visitors now promenading the new road is not recorded. On 26 August a car got through to Groudle with Dr Edward

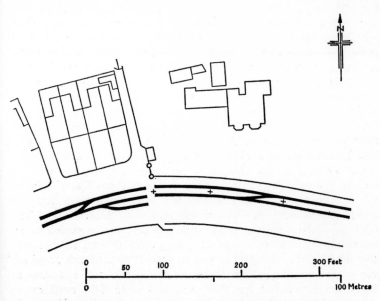

The all-but-end-on-junction between horse and electric tramways crested at Derby Castle in 1894, when the electric line (right) was doubled

Hopkinson, Frederick Saunderson and others aboard, and on Monday, 28 August, more test cars were run, apparently carrying the public. Regular public service commenced on Thursday, 7 September, and lasted for nineteen days. Since Sunday running was unlikely, this saw closure as on Thursday, 28 September, and a reference to the line having closed for the winter appeared in the Press on 30 September, with editorial regrets that no service was to be provided even on Tuesday half-days. Over 20,000 passengers had been carried, at the 3d minimum fare, with 1,689 car (train) miles and earnings of 35.36d per car mile.

Among Mather & Platt's men on site during the trials was a young man of great promise, Joshua Shaw. He was appointed to the I O M T & E P staff in 1894, when only twenty-two, became manager in 1899, and stayed in the island until early 1902, when he became resident electrical engineer to the Mersey Railway and in 1908 general manager and engineer. Although he retired in 1938, he continued on the Mersey Railway board until nationalisation in 1948. He died, in his ninetieth year, early in 1962.

Construction was resumed in February 1894. First, the line to Groudle was doubled, using the single track as a construction line and adding a further track on the side remote from the road, while contractor Mark Carine built the substantial Groudle viaduct of three 20-ft spans and a culvert over the Lhen Coan. A large rustic station, 47 ft 6 in by 12 ft, was added at Groudle a year or two later. By April, it was expected that the double line as far as Groudle would be completed a week before Whitsun. From Groudle to Baldromma-Beg, the contract specification required a single line on a 19-ft formation adjoining a 21-ft roadway to be completed by 1 May 1894. This was a construction line, to be used by Douglas Bay Estate from 12 May in carrying the line northward.

On completion, the Howstrake tramway and its plant were to become the property of the Douglas & Laxey Coast Electric Tramway Company, and the tramway was transferred by a £38,000 agreement between the two parties dated 30 March 1894. The land remained with the estate company and was regarded as an easement, recorded in a deed of 9 July 1895. Beyond Baldromma-Beg, Douglas Bay Estate Ltd was to hand over the lands acquired, the completed tramway thereon, all the plant, and a station at Laxey on which not less than £1,000 was to have been spent; this transfer was made by a deed of June 1896. The Howstrake company was also to lay out the fifty-acre Howstrake Park and hand it over to the tramway, but this was bought back by the Douglas Bay Estate & Groudle Glen Ltd in June 1896. It is now the site of Howstrake Holiday Camp.

The Groudle line reopened on Whit Saturday, 12 May 1894, after successful trials on the Thursday, and by July was carrying 78,000 passengers a week. Three cars were used, and these were fitted with a new and more successful type of bow, as shown in the photographs. Dr Edward Hopkinson had patented the springing now applied to his brother's original rigid design, the effect being that the bow now had a greater height-range and flexibility, though it still left the wire at each supporting pole. Construction continued apace beyond Baldromma-Beg, still by the Douglas Bay Estate Company, and the governor for the first time sought the assistance of the mainland Board of Trade in appointing an inspector. In practice, two inspectors were necessary, one for the civil engineering aspects and one for the electrical, and Colonel Rich and Major Cardew visited the new line on 27 July and reported next day.

Colonel Rich, lately senior inspector of railways at the Board of Trade, implied satisfaction, though at facing points at the termini he sought to have pointsmen equipped with flags and (at night) lamps. He also wanted protective guards at either side of the road crossings, together with notices warning against the danger of touching the overhead wires. All these requirements Bruce and Saunderson undertook to fulfil.

Major Cardew reported at much greater length. He acknowledged Dr Hopkinson's (and Mather & Platt's) foremost position in this field and dwelt on the arduous duty placed on the electrical equipment. The battery house at Groudle was fully described as were the storage cells themselves—unfortunately his description of the cars' control gear was more ambiguous—and he thought highly of the modified Hopkinson bows. His chief qualms were at the use of 500 volts supply, although he knew of its common use in the USA. The line was divided electrically into six parts and BoT regulations for the return circuit had been complied with. In all he was well satisfied, provided adequate records of the earth return circuits performance were kept and the safety measures sought by Rich executed.

With success achieved in the government inspections of Friday, 27 July 1894, the formal opening took place on the following afternoon, a special car carrying the directorate through to Laxey.

The following Saturday's *Isle of Man Times* gave the event a full page, Bruce and Saunderson being specially praised, together with Dr Hopkinson and his assistants, Ramage and Wood, also Joshua Shaw (overhead specialist) and Barnard of Callender's. The official party's arrival at Laxey station (a 65 ft 6 in by 15 ft building sited opposite the present Laxey car shed) was a memorable occasion, with the combined Laxey and Laxey Temperance bands

ISLE OF MAN
TRAMWAYS AND ELECTRIC POWER C?Y L?D
DOUGLAS AND LAXEY ELECTRIC TRAMWAY.
OPENED JULY 28TH 1894.
CONSTRUCTORS OF ELECTRIC PLANT
MATHER AND PLATT, L?D, ENGINEERS
MANCHESTER.
ALEXANDER BRUCE, J.P. CHAIRMAN
FREDERICK SAUNDERSON, C.E. ENGINEER
EDWARD HOPKINSON, D.Sc.
CONSULTING ELECTRICAL ENGINEER

Commemorative plaque at Derby Castle, formerly on the north wall of the engine house but now on the west. It was moved when the elevated switchboard was built in 1898

playing 'See the conquering hero comes' and a triumphal arch bearing the words 'E.T.C. Welcome to Laxey Glen' on the one side and 'Shee dy veagys, glion Laxey' (Peace and plenty to Laxey Glen) upon the reverse.

Bruce, speaking from a lineside platform, was received with cheers, and made witty references to the line's absent contractor

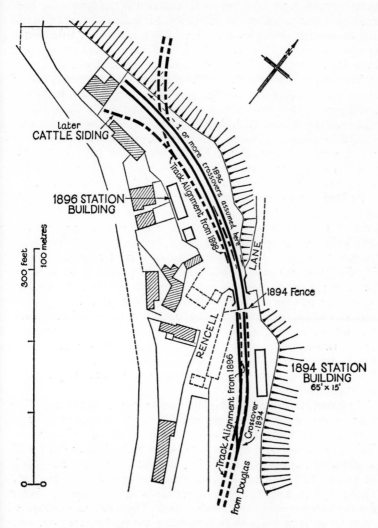

later
CATTLE SIDING

1 or more crossovers

1896
Track Alignment assumed here

1896 STATION
BUILDING

Track Alignment from 1896

300 feet   100 metres

1894 Fence

RENCELL

LANE

1894 STATION
BUILDING
65' × 15'

Track Alignment from 1896

Crossover
1894

from Douglas

Laxey stations and trackwork south of Glen Roy, 1894-7

Brebner, the local MHKS, landowners, Dr Hopkinson, Saunderson and others, hearty laughter greeting his sallies. He had previously been read a welcoming address by the Rev J. M. Spicer of Christ Church, the proceedings being conducted by Thomas Corlett, MHK. Other speakers were Dr Hopkinson, C. B. Nelson, and Saunderson, and then Dr Farrell, who gave his customary classical oration.

The technical press both in Britain and the United States carried considerable references to the new line, the *Electrical Review* stating that no electric traction scheme carried out in Great Britain had involved heavier engineering works. The additional generating equipment requires further reference, for the extension to Laxey saw considerable enlargement of the generating facilities and the creation of a proper feeder system. In these early years, the line was a veritable proving ground for the British electrical industry.

At Douglas, a third boiler, engine and generator and new switch-gear augmented those of 1893. The extra generator, of the newly evolved Hopkinson type, differed materially from its predecessors. The field coils were now positioned above the armature instead of on either side, forming a magnetic circuit in the form of an inverted U. The relative losses (in magnetic terms) proved to be about 24 per cent against 33 per cent for the less efficient Manchester type, in spite of leakage through the base. A further shed for eight cars was also added, being 166 ft long, 22 ft 6 in wide and 18 ft high, and the staffing of the power station and sheds was increased to a smith, two station foremen, a fitter, two carpenters, three general hands, an engine driver and fireman, and several switchgear men. There were also eight apprentices, drawn from families prominent in Douglas life.

At Laxey, a further power plant was erected, on a site some little distance below the line, on the south bank of the combined Laxey and Glen Roy rivers and close to the steep south side of the valley. The boiler house and engine room were built of local stone, with a corrugated-iron roof, and an iron chimney 60 ft high and 5 ft in diameter. The two engines and dynamos were also of the same type as the 1894 set at Port e Vada, the switchgear likewise. Water for the boilers came from a concrete tank. The boiler room measured 65 ft by 27 ft and was 19 ft high, while the engine room was 58 ft 3 in by 24 ft and 24 ft 6 in high, again built so as to allow room for expansion. A short feeder led to a point about one-third of the way up the gradient from Laxey terminus, and a single feeder ran southwards to Fairy Cottage and possibly beyond; elsewhere,

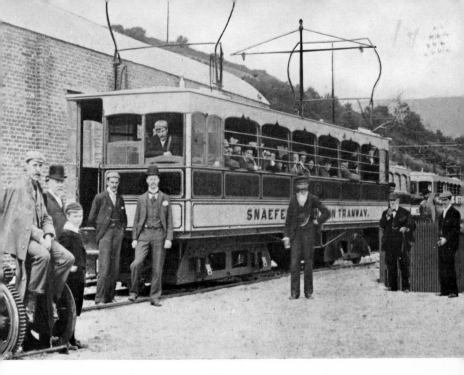

(above) *Snaefell Opening Day, 21 August 1895. Dr Edward Hopkinson is seated on the terminus sector plate winch, George Noble Fell stands against the car, with foot on rail, and Bruce is immediately behind Dr Hopkinson;* (below) *Snaefell track at Lhergy Veg, 1895. Buttressing was added to the wall in 1906*

(above) *Looking downhill past the mountain power station, 1895;* (below) *Snaefell Summit station, 1897, showing the catwalk leading to the hotel. The station measured 50 ft by 13 ft, but was only 7 ft 3 in high*

the double overhead evidently sufficed for the rest of the northern section. From Douglas, an underground feeder with intermediate section boxes led to Half-Way House, using a lead-covered steel-tape armoured 37/14 cable by Callenders, still in peak load use in 1969. In all, there were six electrical sections between Douglas and Laxey.

The wooden Groudle battery house represented an early attempt to deal with the fact that while the average load to keep two cars in service was negligible, a coincidence of two uphill starts would overload any one of the three Douglas generators. To quote the *Electrical Review* of 24 August 1894:

'. . . there are 240 cells of the Patent Chloride type made by the Chloride Electrical Storage Syndicate . . . 120 unprotected cells and 120 protected cells with teak and asbestos separators . . . capable of being discharged at the rate of 500V at 140A for three hours, at 90A for six hours, at 70A for nine hours . . . The working of these accumulators will be watched with the closest interest, both by reason of the comparative newness of chloride cells, and the fact that fixed accumulators have been rarely used to supply power for traction purposes . . .'

The Groudle storage battery was charged once or twice a week, and for the remaining days cars drew on the stored current; the capacity was ample for any possible demand. A 12 kW booster by Mather & Platt was installed for charging, converting 450V 35 amps to 150V 90 amps, and this could be used at other times to raise the line voltage, functioning as a series generator. By 1899, the original cells had been replaced by Chloride 'R' type, with a 50 per cent higher discharge rate. This storage system was copied in several early mainland installations, to cope with fluctuating day loads, but later became obsolescent. On the Manx Electric it survived until 1944, and was thus one of the last British traction examples, save for the Mersey Railway.

Althought the six new electric cars bore the title 'Douglas and Laxey Electric Tramway', a further change of owning company had already taken place in the months between the end of 1893's experimental service and the resumption of traffic in May, 1894. The Douglas & Laxey Coast Electric Tramway Company Limited had made a successful bid for the Douglas horse tramway (£38,000), and on 30 April 1894 changed its name to Isle of Man Tramways & Electric Power Company Ltd, with a capital stepped up from

I

£50,000 to £150,000. The prospectus appeared early in April, and invited subscriptions to a total of £125,000, with £50,000 in debentures. The lists were to close on 14 April, and by 21 April it was reported that the capital had been 'more than realised'. The actual total realised was £140,000, plus £50,000 in Series A debentures. The memorandum and articles were those of the D & L C E T company, and the office was at 7 Athol Street, Douglas.

The directors of the new company were Alexander Bruce, A. J. Lusty (by now a director of the Madras Electric Tramway Co Ltd), F. G. Callow, Dr Edward Hopkinson, J. A. Mylrea JP (of the Isle of Man Steam Packet Co), W. P. J. Pittar, and Dr R. Farrell. W. E. Young was secretary, Saunderson was engineer, and standing counsel was the Attorney-General. The horse tramway was handed over on 1 May 1894, and the two lines thereafter ran as a combined undertaking, with J. Aldworth as manager.

The words 'Electric Power' in the title revealed that the company intended to furnish a public supply. The first customer (1894) was the brand new Douglas Bay hotel, with some 250 lamps, and the company installed at Derby Castle a 1000V Mather & Platt 30 amp alternator, on hire, powered by a 500V motor. In 1896 a Bellis/Mather & Platt 75-hp direct coupled steam-driven set (No 458) giving 50 amps output was added, both machines feeding a combined switchboard which permitted them to work independently or in parallel. By 1900 the public supply side of the undertaking comprised six high-tension and four low-tension mains, with seven transformers totalling 71 kW. The consumers included the Derby Castle Opera House, the Douglas Bay hotel, and private houses, together with a number of Brockie Pell 15 amp arc-lamps which lit parts of Onchan village and much of the Douglas end of the tramway. In 1900 this interesting example of an early public AC supply totalled some 3,190 lamps of an average eight-candlepower, the company charging sixpence per Board of Trade unit. Some pavement mains inspection covers still survive in Onchan today, lettered I O M T & E P.

Bruce's object in taking over the horse tramway was clearly to seek powers to electrify it and thus extend his new electric line to the centre of Douglas: the complex negotiations which ensued are described in Chapter 2. Negotiations for electrification were resumed early in 1897; Douglas town council had written on 17 February asking for terms on which the company would light the promenade from 1 July, and I O M T & E P replied with a composite offer to light, free of charge, all the promenades and much of the Upper Douglas route in return for permission to sell current in Douglas to private consumers and to electrify the bay line using overhead wires, and to extend it to the I M R station. Bruce also offered to take a six-man corporation party to Bristol, Rouen and Hamburg, and stated that the tramway conversion would cost the company £20,000.

A 250-page report was produced by T. H. Nesbitt, town clerk, on 1 December 1897. By 19 March a special committee had been set up, and on 23 March the company agreed to pay for six of a corporation party of ten (eight committee men, surveyor Taylor and town clerk Nesbitt) on the proposed mainland and Continental tour. The council accepted this on 30 March, and planned a tour of London, Paris, Frankfurt, Dresden, Berlin, Hamburg, Cologne, Brussels and Rouen, returning by way of Brighton, Bristol, Dover, Prescot and Liverpool.

Departure was by the ss *Snaefell* on Thursday, 1 April, and from London by S E & C R next day. Visits to Paris, Versailles, Frankfurt, Leipzig, Dresden, Berlin, Hamburg, Cologne, Brussels and back to London were achieved by Monday, 12 April, a sequence involving much overnight travel and such odd nocturnal spectacles as Aldworth, Nesbitt and Taylor staring at gas lamps in the Champs Elysées in Paris during an evening downpour. Rouen, Brighton and Dover had to be left unvisited, but the sights seen included a Simplex conduit line at Prescot and practically every variety of traction in Paris; the list is interminable. Three thousand miles had been covered, and all participants had severe colds. In London, they had an interview with a leading authority, Professor Kennedy, and his later written replies to questions drafted on 21 April were wholly in favour of electric traction on the overhead system. The committee endorsed this choice with enthusiasm; conduit tramways had a strong hold on their affections, but their expense was feared.

In answer to council requests during July and August 1897, Aldworth sent details of proposed overhead construction, and mentioned the intended use of single-deck motors about 25 ft long and 6 ft 6 in wide, hauling trailers chosen initially from the best of the horse cars. A cross-section of a car passing another at a centre refuge, and more detailed data followed. On 31 August the committee voted 6 : 1 in favour of recommendations which would permit electrification of the bay line.

On Thursday, 7 September, the council was faced with a protesting 'memorial' signed by thirty-two house occupiers on Loch Promenade, and adjournment to 7 October was followed by two more memorials, one of seventy-one signatures by car proprietors and drivers, another of fifty-eight signatures from hotel occupiers. A further adjournment followed until after the November elections, and when the new council met on 22 November they were read a letter from company secretary Young announcing that the offer of 6 March was withdrawn. Once more, prejudice had triumphed over reason.

GEORGE F. MILNES & Cᵒ
BUILDERS
○ TRAMWAY & LIGHT RAILWAY ○
CARRIAGE WORKS
BIRKENHEAD, ENGLAND.

CHAPTER SIX

The Snaefell Mountain Railway

The mountain . . . commands a prospect from its summit which for extent and beauty it would be difficult to match in the United Kingdom . . . *The Barrow Route to the Isle of Man,* 1883.

With their visitors and business prospects completely transformed by the new electric tramway, the people of Laxey village honoured its promoters by inviting a director to open the church bazaar, late in 1894. Dr Farrell came, and in his speech he made the first public mention of the company's next ambition. 'My friends,' he said, 'I will let you into a secret. We are going to put an electric tramway to the top of Snaefell.'

The Snaefell mountain, 2,034 feet high, is the centrepiece of the mountainous northern half of the Isle of Man and the island's highest point. On a clear day, the visitor can see not only the entire island, but can look right across the Irish Sea to four kingdoms, and pick out the mountains of the English Lake District, the Mull of Galloway in Scotland, the hills of Anglesey and North Wales, and the Mountains of Mourne to the west, in Ireland. This was to be the site of Britain's first mountain railway.

A survey for a steam-worked mountain railway had been made in 1887-8 by G. N. Fell, as part of the 'Douglas, Laxey & Snaefell Railway' described in Appendix 1. George Noble Fell (born 8 May 1849, died 13 April 1924) was the son of John Barraclough Fell (1815-1902), originator of the Fell centre-rail system for mountain railways, which had been adopted on the Mont Cenis and in

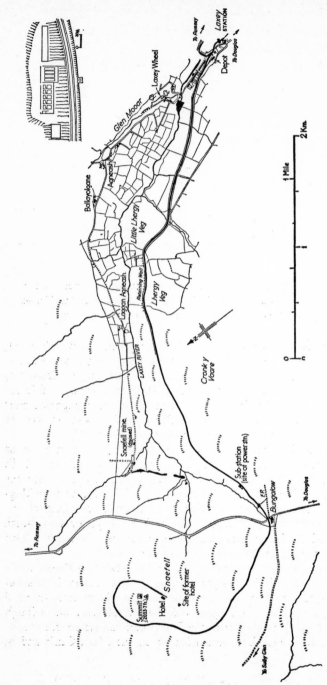

The Snaefell line: (inset) plan of the power station

Brazil and New Zealand; these lines are described by L. T. C. Rolt in *A Hunslet Hundred* (David & Charles, 1964). The family had Manx connections, and with his father's retirement from practice, George Noble Fell became active on his own account in pressing the merits of the Fell system for mountain lines. He was also a light railway engineer, and from 1896 was an associate member of the Institute of Civil Engineers.

By 1893-4 a Snaefell Railway Company still existed, with offices in Athol Street, Douglas. Fell's Douglas-Laxey survey was used in part by Saunderson in 1893-4, as parts of his route appear on Saunderson's initial survey plans, and by 1894 Fell must have been in direct contact with Bruce, who was at once attracted by the possibilities of a line up Snaefell, using the Fell system with electric propulsion. Fell's ready-made survey of 1888 was evidently employed, and the whole line came into being in the incredibly short time of about seven months. The line was solidly built and soundly engineered, and is still in full use today.

The line avoided the usual legislative delays—by being built on lands purchased or leased by voluntary agreements, without any need for the authority of Tynwald or any other statutory power, as no property had to be taken compulsorily. The land occupied by the lower end of the line and its depot was mainly purchased by Bruce, between 26 January and 2 March 1895, and that higher up the mountain was bought by the Snaefell Mountain Railway Association from the Trustees of the Commons. This purchase, sanctioned by Tynwald on 9 July 1895, comprised the trackbed, the sites of the summit station and hotel, the power station, Sulby pumping station, and rights of way thereto, and a fifty-year lease was taken of the remaining land within a radius of 440 yards of the summit. The trustees were to receive one penny per passenger (minimum £260 per year) and certain levies arising from profits on the hotels.

The Snaefell Mountain Railway Association was a private grouping of Bruce and his colleagues, formed on 4 January 1895. The only signatories of its constitutional documents were Alexander Bruce, J. D. Rogers, C. B. Nelson, William Todhunter, Francis Reddicliffe and J. R. Cowell, the other fourteen remaining anonymous. Cowell and Bruce were now chairman and vice-chairman respectively of the Board of Advertising, a new tourist publicity body. No public record is known to exist of the Snaefell Association's proceedings.

Meanwhile, on Wednesday, 20 February 1895, the first annual general meeting of the Isle of Man Tramways & Electric Power Co was held at the Strathallan Crescent offices, Bruce presiding. Net profits were stated as £10,507 8s 10d, and the October dividend of 6 per cent on preference and 7½ per cent on ordinary shares was repeated for the second half-year. Four new cars (Nos 10-13) were on order from G. F. Milnes & Co for the coastal line, the electrical equipment to be put in by I O M T & E P at Derby Castle, Joshua Shaw having now joined the company. Three weeks previously the line had been snowed up, but had reopened on 2 February and carried the mails free for both Laxey and Ramsey. The Howstrake Park was to open in 1895, and part of the estate was being laid out by Douglas Bay Estate as an eighteen-hole golf course; through golfers' return tickets were to be issued for 6d from the Jubilee Clock. The directors' report referred to plans for improved station facilities at Derby Castle and Laxey.

Laxey terminus in 1896, with the 1894 station in the left foreground and the 1896 station behind the cars

Dr Farrell, given two minutes, made a lengthy speech with some Manx anecdotes. His book '*Beyond the Silver Streak in Manxland —The Great Electric Railway*' was about to be published by John Heywood of Manchester, and is commended as a unique piece of tramway promotional literature. He recited a 'remarkably high encomium' allegedly passed by two rural Manxmen boarding a car at Ballabeg one wet winter's night :

'By gosh, Quilliam, it looks lek stepping into a fust class pub', said one.

'My word', replied his companion, 'bud the derachthors are plucky buoys'.

'Garn man; they say that every sowl on the boord is from a different nation'.

'Lor' a massey, is that thrue?'

'Thrue as Gospel'.

'Well, that beats Owld Nick; there's not the lek of it in the unyvarse' (loud laughter).

The choice of the 3 ft 6 in-gauge for Snaefell seems to have been directly influenced by Fell's Mont Cenis experience, since the three New Zealand lines and that up Snaefell were built to virtually the same gauge as Mont Cenis. A double-headed bull-head brake rail is used as the working surfaces for a powerful calliper brake, whilst the flanges of horizontal guide wheels fit below the heads of the rail. On the steam Fell lines the horizontal wheels were driven by separate cylinders and could be forced against the rail by spring pressure to obtain adhesion far greater than in proportion to the locomotive's weight. A further refinement, patented by engineer Hanscotte of the Fives-Lille locomotive works, was to apply pressure to the horizontal wheels by compressed air, the pressure varying with the gradient, and this variant was used for the only true mountain railway built as a steam Fell line, the Chemin de Fer du Puy de Dome at Clermont-Ferrand (1907-26). The elder Fell had advocated the use of his system in the Channel Tunnel, and G. N. Fell later adapted these plans for electric traction; in 1913, when working on a scheme for a line from Lons-le-Saunier to Geneva, he sought permission to carry out some trials on the Snaefell line. At the time of his death in 1924 he was still actively working on a scheme for a Franco—Italian link over the Monginevro pass.

At Snaefell, the inherent limitations of DC supply meant that a new generating station had to be built near the mid-point of the line, and a stone-built power house was erected high up the river valley on a dramatic mountainside perch, 2.8 miles from Laxey. The whole of the equipment had to be taken out by the mountain road, which was crossed on the level, and then lowered down the mountainside by ropes and tackle; this took fourteen days, during which Mr Willis of Mather & Platt, the contractors, slept in a hut on the mountain. Mr Willis also erected the ten miles of single overhead line in a mere eight days. Coal for the power station had to be brought up by the tramway from Laxey, and water was pumped up through a two-inch pipe from a pumping station on Sulby river, equipped with a Galloway boiler and a 4-hp Tangye engine and pump.

The Snaefell power station was the most powerful generating plant yet built in the island. The boiler room, 36 ft by 43 ft and 16 ft 3 in high, housed four Galloway's 120 lb/in² boilers 26 ft long and 6 ft in diameter, with feed pump and injectors. The 60-ft iron chimney of 5 ft diameter was on the other side of the line, and the flues passed beneath the track. The boilers supplied steam to five 120-hp Mather & Platt horizontal compound engines, each with a 7-ft flywheel and a speed of 150 rpm; the cylinders were of 16-in stroke, cylinder diameters being 12 in for the high-pressure one and 20 in for the low-pressure. Each engine was coupled to a 60-kW Hopkinson dynamo, the whole installation being housed in an engine room measuring 72 ft by 30 ft, and 12 ft 3 in high. The switchgear was mounted on a frame of polished ash.

From the power house, an underground feeder of the type supplied by Callenders in 1894 for the coastal line ran downhill again and supplied the overhead line at intervals of one mile. At Laxey depot, it entered a wooden battery house with 250 chloride cells and a capacity of 560 ampere-hours; this building measured 75 ft 3 in by 20 ft and was 8 ft 3 in high. The plant was over-generous, and later much of the power produced from coal laboriously transported up 1,130 ft of mountain returned to feed the coast tramway, through a further feeder connecting the battery house to Laxey valley power station. This feeder, which ran through the Laxey stationmaster's office, was used in reverse in winter to give the Snaefell line's battery a periodic charge from a 12-kW booster installed in the Laxey power station.

The contractor for the Snaefell track was Mr Herd of Douglas, and a later description of it is taken from the inspector's report. Fell and Hopkinson personally supervised their respective branches of the work. By an agreement of 23 April 1895 the Manx Northern locomotive *Caledonia* was hired at £20 per week, and was shipped from Ramsey to Laxey in the *Porpoise* and used with the aid of a temporary third rail. M N R timber trucks Nos 20 and 21 were also hired, at 3s each per day, and the agreement specified that the engine was to be properly housed at night and that the Snaefell Association were to pay the driver 6s 6d and the fireman 4s 2d for a ten-hour day. In mid-August, *Caledonia* took up a trainload of dignitaries of the L N W R and L & Y. Orders had been placed for six electric passenger-cars, and to house these a six-car brick shed with a curved iron roof and pits for all six cars was built at the lower terminus, 119 ft long, 20 ft 6 in wide and 18 ft high.

This depot, which is still in use, was adjoined by the original and short-lived station, a 63 ft 6 in by 20 ft 3 in building approached by a long flight of steps which intending passengers had to climb. In place of points, the line used sector tables, that at the Laxey terminal stub being worked by a two-way winch that appears in opening-day photographs. In 1897, the sector table at the summit was removed, its pit filled in, and a special type of point installed in which a pivoted section of rail was swung across from one side to the other where the two tracks came together. The summit was provided with a wooden station building measuring 50 ft by 13 ft 6 in, and a single-storey wooden hotel, 65 ft by 70 ft, the latter approached by a long catwalk.

The original Snaefell Summit hotel of 1895, with the addition (right) made in the following year

By 16 August 1895, the work was sufficiently complete for formal inspection, again by Colonel J. H. Rich and Major P. Cardew, who reported next day. It was not a legal requirement, but the government regarded the Snaefell line for this purpose as an extension of the coastal tramway. A former Mather & Platt engineer recalled that at 6 am on the day of Major Cardew's inspection, a linesman shorted the switch panel across the already charged traction battery, converting the switchboard into a major electrical bonfire. In four hours, the charred wood was cleaned off, painted with Brunswick black, and the refurbished switchgear mounted with the paint still wet—the inspector himself saying 'I haven't seen a better job!'

The second Snaefell line station at Laxey, with depot and original station in the background and an advertisement board concealing the former access steps

Colonel Rich described the line as 4 miles 5 chains in length, with a 21-foot formation, two-thirds cut into hard ground or rock and one-third on soft material 'thrown out'. The inter track spacing (as on other I O M T & E P lines) was 7 feet. The '50-lb' (actually 56-lb) rails were fang-bolted to 9 in x 4½ in creosoted sleepers 7 ft long, and were in 24-ft lengths. The Fell rail weighed 65 lb per yard. The line climbed 1,820 feet, for 85 per cent of the distance at 1 in 12; level stretches existed at the termini and two intermediate points (see profile). Most curves were of 10 ch radius but near the summit there were some of 7 and 5.

Apart from a wish to see more drainage and a watch kept on the formation for settlement, plus provision of lamps at the stations and the fencing of 'turntable' pits, Rich was satisfied. He, incidentally, explained the adoption of right-hand running in order to keep the ascending cars on the soft part of the formation.

Cardew saw the electrical equipment as basically similar to that

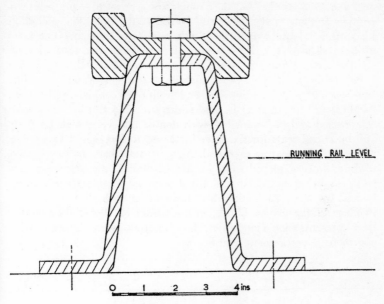

RUNNING RAIL LEVEL

0   1   2   3   4 ins

Fell rail detail, Snaefell mountain line

of 1893-4 on the coastal line but, of course, the cars were higher powered. The four-motor tractive effort of 3,500 pounds set against the 1 in 12 opposing forces of 2,850 pounds meant that a single motor failure would incapacitate a car. Current proposals for regenerative braking involved running downhill at 12 mph, if the cars were unaltered electrically and he wanted extensive proving trials before approval was given. He was alarmed at the proposed 550-volt supply and suggested 520 as the station maximum, considering the power station to be 'uneconomically' sited.

The voltage was evidently adjusted, for the governor gave permission to open the line, and a special car carrying government worthies followed on 20 August. Opening on Wednesday, 21 August, the line carried an average of 900 passengers a day for the remainder of the season, at a return fare of 2s. A Mr Cartner was appointed engineer by the parent Snaefell Association.

It is convenient to deal here with the six cars of the Snaefell line, which have remained in sole charge for more than seventy years and are still largely in their original form. The bodywork and bogies were by G. F. Milnes, the electrical equipment by Mather & Platt to the designs of Dr Edward Hopkinson, including his sprung adaption of his brother's rigid bow collector. The form of Snaefell Nos 1-6 was basically derived from the 1894 cars on the coastal line, but they were less expensively finished, the interior being entirely of pitchpine, including the elaborately panelled bulkhead. Their dimensions were: length over couplers 35 ft 7½ in, height over roof 10 ft 4½ in, and width overall 7 ft 3 in. They were ash-framed and teak-panelled, with double transverse seats for forty and bulkhead seats for six, later increased to forty-eight by adding a single corner seat at each end. As built, they had shallow arched roofs and were glazed only in the vestibules, the six main side windows being unglazed and fitted with adjustable striped roller blinds. By April 1896, they had been fitted with sliding windows in place of the canvas blinds, in the winter of 1896-7 they gained their present roof clerestories, and in 1900 were 'graced' with enormous advertisement boards.

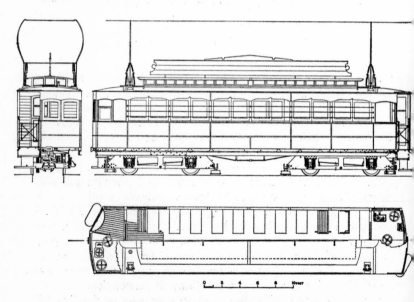

Snaefell passenger car, present-day condition

The two-motor bogies were of a special long wheelbase type (6 ft 10 in) to incorporate the Fell brake equipment and their two Mather & Platt type 5A 25-hp motors. These motors, still in use today, are of an archaic form with extended pole pieces and an enormous single field coil. The armatures are of the ancient series wound type, and the techniques now perfected for rewinding them, using modern glass fibre insulation, are a typical revelation of Manx Electric technical skill. The original control system provided for series-parallel working from the upper end, and series only (with five notches) from the lower end. Trials were carried out in 1895 with a car wired for regenerative braking, which returned up to 50 electrical horsepower to the line and saved a good deal on brake blocks, but Joshua Shaw thought it demanded too much driving skill and altered the motor circuits back from shunt to series. The idea was discussed again with Sir Philip Dawson in 1904, but not adopted. About this period, KH controllers were fitted at the upper end.

About 1906, two stiffening channels were bolted to the lower faces of the original underframes, and the guiding wheels were relocated to a position outside the inner bogie cross member. A rigid bogie brake screw column replaced the original type, which was flexibly jointed to a staff mounted on the platform. About 1954 the uphill end controllers were modified to Form K 12 and new G E C main switches were fitted, replacing the original ones and their 0-500 ammeters.

The other three items of rolling stock comprised an un-numbered tower wagon trailer, a small un-numbered goods wagon built in 1895 by Hurst Nelson to carry supplies for the hotel, and a coal car numbered 7 and nicknamed *Maria*. This last is a double-cab six-ton wagon-bodied underframe, of unknown date and parentage, which acquired trucks, equipment and bow collectors from a passenger car each winter and took the next season's stock of coal up to the generating station. It was certainly in use in 1900, and may be original (1895). After generation ceased at Snaefell power station in 1924 it was used only for construction work, the last occasion being some Air Ministry work at the summit in the winter of 1954-5. In 1898-9, attempts were made to secure winter mineral traffic from the Snaefell lead mine, and sections of a light railway plan by John Todd survive bearing the date 5 October 1899. This would have included major inclined planes.

The Snaefell Association now proceeded to sell their line to the

Isle of Man Tramways & Electric Power Co, as intended from the start. At the I O M T & E P annual general meeting on 28 February 1896, the directors' report explained that a debenture issue was needed to finance the cable tramway and the Snaefell purchase, and a private meeting followed at which the Snaefell line's purchase for £72,500 was agreed, on a motion by R. M. Broadbent. The agreement called for £32,500 in cash, the rest in equal amounts of 6 per cent preference and ordinary shares of the tramway company. The amount clearly included a profit to the Association's members but it later transpired that the real cost of building the line had only been about £40,000, and that the £2,000 put into the S M R A by I O M T & E P had brought a return of 100 per cent! The Snaefell Association was wound up later in 1896, after presenting Bruce with an engraved service of silver plate and a gold watch bearing his family crest, together with presents of jewellery for his wife and three daughters. These were presented by J. A. Mylrea at a ceremony at Dumbell's Bank on 21 August.

The two termini in Laxey were a good distance apart, and the long climb up to the Snaefell line's station was a deterrent to visitors. In the directors' report presented on 20 February 1896 it emerged that the coast tramway, which in 1894 had ended opposite the present Laxey car shed, had been extended in the winter of 1895-6 by a bridge across the Rencell road, to a station just short of the future viaduct. This was a new single-storey building, 43 ft 3 in by 19 ft 6 in. From here, through passengers could walk across the road bridge towards the Snaefell line's steps.

However, by February 1897 land had been purchased alongside Dumbell's Row to bring the line to a new low-level terminus. The earthworks involved cut right through the original flight of steps, which survive today as a fossilised slope between two heavily overgrown walls. On reaching level ground, the up and down tracks came together in a pivoted switch of the type now also installed at the summit, and a rustic station building was erected, measuring 46 ft 6 in by 17 ft. This replaced the somewhat larger station on the hillside, which now stood disused—*vide* our earlier drawing.

The line to the depot now diverged from the downhill running line on the gradient, and a special turnout of unique design was installed with four moving sections that provided a five-stage 'curve' on the turnout, complete with Fell rail. This survives today, but the centre rail is not used for normal braking, as the crew slacken off the rear brake on approaching the point and apply the front

(above) *Douglas engine room looking south, 1894. 1893 generators at left, 1894 type at right. The engine footplating carries makers' plates inscribed 'Patented A. D. 1890 No. 4244' and, further along, 'Manchester 1893'*; (below) *the Snaefell generating plant, 1895*

Page 162

*Ballaglass boi[l]
room in 1922*

*The Robb
Armstrong
engines, with
their* ECC
*dynamos, in
Ballaglass
power
station*

*Laxey power
[sta]tion 1922. Be[lliss]
Morcom sets
centre and swit[ch]
gear platform [at]
right. Mr Bertr[am]
G. Kelly, c[hief]
assistant engin[eer,]
standing near [a]
turbine-driven [al]
ternator*

one immediately after passing it. Access to the depot building was still by a sector table, which survived until about 1932; Mr Gale of the M E R recalls a car falling into its pit!

It is not clear why the sector tables ('turntables') and the replacing pivotal switches were adopted, for the Fell gear was above the level of the running rails and in later years conventional turnouts were installed at several places. Apart from these, the 1895 operating rules are still applicable today, though the line also has a level crossing with the road through Laxey village, and there are red and green light signals controlled from Laxey station to govern entry to the single line. The present rulebook also contains an injunction to post a flagman in rear if an involuntary stop is made on the descent; this results from a 1905 collision, described later.

The creation of the present station of 1898 belongs to the Ramsey line story in the next chapter, but meanwhile the Summit hotel had been extended, and another large 'hotel', known as The Bungalow and measuring 90 ft by 80 ft, was built at the crossing of the mountain road at the Half-Way Hut. The construction of a branch from here to Tholt-y-Will was seriously contemplated, and appears in company literature of 1896-7. From 1907 the trip could be made by motor charabanc, as described in Chapter 8. Dr Farrell had by this time taken to acting as impromptu guide to those travelling up Snaefell, and at the summit would declaim:

'Here you see seven kingdoms—England, Ireland, Scotland, Wales, the Isle of Man, (the kingdom of) Man and, where is the seventh?—Ah—the Kingdom of Heaven!'

The line was solidly built, and after a landslide on to the track in the first winter the only major repairs needed were at Lhergy Veg in 1905-6, when the retaining wall slipped and had to be reinforced with substantial buttresses, which bear the dates of erection on their tops; the cost was £844. Apart from periodic erosion slips near Bellevue on the Ramsey line, caused by poor shore defences, this was the only physical instability recorded on the entire group of lines until the Bulgham slip of 1967. A new battlemented Snaefell Summit hotel, with a 100-ft frontage, a depth of 60 ft and a round tower 25 ft high, was opened on 10 August 1906, having been built in only four months. The original wooden hotel was then demolished.

(*continued on p* 166)

K

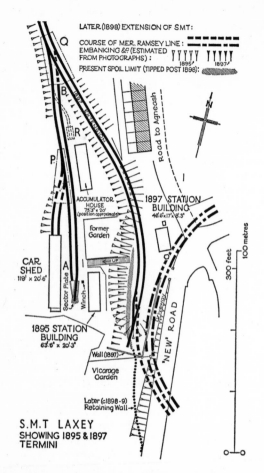

Snaefell line stations at Laxey. The depot pointwork (at P) is that existing today. The original arrangement, to about 1931, seems to have used a further sector plate, whose operating winch survived until recently. Track A and the sector plate beyond this point were removed at some date after 1896, track from B to sector plate and track shown dotted in outline Q removed in 1897. R indicates the present Ministry of Defence railcar shed and access track

SNAEFELL MOUNTAIN ELECTRIC TRAMWAY Co.

INSTRUCTIONS TO DRIVERS & CONDUCTORS

1.—Drivers and Conductors must not allow any person (excepting an Official of the Company) to travel in their compartments, or to occupy the platform or steps, neither shall they enter into conversation with any person while the Car is in motion.

2.—No Driver shall start his Car without the proper bell-signal from his Conductor.

3.—When the Car is in motion, the Driver shall always be on the Front Platform, and at no time, either when shunting or otherwise, shall a Car be driven or controlled from the back end.

One Ring from the Conductor means STOP.
Two Rings from the Conductor means START.

.—Both Driver and Conductor are responsible for the proper working of the Brakes of the Car, and great care must be taken to have them properly adjusted to the wheels and to frequently use and test the Centre Rail Brakes, and any defect, however slight, must be immediately reported to the Car Inspector, in addition to entering the same in the Report Book.

5.—Care must be taken that the Centre Rail Brake-blocks are sufficiently apart to clear the Centre Rail before every start, and the front Centre Rail Brake must not be used for stopping, except in special cases of emergency.

6.—In case a Driver requires the rear Centre Rail Brake applied to the Car he must give One Ring, and if not applied sufficiently tight, he must continue to give Single Rings at distinct intervals.

7.—When the Driver wishes it released he gives Two Rings.

8.—No Car shall be driven quicker than 8 miles per hour, and under no circumstances must the Journey from Snaefell be done in less than 40 minutes.

9.—Every Car on the Down Journey must stop at the Signal Board before reaching the Hut.

10.—Drivers must use special caution in approaching the Turntables at Laxey and the Switch at Summit.

11.—Drivers must see that their Outfit of Tools or Fittings is on the Car before starting each Journey, and that their Sand-boxes are properly filled and Pipes in working order.

12.—Any Driver taking the Tools or Fittings from another Car will be instantly dismissed the Company service.

13.—In the event of an accident happening in connection with the Car, no matter how slight it may be, a full written report of the same must be given on the form provided for the purpose and be delivered to the Station-Master at Laxey immediately on arrival, and every care must be taken to obtain names and addresses of reliable witnesses of the occurrence. Drivers neglecting to do this will be held responsible.

14.—Under no circumstances shall a Driver enter a Public-house, or use intoxicating drink while on duty.

15.—Before going off duty, a written report of the state of the Car must be made in the Report Book provided for the purpose.

16.—The Conductor shall take his order to start the Car from the Station-master only, and shall then communicate the same to the Driver by the proper signal—namely, Two Rings.

17.—Conductors before leaving Snaefell must see that the Centre Rail Brake is sufficiently off to clear the centre rail, and on starting when the centre rail is entered they must apply the Brake so as to bear slightly upon the rail, and then await the orders of the Drivers as directed in Instruction No. 6.

18.—Always before re-starting they must make sure that the Brake is sufficiently off to clear the centre rail.

19.—Conductors must stand by the rear Brake all the Journey while the Car is in motion, ready to apply the Brake when signalled, and must only collect Tickets while the Car is stopped at the Hut.

Any Driver or Conductor infringing these Rules, or any of them, will be instantly dismissed.

The Directors earnestly request the Officials to see that these Rules are strictly complied with, and that any departure from or neglect of the same be at once reported to the Manager.

H. Harrison. **MANAGER.**

Snaefell line working instructions. Note the erroneous company title

On 14 September 1905, the Snaefell line saw its only serious accident, a rear-end collision. During shuttle working to Bungalow (for a motor race!) an ascending car stalled at Lhergy Veg from either a motor fault or loss of wire contact, and the third of a convoy of three cars later descending on the same track failed to stop in time. The compensation paid to injured passengers was considerable, and seriously affected the year's profit. The Fell rail has proved fully effective in preventing derailments or runaways, and no other incidents of this kind are on record.

Finally, a description of a ride up the mountain. Immediately on leaving the Laxey station, the car takes the right-hand track and begins the curving ascent to the rear of Dumbell's Row, soon passing the downhill road's facing connection to the depot, with its special point. Next comes a fine view across the valley to the 1854 Laxey Wheel, and the ridge on which stands the ancient village of Agneash, and behind them the hidden valley of the Mooar. The northwest limits of Baljean see the line climb over a rocky spur before a brief descent to the buttressed stone embankment at Lhergy Veg, the only point other than Bungalow at which the descending cars disengage their slipper brake. The field enclosures here are lost in wild vegetation.

Above Lhergy Veg, the line runs on the lands of the Commons Trustees, and is unfenced. The view across the Laxey valley is increasingly impressive, and includes the tree-enshrouded ruins of the Snaefell mine, and then Snaefell itself, skirted by the mountain road. Most of the formation consists of a cut and tipped shelf, and on this section the car passes the remains of the mountain power station. Soon the gradient slackens, and the car leaves Laxey valley to cross the mountain road and stop at the Bungalow, the former hotel's site now hardly recognisable; here the line passes into Lezayre parish. The remaining spiral climb round Snaefell is evident from the map and, given a fine day, this ascent with its increasingly spectacular views is certainly the most rewarding inland ride in the island.

CHAPTER SEVEN

A Tramway Colossus and Its Cost

Your safe and commodious cars which traverse a piece of coast and mountain scenery which suggests the great new road from Sorrento to Amalfi . . . are, in my view, great contributors to the education and happiness of the thousands who make the Isle of Man their annual resort—Hall Caine, writing to manager Harold Brown, c 1904

The expansion of the undertaking between 1896 and 1899 was founded on the good results achieved by the coast tramway. The profit of £10,507 in 1894 increased to £14,467 in 1895, and the half-yearly dividend of 6 per cent on the preference and 7½ per cent on the ordinary shares was followed by a repeated 6 per cent on preference and 8½ per cent on ordinary for the second half-year. At the annual general meeting on 28 February 1896, Bruce's entry was marked by loud cheers!

The year's total mileage on the horse and electric lines in 1895 (excluding Snaefell) was 302,121, and 1,923,316 people had been carried, the electric line's best one-day figure being 10,477. Laxey had had 7,148 cars that year. Winter receipts per journey were between 9s 2d and 15s 1d, contrasting with 47s 5d in August. The working expenses were given as only 34 per cent of receipts (11.64d per train mile), and 2,300 tons of goods had been carried. Mr John Mather questioned the aggregation of items and lack of allowance for depreciation, but Bruce explained that repairs and renewals had been charged to revenue. To pay for the Snaefell and cable lines, the company's capital was increased to £315,000,

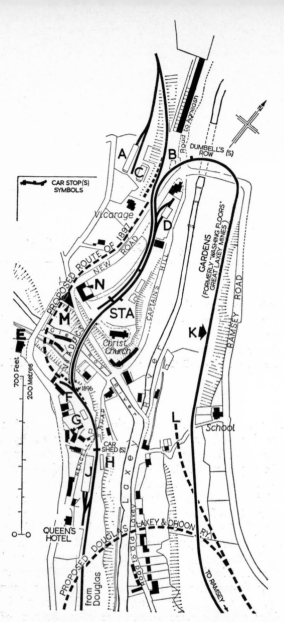

Tramways at Laxey since 1897, showing Snaefell depot (A), site of 1897 Snaefell terminus (B), site of 1895 Snaefell terminus (C), goods shed (D), Commercial Hotel (E), cattle dock (F), 1896 station building (G), site of 1894 station (H), Laxey car shed (J), the Workmen's Institute (M) and the Laxey Industrial Co-operative Society's shop (N). K is the official starting point of the extension to Ramsey (F to K being regarded as a branch) and L is the trailing connection from the proposed Douglas, Laxey and Dhoon Railway to the former lead mines' washing floors, now occupied by gardens and dwellings. Symbols are standard with those of the route maps in Appendix 6

of which increase £25,000 was in preference shares and £100,000 in series B 1896 debentures at 4 per cent.

The running time from Douglas to Laxey was about forty minutes, and all cars were kept at Douglas, as shown by the winter 1896 timetable. Weekday departures from Douglas to Laxey were at 6.20, 8.15, 10.0, 12.0, 2.30, 3.30, 4.30, 5.30, 6.30, 7.30, 8.30 and (Sats) 9.0, returning from Laxey at 7.20, 9.0, 11.0, 1.0, 3.30, 4.30, 5.30, 6.30, 7.30, 8.30, and (Sats) 9.45. On Sundays, cars left Douglas at 10.0, 1.0, 2.0, 3.0, 4.0, 5.30, 7.30 and 8.30, returning from Laxey forty-five minutes later.

The year's profit of £17,822 announced at the next I O M T & E P meeting on 8 March 1897 reflected the season's bad weather and the struggles of the cable line. Nevertheless, the same dividends were paid as in 1896. On the electric lines, passengers had reached 591,163 and car miles 153,897, whilst the entire system of four lines had carried 2,398,559. The Douglas car sheds had been twice extended, first by a new six-car shed in 1895 (125 ft 6 in long, 21 ft 6 in wide and 17 ft 6 in high), and then in 1896 by a shed for fifteen trailers, 166 ft long and 27 ft wide but only 10 ft 6 in

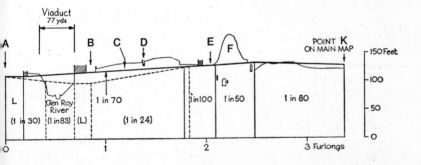

Profiles for the 1897 proposals at Laxey. The solid line shows the original proposal, crossing the road junction (B) on the level, and the broken line shows the later underpass scheme, with gradients in brackets. A is the divergence of main line and cattle dock sidings, C is the location of the accompanying section through the cutting, D is the vicarage garden entrance, E is the Agneash road crossing and F the mines' spoil heap. The first scheme would have involved a two-arch viaduct 77 yards long and the second a similar but lower viaduct, plus an underpass 22 ft wide

high. A rustic ticket office, 12 ft 6 in by 8 ft, was built at the Douglas terminus early in 1897.

Bruce now sought a line to Ramsey, an aim equally shared by Ramsey shareholder J. R. Cowell, a director of the Manx Northern Railway! On 9 April 1896 a rival London consortium had sought leave to introduce a Bill in Tynwald for a Laxey—Ramsey railway, and had engaged G. Noble Fell to survey it, but by 28 October the I O M T & E P petitioned Tynwald for leave to present their own Bill. This proposed separate termini in Laxey for all three lines (Douglas, Snaefell and Ramsey). By 10 December the other group had withdrawn by consent, and the I O M T & E P's scheme was itself withdrawn 'to allow of an improved plan, with communication between both tramways'. This was by a so-called branch (actually an end-on connecting line) between the 1895-6 terminus and the point K shown on our Laxey area map on p 168.

In a new petition on 25 March 1897, Ring, Brown and Nelson appeared for the I O M T & E P. The connecting line was to cross Glen Roy from the second terminus of the Douglas line, pass through the Workmen's Institute, and then cross the four-road junction on the level to enter a roadside reservation leading to the second Snaefell station, which would become joint for both lines. Following opposition, this was withdrawn on 13 April in favour of an altern-ative plan by I O M T & E P's new engineer, William Knowles, CE (formerly of Liverpool tramways), for the line to cross Glen Roy descending to 19 ft 3 in below road level, then tunnel under the road intersection with a girder roof, and climb at 1 in 24 into the Snaefell terminus. The station south of Glen Roy remained the main one, and the rest of the line to Ramsey was much as later built. The anticipated cost of the line and equipment was between £95,000 and £100,000, and the earnings £11,000 to £12,000 per year, with working expenses estimated at 45 per cent.

The Douglas & Laxey Tramway (Extension to Ramsey) Act 1897 was passed on 13 May 1897 and promulgated on 20 July. It provided for the new line to be a separate undertaking with its own capital, revenue and accounts. I O M T & E P were allowed to contract for the line's construction (a meeting to approve this was held on 7 February 1898) and a capital charge of up to £30,000 on the general undertaking was permitted. Meetings of both con-cerns prior to the opening were to settle the division of revenue. The tolls were fixed at 2d a mile, with a 3d minimum, and four cars per day were made obligatory, two in each direction. Goods

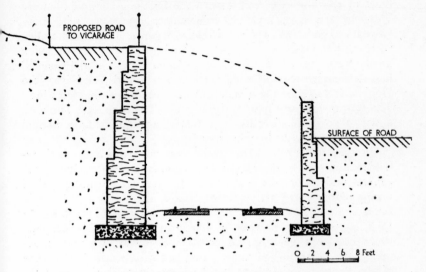

Section through intended roadside cutting at Laxey, from an original
initialled by Knowles and Goldie-Taubman

traffic and mails were provided for, being now an established traffic,
though purely passenger cars were not expected to carry mails
unless in the charge of a Post Office officer.

Compulsory land purchase by arbitration was included, and
liabilities to adjoining landowners included fencing and providing
new water troughs for cattle. The underpass in Laxey was to be
able to carry road traffic equivalent to a 20-ton traction engine
pulling two loaded trucks, and gradients were limited to 1 in 23,
with 90-ft radius curves. Speed was limited to 4 mph across the
Agneash road at Laxey, on the washing floors embankment, and
on Ballure Glen bridge. At Bulgham, the line was to occupy the
cliff-edge location of the old road, and any new road constructed
as the result of such re-alignment had to have the same width,
length and gradient as its predecessor. The line was to be built
within two years of promulgation.

Shaw and Aldworth went to the Continent in 1897, comparing
notes with other undertakings, and the company also obtained
advice from Granville Cunningham of the City of Birmingham

Tramways. Possibly in consequence, before the 1898 season, trolley bases of the Boston Pivotal type made by the Anderson Co were fitted to the cars, and non-insulated trolley poles with non-swivelling heads replaced the Hopkinson bows. The round trolley wire, of BWG section 0, was henceforth suspended by orthodox arched ears instead of the original Aetna type. On the Snaefell line, a heavier wire of BWG section 3 was used, and here the Hopkinson bows were retained, probably because of the high winds. The Ramsey line was equipped for trolleys from the start, and used a new type of Blackwells stepped pole, again with both normal 6 in/4 in and heavy 7 in/5 in types.

On 3 September 1897 the I O M T & E P put out a letter to share-holders announcing the intention of augmenting the capital of the general undertaking by £25,000 in £1 preference shares, and of issuing £100,000 of 1897 preference and 1897 ordinary shares in the separate undertaking. By the date of the next AGM on 10 March 1898, 35,000 1897 preference shares and 15,000 1897 ordinary shares had been taken up, raising £18,781 towards the new under-taking, but £21,343 had already been spent on works. The capital of the general undertaking stood at £315,630. During 1897 the electric lines had carried 602,068 passengers with 155,927 car miles, earning 27.68d a mile, expenses being 43.34 per cent of re-ceipts. The year's passengers on the whole undertaking reached 2,712,114, and the reduced profit despite larger numbers carried was put down to the fact that people had only made short journeys in the season's bad weather.

The date officially quoted for the start of the work on the Ramsey extension was 1 November 1897, though preliminary work began in August: the meeting which formally approved I O M T & E P's contract took place on 7 February 1898. It was engineered on a grand scale, spoil removed totalled 250,000 tons, and 60,000 tons of ballast were put down. A well-designed rail was used, weighing 62½ lb/yd. A force of from 1,000 to 1,100 men, were paid 4d an hour; at one stage they demanded 4½d and threatened to strike. Thirty horses were borrowed from the Douglas tramway, and I O M T & E P bought a steam locomotive and forty-five ballast wagons, plus sundry other vehicles. The engine was an Andrew Barclay 0—4—0 saddle-tank originally built in 1892 (works number 713) to the order of contractors Morrison & Mason of Glasgow; it was resold in October 1900 to Douglas Corporation (with the wagons) for their West Baldwin reservoir railway, and remained

I O M T & E P's locomotive, later Douglas Corporation Water Department's *Injebreck*

there until 1904. At West Baldwin it acquired the name *Injebreck*.

Two more locomotives were hired. From the I M R came No 2 *Derby*, which worked from Laxey after being shipped from Ramsey and brought up to the line on a wagon hauled by traction engines. Meanwhile, a separate gang built south from Ballure, using the M N R's No 1 *Ramsey*, which was brought to Ballure using baulks and rollers laid through the streets of Ramsey. The agreement of 12 April 1898 with the Manx Northern was £2 10s rent a day for the engine and 3s each for open wagons Nos 20 and 21 and low-side ballast wagons Nos 24 and 29. The wages were 5s 6d and 4s a day for the driver and fireman, and 3s 2d a night for a cleaner, paid by the M N R and claimed back from the I O M T & E P.

Work at Bulgham began on 15 November 1897, after the Highway Board on 11 October had agreed to close the road for three months. In places, the road was diverted some thirty feet inland and the tramway built on its former drystone walled embankment, but at one point it was built out on a partly cantilevered shelf. A proposed 45-yard viaduct was not built, the older road's retaining wall being used instead to support the new formation. By 19 April the road was still closed and even when reopened it was not properly metalled, nor was this completed to the satisfaction of the Highway Board until 26 April 1901. An angle-iron railing contrived to look like a solid bar was added to the parapet wall in 1899 to reassure nervous passengers alarmed at their 600-ft high vantage point.

Work at Laxey was meanwhile held up by a change of plan. By March of 1898, the Highway Board had consented to a road crossing in Laxey, and the church authorities had agreed to the line passing through the churchyard to a station in mine-captain Reddicliffe's garden; his house survives in part as the station hotel. This eliminated the unpopular underpass, but meant that the Snaefell line would have to be altered yet again to bring the two lines into today's common station. Work began on 14 March 1898, and con-tractor Mark Carine then built the curved four-arched viaduct in only four months. On the far side, after a girder underbridge end-on to the viaduct, a joint station was laid out for the coastal and Snaefell lines, bordered by a triangular grass plot laid out with rustic seats and kiosks. The station building was moved across from the 1897 Snaefell terminus and re-erected, the board over the veranda now announcing 'LAXEY JUNCTION—change for Snaefell'. In 1899, a huge wooden refreshment room with restaurant and bar was built alongside, 140 ft by 40 ft; it was destroyed by fire on 24 September 1917.

Beyond Bulgham was Dhoon Glen, later provided with a rustic building that included a stationmaster's office. The glen was rented by I O M T & E P, who charged 4d for admission and paid 1¾d to the owners; a similar charge was made at the other four glens, Groudle, Garwick, Laxey and Ballaglass. Small waiting-rooms were provided at Glen Mona, Ballaglass and Port Lewaigue. North of Dhoon Glen lay the 53-acre Dhoon granite quarry, leased by Bruce in October 1895, whose prospects were a factor in the Ramsey line promotion, and whose setts had paved the Upper Douglas cable line. Bruce had imported men from Dalbeattie, the Scottish granite centre, to develop the project, and his aim (soon realised) of ex-porting setts to the mainland gave added point to an 1897 plan for a line ending at Ramsey harbour. There was also a quarry and siding for building stone at Ballajora.

The original plan at Ramsey was to cross Ballure Glen and end at the Pavilion, but meanwhile the town commissioners had pro-posed a new line along the shore from Port Lewaigue, to a point near the Queen's pier. A ratepayers' meeting had approved the idea, even though it would have involved a 1d or 1½d rate. I O M T & E P duly met a Tynwald committee, while some preliminary work was done at Port e Vullen.

Drawings by Knowles show that the promenade from Port

Lewaigue was to be 50 ft wide, with a 4-ft footpath, 20-ft tramway, 16-ft roadway and 10-ft seaward footpath, all to be built by IOMT&EP with a £2,250 contribution from the Ramsey town commissioners, agreed on 29 June 1897. Tynwald approved the alteration on 7 August and revealed plans for a further extension

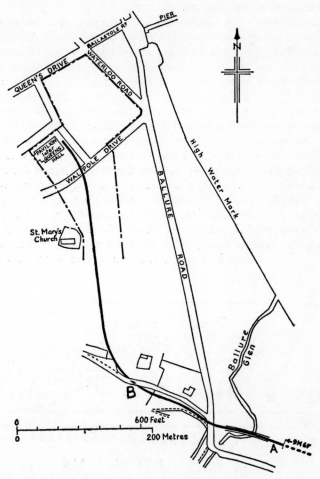

Ramsey entry as proposed in 1897, with underpass at B. Limits of deviation at the terminus are shown in chain dotted line. During 1898 the line ended at point A

along the existing south promenade to Ramsey harbour, with approving comments. Just when and why the company abandoned this scheme was never publicly stated, though it emerged later that Bruce had told the Ramsey town commissioners in the spring of 1898 that the scheme would have to be dropped, reportedly for geological reasons. The initial deviation is shown on our route map, commencing at Close 262.

Notwithstanding its enormous commitment, the IOMT&EP also now became involved in behind-the-scenes moves for taking over the Manx Northern Railway, whose traffic would be affected by the new line. By 24 January 1898 IMR chairman Sir John Goldie-Taubman had got wind of this, and wrote to MNR chairman J. C. Lamothe deploring any such merger and suggesting that the MNR put their line up for sale on the open market. Lamothe admitted negotiations and said that the MNR's only object was to get the best price, and Bruce confirmed to IMR director Stevenson (chairman of Dumbell's Bank) that it was the MNR who had approached the IOMT&EP, and not the reverse. On 3 February offers from any party were invited, and on 22 February MNR acting chairman Todhunter offered to sell to the IMR for £72,500, with a 28 February deadline. Nothing came of this, but a typewritten IMR analysis survives of the whole affair, revealing that IOMT&EP were prepared to electrify the MNR and build their own electric line from St Johns to Douglas. It ends with the words

The site of Ballure depot, 1898-9. The junction was about 145 ft from the bridge

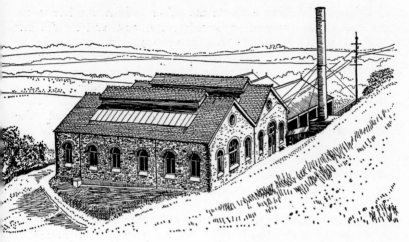

Ballaglass power station, 1898

'The promoters of the Electric Company are very popular in the Island and have immense influence, both legislative and financial. . . .'

By July 1898 the new line had been built as far as Ballure, just short of Ramsey, but with only a single line through the cutting at Ballagorry. Once again Colonel Rich and Major Cardew came to inspect the new line, reporting the same day, 18 July.

Colonel Rich found the 3 ch 4f connecting branch tramway incomplete, as was the line into Ramsey beyond Ballure. At Ballagorry, the deep cutting contained only a single line—otherwise double track was complete throughout. The rails of 62½ lb/yd section were in 31 ft 6 in lengths, on 9 in x 4½ in sleepers 6 ft long. Fang-bolts were used in addition to spikes. Laxey's brick arched masonry viaduct had four 30-ft spans and there were also listed the similar span at Minorca, two girder underbridges, the 18-ft culvert at Ballaglass and other smaller structures. The gradient maximum was 1 in 24, and the minimum curvature, 2½ chains.

Rich, taking exception to the lack of numerous finishing touches and, more seriously, of protective devices at Ballagorry's single-line section, refused his approval. Cardew was much more satisfied with the electrical side of the undertaking and merely sought a later check on the performance of the new cars and the return circuits.

Following intensive work on the points at issue, the line to the Ballure railhead opened on Tuesday, 2 August, and for the first time I O M T & E P received full governmental recognition of its efforts. The opening was attended by the Lieutenant-Governor, Lord Henniker, accompanied by the Lord Bishop, Ramsey's High Bailiff, J. M. Cruikshank, the chairman of the Ramsey town commissioners and other gentlemen, not forgetting Messrs Bruce, Knowles, Saunderson, Mylrea, Aldworth and Dr Farrell. The governor and the lord bishop travelled from Douglas by the shareholders' 'special', made up of two new motor-cars and all stations en route were flag-bedecked. Brief speeches at Ballure were followed by a drive to the Pavilion, for a splendid repast and further speeches. Cruikshank referred to probable losses by the Manx Northern due to the new line, but the governor, in a further speech, made the point that both lines might become part of a route all round the island. He saw the M N R route advantageous for the tourists' return journey. Bruce replied to a toast to I O M T & E P by summarising the work from its inception, and the special then returned to Douglas in eighty minutes.

Public traffic to Ballure began on the same day and continued until Monday, 24 October, when the extension was closed again for completion. Fares during the 1898 season from Douglas were 3d to Groudle, 6d to Garwick, 9d to Ballabeg and 1s to Laxey, with return fares of 3s 6d to Snaefell and 3s 6d to Ballure (for Ramsey). No depot yet existed at Laxey for the coastal line, but a shed for six cars with pits for three was built at Ballure, 126 ft 8 in long and 21 ft wide. In 1899 it was dismantled and re-erected at Parsonage Road.

The new generating equipment again used steam power and accumulators. In the new distribution system, the 1894-5 switchgear at Douglas was replaced by a larger installation with five slate panels, and a new seven-panel board was installed at Laxey, together with an additional Robb Armstrong engine with direct-coupled generator and an additional Galloway's boiler. A new feeder cable of the 1894 pattern was put in from Half-Way House to Ramsey, with feeder pillars at half-mile spacing, and a combined pilot and telephone cable was added between Laxey and Ramsey, all at the expense of the separate undertaking.

At the new steam power station at Ballaglass, $12\frac{1}{2}$ miles from Douglas, a fast flowing stream, the Corony, brought water to the very door, and the tramway passed high on an embankment down

(above) *The 1897 Snaefell terminus at Laxey, with access ramp to Vicarage on right and Dumbell's Row immediately beyond the car. The spoil heap, locally known as 'the deads', was from the lead mines;* (below) IMR *No 2* Derby *near Feeder Point 16 on the Ramsey line during construction, winter 1897-8*

Page 180
(above) *No 19 posed on Ballure bridge, winter* 1899; (below) *Bonner road-rail wagons in service at Laxey,* 1899

which coal brought by tram from Ramsey readily fell to the bunkers at its foot. The station was most ornate, with walls panelled waist-high with varnished pitch pine cut 'on the quarter', and the tiled floor patterned round each piece of the plant.

The building is of stone with a slate roof, and consists of two large halls placed north—south, with a boiler house and coal store placed end-on. One hall was the engine room, measuring 73 ft by 32 ft 6 in, the other was a battery room 65 ft by 32 ft 6 in; the boiler room and adjoining coal store were each 56 ft by 31 ft. Two boilers (again by Galloways) were installed, 26 ft long and 6 ft 6 in in diameter, the same as the new boiler at Laxey. The boilers had feed pump and injector equipment, and also Ledward's No 8 ejector condensers and centrifugal circulation pumps driven by a 10-hp motor supplied by the Electric Construction Company. The exterior view today differs little from that in 1898, lacking only the iron chimney; this was 60 ft high and 5 ft in diameter.

Contractors for the generating equipment were now Dick, Kerr & Co, who installed two Robb Armstrong tandem compound engines direct coupled to ECC six-pole multipolar generators. The engines, fed with steam at 120 lb/in^2, were of 180 indicated horsepower at 175 rpm, and each generator produced 240 amps at 500 volts. The makers' numbers for these two generators and the similar new set at Laxey were 4332-4, and the armatures measured 51 in by 16$\frac{1}{2}$ in. Other equipment in the engine room included a booster set, comprising a 500V/150V shunt wound motor generator (ECC No 4476) for charging the batteries, and a 150V series generator (ECC No 4477) used for raising pressure on the new feeder system. An additional feeder ran two and a half miles northwards from Ballaglass to assist in maintaining voltage on the steep grades. Switchgear totalled seven slate panels (two for the generators, two for battery circuits, two for testing and one for booster), and the battery room contained a Chloride battery of 260 type 'R' cells rated to give 140 amps for six hours.

The results for 1898 were announced at the company's meeting held at Stathallan Crescent on 31 March 1899. Car mileage for Douglas—Laxey was 132,169, with costs of 10.66d/mile against receipts of 28.13d. Snaefell earned 33.37d/mile against costs of 20.24d, and car mileage for the whole system was 443,409, with a passenger total of 2,711,696. The 'separate undertaking' had raised £28,703 in shares and had an 'advance re debenture stocks' of £65,000; its capital now amounted to £106,535. Income from

L

revenue account had been £71. The general undertaking had a healthier aspect and 6 per cent was paid on both classes of share, but this was later found to be via 'shop-window' accountancy. Bruce looked towards the coming season as that in which the new line would begin to earn, and gave its cost as £6,000 per single-track mile, as against the £11,000 of the Blackpool—Fleetwood line of which he was also a director. All had previously ridden to Ballure, and a group photograph had been taken at Ballaglass.

At Ramsey, the stated aim was now to end at the Pavilion, but in June 1898 provisional agreement had been reached to extend beyond, and the company had bought the Palace concert-hall (a miniature of the one in Douglas) to use its grounds for a new terminus, the building being let off. By 16 May 1899, Ramsey town commissioners dictated their revised terms for this extension—that IOMT&EP should pay them 5 per cent of the gross earnings of the tramway within the town for twenty years, commencing in 1904. The length of town tramway for this calculation was put at a half mile, out of a ten-mile total. Bruce refused, bought further land at the Pavilion, and ordered four Bonner road-rail wagons with which he could haul goods from any part of the town 'without the assistance of tramlines'. A line would still run on to Mr Cruikshank's garden (see map), but only for goods and boat traffic.

The commissioners now retreated and on 1 June 1899 agreed to a line from the Pavilion to the Palace and beyond to the quay, without the proposed toll but with a flat rate charge of £10 per year against IOMT&EP, who were also to light the street inter-sections. The commissioners' debates revealed the proposed route to the quay as 'across Parsonage Road and the old Pump Road and then below Mr Cruikshank's house, skirting round here and going down to Casement's on the Quay'. A line along Queen's Drive to the Queen's Pier was also agreed, subject to Tynwald approval.

Meanwhile, much of the Douglas—Laxey section had been planted with ornamental shrubs, and further waiting rooms had been built (or planned) at Half-Way House, Garwick, Ballabeg and South Cape. Most of these still exist, but the Half-Way House shelter was later moved to Minorca. New cars for the Ramsey service arrived on 13 May. The cutting at Ballagorry had been widened to take a double track and, by early June 1899, work was in full swing on Ballure bridge. This had two spans, formed by four girders 80 ft by 9 ft in pairs, placed 10 ft apart, with one girder under each track. The southern abutments carry on a cast-iron plate the names of the manufacturer (Francis Morton & Co of Garston, Liverpool) and the erector, William Knowles, CE, and the date, 1899.

At last, on 17 June, the line was reopened to Ballure, with an

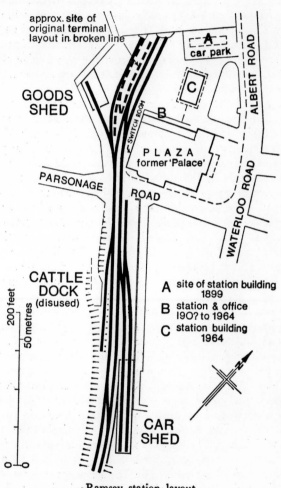

Ramsey station layout

hourly service. Track had been laid by 6 June to Parsonage Road, including some stretches in grooved rail at the behest of the land-owners concerned, and on 9 June the town commissioners (all forgiven!) were taken to Snaefell, under the guidance of Dr Farrell. Then, on the afternoon of 3 July 1899, a saloon car bearing Bruce, Farrell, Joshua Shaw and Knowles, ran through into Ramsey, and mail service began on 11 July. At the governor's invitation, Colonel Rich and Major Cardew officially inspected the new line, Rich on 21 July, Cardew on the 20th. Their reports are dated 22 August (!) and 27 July respectively. The 1,266-yard extension from 1898's terminal, the doubling at Ballagorry, and the new bridge all found approval, as did the new cars' performance. Cardew merely sought a regular earth return check in Ramsey town.

I O M T & E P advertisements announced the opening for 22 July, but the actual opening took place on Monday, 24 July 1899. An advertisement in the *Ramsey Courier* of 28 July specified out-of-town service from 7 am half-hourly until 9 pm, Sunday 9.30 am until 8 pm. The return fare to Douglas was 3s 6d (sixpence dearer than by carriage), and fell to 2s 6d after 4 pm. It was still 3s 6d in the winter of 1965-6! On bank holiday Monday, 7 August, bookings had to be suspended for a time because of the rush, and on Wednesday, 16 August, the line brought about 4,500 people from Douglas. Bruce had invited the six battalions of the West Yorkshire Infantry Volunteer Brigade to hold their annual camp near Ramsey, on the Milntown estate, and their manoeuvres around Snaefell culminated in a full-scale mock battle on 9 August held at a point only accessible by electric car and which the public were invited to witness! The Palace station, a single-storey building 55 ft by 12 ft 3 in, was completed by 25 August, and on 26 September the Bay Regatta had as its first prize a cup presented by I O M T & E P. Former governor Ridgeway visited the line on 13 October.

On 1 September 1899, three road/rail wagons from the Bonner Wagon Co of Toledo, Ohio, USA, entered service. Carried on a four-wheel 3-ft gauge truck, or on their own road wheels, the transition was effected by means of a simple trackside twin ramp which, by transferring the load to the road wheels, left the rail truck free to be withdrawn. The appearance was that of an orthodox high-sided, five-ton, two-horse cart, measuring 13 ft by 6 ft by 2 ft 6 in, with all four sides lowerable. The Bonner wagons were intended for a shuttle service, taking coal from Ramsey harbour to Ballaglass power station, and returning with setts from Dhoon quarry for export, but loading ramps also existed at Derby Castle and Laxey. Soon after the service began on 1 September complaints arose in Ramsey at the noise caused during the night, and this was solved

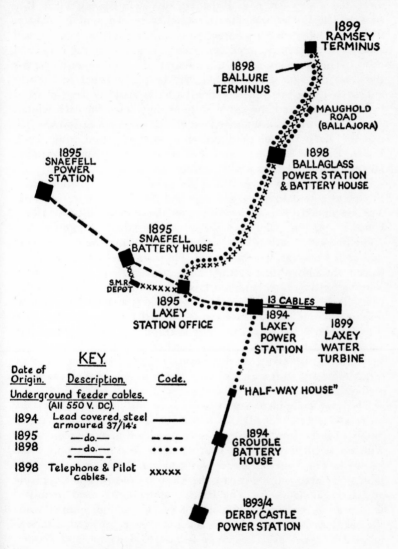

The electrical feeder system as evolved by 1899

from 5 September by making the road/rail transfer at Queen's Drive instead of Ramsey station, with a portable ramp.

Meanwhile, there was fresh activity in the Laxey valley. Here meet the Laxey river and the equally swift-flowing Glen Roy stream. The former was already exploited by the mining industry, whilst the latter drove a large corn mill, but an opportunity still existed for a water-powered generating station using the combined waters. The company saw in this a source of cheap winter power for the cars; the 1898 feeder system had been completed, and it was anticipated that all three traction batteries could be kept charged by the turbine, and the steam stations shut down for each winter. At this time the peak summer load on the three power stations had reached 2,200 hp, all produced from coal imported from South Wales. Even so, further extensions were contemplated, including an enormous brick chimney to be duly dated '1899'.

The turbine power plant was designed by Joshua Shaw, with F. Nell as consultant; Nell also supplied the turbines and pipework. The associated civil engineering was the responsibility of Harry Curphey, AMICE, who had been one of the company's 1894 apprentices. A headwork consisting of a concrete weir 40 ft long and 4½ ft high was first built across the river, after which the water passed through a first settling tank, then 826 ft of head race, a second settling tank, and 820 ft of 3 ft diameter x ⅛ in steel pipes. Considerable trouble was taken to avoid the entry of mineral residue. A total fall of 41 ft was obtained by taking water some distance above the steam power plant and discharging direct into Laxey harbour. The fall from the level of the weir to the centre of the turbines was 26 ft, the remaining 15 ft fall being obtained by 'draft tubes'. A 10-ft wide tail race, 624 ft in length, took the water to the harbour.

The new equipment was housed in a turbine house, 30 ft by 16 ft and 13 ft 3 in high to the eaves. Two independent Victor 70-hp 12-in horizontal turbines were provided, in a common casing with the shafts direct-coupled; at low water one turbine only could be used. The running speed was 720 rpm, driving a combined bipolar dynamo and booster by the Electric Construction Co, giving 160 amps at 520 volts. The friction clutch drive used permitted its use as an ordinary motor-driven booster in the summer when the river was very low. All the machines were provided with self-lubricating bearings. The mains from the generator and booster, and their regulating wires (totalling fifteen cables) were carried overhead to the steam power station 1,100 ft upstream, from which the turbines were initially controlled, two Lundell ¼-hp motors (powered from a small battery) being used to open and close the turbine regulators. Switch panels for the plant were thus included in the main switchboard in the steam station. (See *The Electrician* of 26 January 1900 for a detailed account.)

The turbine plant was normally worked in parallel with the three battery substations, each now containing 250 cells of the Chloride 'R' type. The turbine generator thus assisted the batteries when under load, as well as providing charging current. During the night, the booster was put in series with the generator, and the batteries charged at a heavy rate through the underground feeders, enabling a full load to be maintained on the turbines over the twenty-four hours. It was hoped that the steam plant might now be shut down for seven months of the year, but this was found to be over-optimistic. Plans were also prepared in 1899 for a similar plant at Ballaglass, with a weir below the tramway bridge and a 1,470-ft trench leading at 1 in 2,000 to the proposed turbine plant. A further plan of 1899 for a hydro-electric plant to provide power for the cable tramway's winding house has been mentioned in Chapter 2.

On 17 December 1899, Bruce performed what was to be his last public duty by starting the Laxey turbines; within a few months he was to be a dying man. The turbine plant successfully completed a 240 hours continuous test, and regular working commenced on 27 December. In October, a 6 per cent preference and 7½ per cent ordinary dividend had been declared for the six months to 30 June.

Nine months earlier, on 6 January 1899, W. E. Young had resigned the secretaryship, for the company was seriously overspent and he could not stomach the publication of the forthcoming balance sheet. But he kept his complaints private other than to the auditors, and so when, on Saturday, 3 February 1900, at 10 am, Dumbell's Bank suddenly closed, the entire Manx community was taken by surprise. The apparent cause was the withdrawal of an underwriting of 1 February by Parrs Bank, authorised by Bruce when he was already seriously ill at home. At once, I O M T & E P dismissed one hundred quarry workmen.

On Monday, 12 February, J. A. Mylrea had to tell his fellow bank shareholders that the 'absolute, most implicit confidence' placed in Bruce and manager Shimmon had been 'grossly betrayed'. The bank had, in fact, two major undisclosed liabilities. By 17

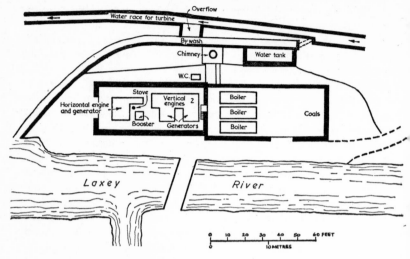

Laxey steam power station of 1894, with additions of 1898-9

March it emerged that the loan of £65,000 to the Laxey—Ramsey 'separate undertaking' had come not from England, but from Dumbell's, who then borrowed a like sum from the English bank concerned, and the whole landslide apparently started when the mainland bank wanted its money back from Dumbell's. By 12 May the true cost of the I O M T & E P lines emerged—£518,000, of which only £366,000 had been raised. The general undertaking's share capital was only £165,000, and I O M T & E P owed about £150,000 to Dumbell's Bank, whilst Ramsey-line land claims awaiting arbitration still totalled some £20,000. To help appearances, Bruce had dispensed some £15,646 in dividends out of capital.

By 9 June, warrants were issued for Nelson, Bruce, Shimmon, W. & H. Aldred (the tramway auditors) and J. D. Rogers. Bruce (in bed since March) had been showing signs of recovery, and had written letters in his own defence, but now he experienced a severe relapse and the high bailiff accepted without question evidence that his arrest would be fatal.

The I O M T & E P board had met on 7 February and, frightened by their financial position, called upon Turquand Young & Co to make a special audit, which took fifty-nine days. This 51-page

audit was based on the working for 1899, and it was a gloomy one.
Dividends had been paid 'other than out of profits' since 1896, and
in December 1897, when securing the £65,000 loan, debentures
had been issued with promissory notes as a charge against the
separate undertaking (one for £35,000 and another for £30,000)
for which latter the general undertaking was charged with £30,000
as collateral security. The year 1899 had seen a working loss of
£402, and the constructional costs for Laxey—Ramsey now emerged
as £153,412, including £38,349 for preliminaries and lands,
£73,400 for civil engineering and permanent way, and £41,662 for
overhead, cars and power. The trolley conversion cost was given
as £2,821. Unpaid calls on ordinary and preference shares totalled
£7,113. No further scandals were uncovered, and the criticisms of
Turquand Young were more an exercise in book-keeping logic.
Despite all this, Aldred Sons & Turner produced an optimistic
balance sheet for 1899 on 5 May.

The company's meeting was held late, on Thursday, 24 May.
J. R. Cowell, a director since March 1899, presided, and with him
were Mylrea, F. G. Callow and Dr Farrell, along with Joshua Shaw
and F. Browne. Dhoon quarry was by now completely closed, and
the hotels let off. Service had been kept going, but all the time
English creditors were proceeding against the company. A minor
point of interest was the repudiation of Bruce's further order to
Colonel Bonner for six more wagons. Cowell explained that while
the audit had been in progress he had sought interviews with
several English banks to whom money was owed, begging more
time and asking for capital in the form of a loan, but this failed,
as did requests for help from London financiers.

In desperation, Cowell had next tried to sell the entire concern,
so as to give a fair return to the shareholders—but potential buyers
could see their chance of getting hold of the line from a liquidator
for less. The total capital needed to put the concern on its feet
was £150,000. Coming to the Snaefell Mountain Railway purchase,
Cowell defended the transaction as a perfectly open and fair one,
though he admitted that the Laxey and Ramsey section's earning
power was inadequate to cover even the money already spent on
it : ill tidings for its shareholders ! He then detailed the various
debts on capital; until 1895 things had been kept straight, but
overspending thereafter had been £533 in 1896, £22,587 in 1897,
£12,010 in 1898 and £51,861 in 1899, a total of £86,991. Excusing
the board's apparent acquiescence, he blamed Bruce for everything,

but praised Joshua Shaw who had latterly 'carried' the whole concern, as both engineer and secretary.

A plausibly-explained rider by Aldred Sons & Turner to their accounts for 1898 was then produced, which effectively exonerated both themselves and Cowell and his fellow directors from blame. Cowell ended by proposing acceptance of the 1899 accounts, and suggested that a committee drawn from shareholders should look further into affairs with the board, which was agreed. Though his speech had been given a quiet hearing, Cowell's proposal to adopt the 1899 accounts was defeated; speakers condemned the board and Bruce repeatedly, but excused Cowell, who had been either busy in America or ill at home for much of 1899. The Snaefell Association had clearly made a very smart deal for themselves, their shares reaching one and a half times their par value at the time of the sale. W. E. Young was present, and the facts of his resignation came out; he had first protested at a profit of £6,000 made by the general undertaking in contracting for the new line, which the board then dropped, but when in September of the same year Bruce announced a £10,000 profit from the same source (and 7½ per cent interim dividend), Young gave notice and left. After more exchanges on the subject of Snaefell, all adjourned until 15 June.

The meeting of Friday, 15 June, was as lengthy as that of 24 May, and even more disjointed. The shareholders' committee had held fruitless discussions with the board, and two factions now emerged; those who hoped to find more capital, and those who favoured liquidation, knowing that a liquidator and receiver would rescue all he could. The latter group, largely debenture holders, were accused of seeking to scuttle in their own interests. Meanwhile, a creditor (Robert Okell) had lodged a petition in court to wind up the company, and it was finally decided to adjourn until Tuesday, 19 June, the day following the court hearing.

On Monday, 18 June, the Clerk of the Rolls presided, and in his dealing with the petitioner showed that the company had at least some sympathy in the insular courts. By this time, however, the company lacked directors, as Mylrea had resigned (His Honour —'Who has he resigned to?'). Farrell, who was in court, later protested that he, Mylrea and Callow were still directors, but to no avail, and the Clerk of the Rolls adjourned the petition until Thursday. At the adjourned company meeting on 19 June Farrell was re-elected to directorship, with newcomers Messrs Ward,

The 1899 station at Ramsey

Harrison, Clare, Shackleton, Hodson, and Dr Edward Hopkinson, and a supporting committee of shareholders.

Appearing at court on 20 June, the new board obtained an extension of grace until 11 July, and were willing that a receiver (W. H. Walker) be appointed meanwhile, though he was not to interfere with Shaw's management of the line, of which all approved. At the court hearing of 11 July no further progress had been made by the company towards self-salvation, and liquidation was enforced, with W. H. Walker as liquidator. His appointment as receiver was confirmed by the Clerk of the Rolls on 25 July, and all the familiar names hereafter vanish from the scene.

The order for sale was not made until 3 July 1901, and by then a historically invaluable liquidator's book, largely the work of Mr Ramsey B. Moore, later Attorney-General, was ready for circulation. Apparently even in mid-1901, the company's paper affairs, especially concerning land purchase, were still in an appalling state.

The bank trial took place in Douglas from 5 to 19 November 1900, and the five offenders present were found guilty. Shimmon and Nelson received sentences of eight years' penal servitude each, and Aldred senior, then seventy-five years of age, escaped with six months hard labour. Bruce was not there, for he had died at 2 am on Saturday, 14 July, the news of the liquidation being perhaps the last blow. His funeral on the Tuesday following was an occasion for public curiosity, and some older Manx folk continue to believe that the coffin contained but stones, and that the culprit had, in fact, escaped. More realistically, and fairly, the Press admitted that 'had Mr Bruce died a year ago, half Douglas would have followed his coffin'.

George J. Milnes & Co. Ltd
BUILDERS
TRAMWAY & LIGHT RAILWAY
CARRIAGE WORKS
BIRKENHEAD, ENGLAND

CHAPTER EIGHT

The Manx Electric Takeover

'The popular OPEN and CLOSED ELECTRIC CARS along the COAST ROUTE, noted for its COAST AND MOUNTAIN VIEWS.'—

M E R publicity folder

At 11 am on 7 September 1901, tenders for the purchase of the liquidated undertaking were opened. The offers, which included one from the British Electric Traction Company, lay between £188,850 and £225,000, the latter for all five lines (horse, cable, and three electric). Douglas Corporation's final offer of £50,000 for the horse and cable lines was accepted on 25 September, but the liquidator was dissatisfied with the others, and things dragged on until January 1902, when a prominent merchant banker of Continental origin (representing himself as 'a Manchester syndicate') offered £250,000 for the electric lines, and this was accepted. The sale was sanctioned by the Clerk of the Rolls on 5 September 1902, the final figure being £252,000, and completion was to be by 14 November.

A new company, the Manx Electric Railway Company, was incorporated on 12 November 1902. Its leading figures were Ernest Schenk (nominee for the purchaser), A. G. Kitching, William H. Vaudrey, and Bernard E. Greenwell, most of whom had interests in overseas railways, mainly South American. The registered office was in London, at 78 Cornhill. Schenk, who changed his name in 1913 to Remnant, had numerous personal directorships including the Crystal Palace Company, the South Manchurian Syndicate, and the Yorkshire Electric Tramways Construction Syndicate. The

Greenwell family were noted London stockbrokers, and took up the lion's share of the new M E R's capital. Boscawen and Vaudrey were later knighted, and Greenwell became a baronet. The purchase price by the new company to the 'Manchester syndicate' on 30 November was £370,000 . . .

Meanwhile, in December 1901, Joshua Shaw, general manager and engineer of the I O M T & E P since January 1899, resigned as mentioned in Chapter 2. His successor as engineer of the future Manx Electric system was I O M T & E P employee Frank Edmondson, then about twenty-seven years of age, and earlier a product of Dr Farrell's Victoria College and of Owen's College, Manchester. Later in 1902, the new owners appointed as manager Harold Brown, a young self-made Manxman who had begun his working career with the steam-packet company and had rapidly risen to take charge of the goods department at Douglas. One of Shaw's last engineering tasks before departure had been the erection in 1901 of a three-span wooden footbridge over the line at Balla-

Royal Journey: inside No 59, 25 August 1902 (from *The Golden Penny*, courtesy: Manx Museum)

gorry cutting, replaced in the 1950s by a neat M E R-built concrete
structure.

On 25 August 1902 the coast electric line, then still administered
by the liquidator of the I O M T & E P, was the scene of a royal
journey. Landing from the royal yacht at Ramsey during their
post-Coronation cruise, King Edward VII and Queen Alexandra
drove in carriages from Ramsey to Kirk Michael, Peel, Tynwald

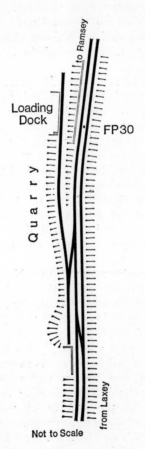

Ballajora quarry siding, as installed in 1898-9. Stone from both Dhoon
and Ballajora quarries was used to reballast the Douglas—Laxey line in
1904

Hill and Douglas, and returned to Ramsey by the electric railway. At Derby Castle, where the double-deck horse cars formed a convenient grandstand at 2d per patron, their Majesties were greeted by a guard of honour, Hall Caine, and a band, plus local dignitaries. Draped in royal purple, the saloon trailer No 59 was coupled to one of the 19-22 series motor cars, with the late Harry Quayle as conductor and William Hunter as motorman, and made a fast run to Ramsey, with Edmondson as accompanying guide. The M E R still possess a handsome brass plate commemorating this visit, and for many years used the 'Royal Route' slogan in their publicity. The royal trip ended at Walpole Drive, whence an open carriage drawn by fishermen conveyed the royal party to Ramsey pier.

The authorised capital of the new Manx Electric Railway Company was £500,000, half in shares and half in debenture stock; of the share capital, half was to be in ordinary and half in 5½ per cent preference shares. By March of 1903, £200,000 of the share capital and £170,000 of the 4½ per cent debenture stock had been raised, largely by the Greenwells. The first statutory meeting of the new company was held in Douglas late in February 1903, under Bernard E. Greenwell's chairmanship. The purchase agreement of 13 November 1902 included retrospective adjustment to 18 August, and since that date £12,239 had been earned and £8,152 spent; debenture interest had absorbed £4,726. Mileage run had been 146,187 for passengers, and 16,556 for goods, including 'company's service'.

Permanent way superintendent Robert Newell reported on the entire coastal line as in early 1903. Alarmingly, there was scarcely one mile of 'good' track between Douglas and Laxey, and no serious attempt at ballasting had been made until March 1900; instead, a dressing of stone had simply been put on top of the earth ballast. The drains had soon filled with earth, due to vibration, and the sleepers had so deteriorated in six or seven years that Newell had already put in 6,000 new sleepers and reballasted accordingly, until stopped by the liquidation. Fencing repairs were another headache, especially as the sharing of responsibility between Douglas Bay Estates and the tramway company was never properly settled. Some of Newell's requirements must have caused rather a shock to the new owners—he wanted 120 tons of rail, up to 20,000 tons of stone ballast, and new sleepers to the tune of 5,200, for Douglas—Laxey alone.

Page 197

(above) *Locomotive No 23 (I) at Derby Castle depot;* (below) *Cattle car No 12 at Derby Castle, about* 1909

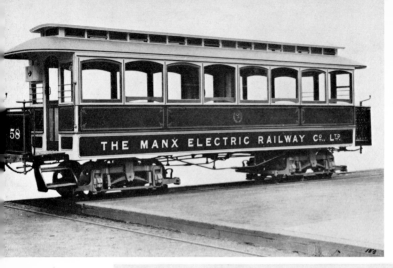

Page 198
Builders' pho-
graph of sa
trailer No

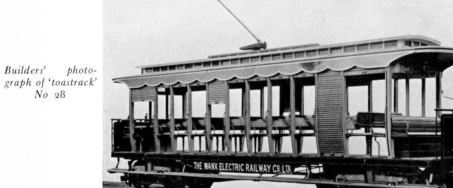

Builders' photo-
graph of 'toastrack'
No 28

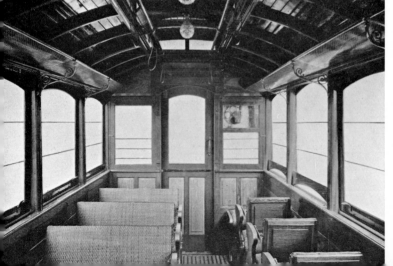

Interior of No
The rattan sea
has now been
placed by moqu
and the lugg
racks remove

On the Ramsey section, less work was needed apart from local ballasting and alignment of the 62½ lb/yard rail, and the sleepers were appreciably better. The new company disliked the partially cantilevered 1898 tracks at Bulgham, and their consulting civil engineer, Douglas Cooper, had met Highway Board officials at Bulgham in the previous October. It was decided to move the tracks on to the solid rock (within today's sinuously curved retaining wall), and to move the public road in by a similar amount by cutting back the cliff. Leave was given to close the road for six months from January 1903, and the work was already under way by the end of February. In the first year £1,240 was spent on this and £3,332 in the next; completion was delayed by a landslip, and was not finally achieved until October 1904. Spoil removed from Bulgham to the end of 1903 totalled 46,735 tons.

How much else of Newell's ambitions were fulfilled is a little difficult to say. He raised and ballasted the Douglas—Laxey track during 1904, and put in some very heavy rails at the various road crossings, about 100 tons of 85 lb/yard rail being bought. He also advocated (and obtained) a crossover at Ballameanagh, where the locomotive had been obliged to run many dead miles in shunting during reballasting. Another request remained unfulfilled; Newell was worried about the lack of catch points on the long upgrades, and when taking a run had made a practice of riding in the last wagon of a train. During the next few years, the drains, hedges and platforms were completed and improved, and several interrupted curves were converted into easier continuous ones.

On the electrical side, the new company was also penalised. By 1902 Ferranti's work on AC supply had utterly discredited DC generation and distribution, and the slow reciprocating steam power plant was equally obsolescent. Immediately on taking possession, the new company asked the engineering consultants, Messrs Kincaid, Waller, Manville & Dawson of Westminster, to report on how to bring the line up to modern (1903) technical standards. Mr Dawson's report, which was accepted *in toto*, recommended a change to AC generation and distribution, and re-equipment of the cars. Tenders were invited, and the major contract was awarded on 16 February 1903 to Witting, Eborall & Co. Other (higher) tenders were received from British Thomson-Houston and from British Schuckert.

Laxey steam power station, which lay nearest to harbour facilities, was selected as the hub of the new AC system, and the gener-

M

ating side was reconstructed in the five months to July, 1903. The Galloway boilers were augmented by two Climax cylindrical vertical water-tube boilers by B. Rowland & Co of Reddish, 12 ft in diameter and 23 ft 1 in high, which could raise 150 lb/in² of steam in thirty minutes and produce 11,000 lb/hour at a pressure of 165 lb/in². Each had a self-contained 75-ft steel chimney 44 in in diameter, and mild-steel steam pipes to the two new engines. The auxiliaries comprised a surface condensing plant by Mirrlees & Watson, and two Weir feed pumps.

The new engines were totally-enclosed Bellis & Morcom triple-expansion machines of 400 horsepower, Nos 1702 and 1956, the three cylinders having respective diameters of 12, 17, and 26 inches and a 13-inch stroke. The working pressure was 155 lb/in², and the running speed 375 rpm. These drove two 300-kW revolving field alternators with star-connected armatures producing three-phase alternating current at 7,000 volts, 25 cycles, built to a special ultra-compact design evolved by the Société l'Electricité et l'Hydraulique of Charleroi, Belgium, forerunners of the present A C E C company. The Galloway's boilers and the Robb-Armstrong engine were retained, as was the water-turbine plant, but the 1894 Galloway/Mather & Platt sets were removed and offered for sale. The new high-tension switchgear was placed in a special fireproof annexe, and was remotely controlled from a nine-panel white marble switchboard erected above the old low-tension board.

On the distribution system, the work was divided between Henley's (underground) and R. W. Blackwell (overhead). The old underground DC feeders were retained as part of the distribution network, and are still capable of use today—a wonderful tribute to their makers. The 7,000-volt supply was taken through the new AC feeders to rotary converter sub-stations at Douglas, Groudle, Ballaglass and Snaefell, and to similar equipment inside the Laxey power station. The sub-stations contained six-pole rotary converters by Kolben & Co of Prague, with a speed of 500 rpm and a rating of 150 kW at 330/550 volts, 25 cycles, designed for alternative compound or simple wound operation, and fed through pairs of 75-kW transformers by Kolben, air-cooled when first installed but converted later to oil cooling. The rotary converter at Laxey was started from the DC side by means of the Groudle battery plant.

At Douglas, the 1893-4 generating plant was taken out of use, and the rotary and its six-panel marble switchboard went into the engine room. The Galloway/Mather & Platt sets were dismantled and offered for sale. The Bellis alternator set used for the public supply was split, the engine being sold and replaced by a 75-hp motor supplied by Witting, Eborall. One rotary converter was

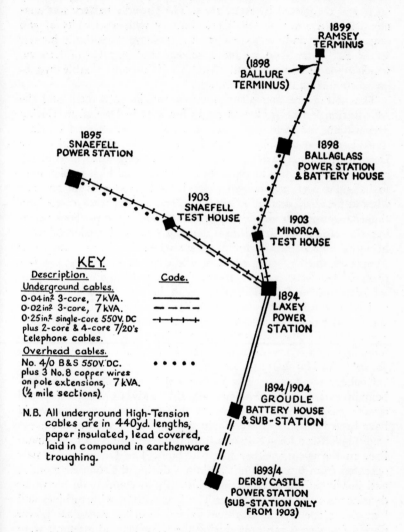

KEY.

Description.   Code.

Underground cables.

0·04 in² 3-core, 7 kVA.
0·02 in² 3-core, 7 kVA.
0·25 in² single-core 550V. DC
plus 2-core & 4-core 7/20's
telephone cables.

Overhead cables.
No. 4/0 B&S 550V. DC.
plus 3 No. 8 copper wires
on pole extensions, 7 kVA.
(½ mile sections).

N.B. All underground High-Tension
cables are in 440yd. lengths,
paper insulated, lead covered,
laid in compound in earthenware
troughing.

1899
RAMSEY
TERMINUS

(1898
BALLURE
TERMINUS)

1895
SNAEFELL
POWER STATION

1898
BALLAGLASS
POWER STATION
& BATTERY HOUSE

1903
SNAEFELL
TEST HOUSE

1903
MINORCA
TEST HOUSE

1894
LAXEY
POWER
STATION

1894/1904
GROUDLE
BATTERY HOUSE
& SUB-STATION

1893/4
DERBY CASTLE
POWER STATION
(SUB-STATION ONLY
FROM 1903)

M E R AC distribution system, added to the DC feeder system of 1899 placed in Laxey power station, and two more (each with a four-panel switchboard) in that at Ballaglass, of which one set was intended for Snaefell. The other two rotary converters were placed in a new stone substation building at Groudle, measuring 44 ft by 30 ft and completed by April 1904. The Groudle battery was augmented by a new 260-cell Tudor battery with a capacity of 560 ampere-hours, and by a new 72-hp 160-amp Swiss-built booster set of R. Thury type by the Electrical Industry Co of Geneva, which remained in use until 1944. An eight-panel marble switchboard completed the new plant here.

The new generating plant was first run in July 1903, and the AC distribution network was ready for tests in December. During preparations for these tests, No 1 Bellis alternator suffered a serious short circuit, consuming five coils; the culprit was found on 22 December, a mouse whose charred remains were discovered in the machine frame. Later in December, the overhead high-tension lines to Ballaglass were commissioned, and stood 7,500 volts for an hour without trouble, despite a wet day. These lines were carried on timber extensions from the overhead standards : the rulebook warning the crews not to mistake the AC overhead feeder between Minorca and Ballaglass for a trolley wire ! The new system was completed during 1904, when one Mather & Platt 1895 set was removed from the Snaefell mountain power station and the spare rotary converter from Ballaglass (with its four switchgear panels and twin transformers) was installed in its place, fed by an already completed 7,000-volt pole-mounted line from Laxey; this line now carries 6,600 volts AC to the present-day rectifiers. (Many of the foregoing details are taken from the *Light Railway and Tramway Journal* of 4 March 1904.)

Coal for the Laxey power station was brought up from the harbour by cart, but in February 1904, Edmondson proposed a special electric railway from the quay to the power station. This would have been isolated from the main system, but in 1906 final surveys were made for a longer branch tramway continuing up to the main line. In the event, neither line was built. The Laxey station now operated from 6.30 am until midnight during the summer months, and in winter was steamed intermittently to compensate for water deficiency at the turbine plant. The longest runs with turbines and batteries alone averaged three to four weeks. Ballaglass power station from 1904 ran only during the summer, and attempts were made (against Edmondson's advice) to sell off the entire Snaefell

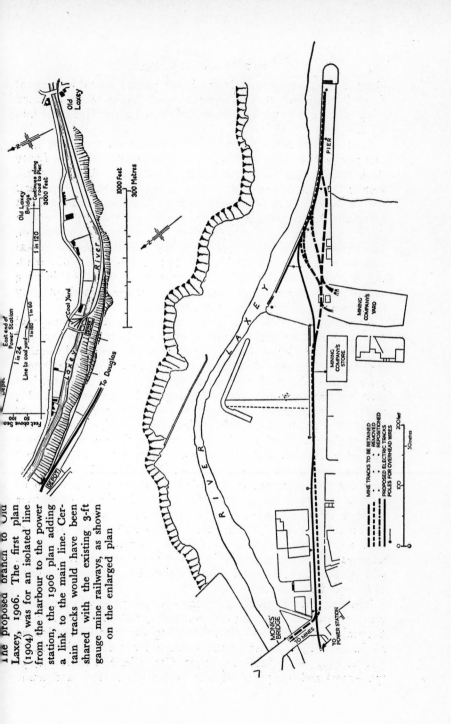

The proposed branch to Old Laxey, 1906. The first plan (1904) was for an isolated line from the harbour to the power station, the 1906 plan adding a link to the main line. Certain tracks would have been shared with the existing 3-ft gauge mine railways, as shown on the enlarged plan

Feet above Sea

Depot

East end of Power Station

1 in 24

Line to coal yard

1 in 160   1 in 60

Coal Yard

DEPOT

To Douglas

1 in 60

1 in 120

Old Laxey Bridge

Continue along road to Pier

Old Laxey

1000 Feet
300 Metres

3000 Feet

River Laxey

R I V E R   L A X E Y

MONKS' BRIDGE
TO MINES
TO POWER STATION

MINING COMPANY'S STORE

MINING COMPANY'S YARD

PIER

MINE TRACKS TO BE RETAINED
REMOVED
REPOSITIONED
PROPOSED ELECTRIC TRACKS
POLES FOR OVERHEAD WIRES

200 feet
100
50 metres
0

plant, but this plan was dropped and partial steam working at Snaefell continued until 3 September 1924, after which a second 1903 rotary converter was transferred from Laxey. This came into use in 1925.

Coal consumption was now reduced to between 2,000 and 3,000 tons per year. Staffing remained at around twenty-three; the Laxey steam station had two drivers (who in winter worked as fitters), four shift firemen, two shift trimmers, two switchboard men and one or two apprentices. Laxey turbine house now had a night attendant, Ballaglass had an attendant for the rotaries, an engine driver, a fireman and an apprentice, Snaefell had one fireman, an engine driver and an apprentice, the Groudle sub-station was manned on a shift basis, and Derby Castle had an apprentice tending its rotary converter and an additional man on the AC lighting supply plant. The staffing of the Snaefell plant seems to imply only partial working, probably on busy afternoons.

Re-equipment of the cars by Witting, Eborall & Co was spread over two years, for the successful summer season of 1903 demanded full use of the rolling stock. A welcome result was a reduction in the standard journey time for Douglas—Laxey to thirty minutes; prior to the advent of the four-motor ECC cars of 1898, the best time had been 35-40 minutes, reflecting the low power of the 1893 and 1894 equipments. The load was then limited to one light trailer or a goods wagon, but not both; Joshua Shaw before 1900 quoted the weight of a train as $8\frac{1}{2}$ tons for the motor-car plus 3 tons of passengers, and a 4-ton trailer with 3 tons of passengers or a $1\frac{1}{2}$-ton wagon with 6-ton payload. The 1898 ECC equipments gave a better performance, recorded on test in 1901 with No 21 hauling two 1899 trailers from Douglas to Laxey at an average speed of 15.23 mph with an average current consumption of 104.72 amperes. If the average was calculated to include the periods of coasting, the consumption on this run worked out at only 65 amperes. Three-car trains, as in this example, are today only run with empty stock (as when pairs of lightweight trailers are hauled to Ramsey for winter storage).

The first winter's working by the new company was somewhat unrepresentative. The new company's financial year ended on 30 September, and the next annual meeting was held in London on 26 January 1904, to adopt the accounts for the period from 18 August 1902 to 30 September 1903. Car miles had been 448,639 (passenger) and 39,237 (goods and company's service), and traffic

overall was 20 per cent up on earlier years. Earnings were £41,000
against costs of £20,435, enabling debenture interest and preference interest to be paid and the equivalent of 3¼ per cent on
the ordinary shares to be carried forward to the following year.

On the capital side, the issued capital had reached £395,098, but
expenditure already totalled £400,042. The bill for new works
now totalled £44,399, plus £3,332 spent on Bulgham and £1,508
in repurchasing Dhoon quarry. A new 16-car depot 150 ft 6 in
by 40 ft (by Carine) and a large goods shed were being built at
Laxey, and a goods shed at Ramsey, where the layout was altered.
New waiting shelters were being erected at out-of-town locations,
new trailer cars had arrived from the Hadley Castle works of
G. F. Milnes, and much of the work on re-equipping the cars had
been carried out. A further £20,584 was spent in the following
year, bringing the total outlay to £420,455. By September 1905,
this figure had risen to £422,605, of which nearly £6,000 was for
new vehicles.

The company meeting of 3 January 1905 must have found the
summer results of 1904 rather disappointing; only 472,556 passengers had been carried as against 557,346 in 1903. Car miles for
1904 were 378,721 (passenger) and 58,901 (goods). No ordinary
dividend was paid, and the year's balance of some £780 was carried
forward. The next year, 1905, was better, with 501,696 passengers
and 359,960 car miles (plus 38,732 for goods), and the expenses/
receipts ratio had improved from 56/44 to 47/53. Preference
shareholders continued to receive their 5½ per cent, and the debenture interest was always paid, but there was still no dividend
on the ordinary shares.

Perhaps fortunately, the majority shareholding, both ordinary
and preference, lay in the hands of the Greenwells, who, indeed,
looked on the line as a family concern. In later years their losses
were considerable, and theirs was a charitable financial dynasty
from the Island's viewpoint. It was thus rather unjust that the line
was now regarded as the disliked 'outsider' in the Manx financial
corridors of power. The 1905 payments of 4½ per cent on £200,000,
5½ per cent on £127,500 and 0 per cent on £100,000 would, if
rearranged as a flat rate, pay just under 4 per cent on the whole
capital as at that date.

There now occurred a second attempt by the electric line to
take over the Manx Northern Railway. By April 1904 the Manx
Northern was rapidly drifting into the hands of the IMR, who had

worked the line, with government approval, since February. Vondy of the M N R favoured the M E R cause, and tried to have the sale to the I M R deferred for a month, though rumours that the M E R had already made an offer were unfounded. Edmondson put up a case for purchase to M E R secretary C. A. Huni, considering that on a capital of £75,000 the line would be valuable as an adjunct to the M E R and would confine I M R activity to the southern half of the island.

Following a wire from Huni, conveyed via Edmondson, Vondy had met M N R chairman Todhunter, talking until ten o'clock at night, and had then arranged a further meeting between Edmondson and the M N R chairman and directors for 12 April. However, they failed to appear, and later that day a shareholders' meeting, fearing I M R withdrawals, rejected any postponement. Edmondson then suggested to Huni that the M E R should advertise the fact that they could have improved on the I M R offer. Director Vaudrey sought to see the Attorney-General, and the I M R, now thoroughly frightened, were rushing their purchase through the Keys with all possible speed. On 18 April Huni wrote to Edmondson to say that the M E R board had decided to withdraw, and the Act of Tynwald allowing I M R takeover was passed on 24 May 1904. The two companies were finally merged as from 19 April 1905, and the price was a mere £60,000, poor comfort for the M N R shareholders who got only 14s for each preference share and 9s for each ordinary share.

The construction in 1903 of goods depots reflected a determined effort by manager Harold Brown to offset the unbalanced working season. At liquidation, there were twelve orthodox goods vehicles (Nos 1-12) and the three Bonner wagons, together with a locomotive (No 23) which ran on bogies borrowed seasonally from a passenger car. Early in 1903, passenger car No 12 was converted to a bogie motor cattle car, and further vehicles were added in subsequent years. During the agricultural peak period each spring, seatless 1893 trailers were pressed into service to carry bagged patent manure. The company were out for business in no uncertain terms, and traders' tickets were issued to Ramsey at 1s 6d return to those who undertook to send all their goods via M E R. An even larger goods shed was built at Douglas in 1908, on the site of the 1893 boiler house, and still stands.

By March 1912, goods stock had risen to twenty-nine vehicles, excluding the Bonner wagons, which were never listed as stock by the M E R, although certainly used for some years; their unrecorded demise is an exasperating mystery. Traffic had grown to cover a wide range of goods, and Mr William Duggan, former goods manager, remembers particularly the cattle rush for the 'Christmas

Edwardian peak traffic

Mart', horses for the Whitehaven boat sailing, up to 200 tons of flour for Corlett's mill at Laxey, and a regular 200-package total of luggage for the steam-packet's sailing on Friday night. The stone traffic from Dhoon quarries continued, usually in trains of two 6-ton wagons hauled by locomotive No 23 and transhipped to road vehicles at Derby Castle terminus close by the booking office. Dhoon granite setts were exported to the mainland and widely used in the island, and the quarries (latterly one on each side of the line) supplied lower-grade roadstone until 1961-3.

In addition to the goods and parcels traffic (including milk) provided by traders and farmers, the line was extensively used by the Post Office. The origins of this service go back to at least 1894, and an 1895 minute to the Postmaster-General refers to 'Kirk On-chan & Laxey Posts; revised service by Electric Tramway'. By 1897 postmen were using the line to travel to Half-Way House, and in 1899 bagged mail traffic was instituted between the Douglas and Ramsey sorting offices. At some date between 1899 and 1904 the contract was extended to include the timed collection of mail from lineside boxes by conductors, as well as a twice-daily bulk loading of mail for both Laxey and Ramsey. In winter, one journey sufficed.

The island's 1906 season was a record, and the M E R carried 535,021 passengers and earned £34,279. Mileages run were 368,152 passenger and 43,541 goods. A reserve fund for special renewals was invested in securities or in South American railway shares; this totalled £4,066 15s by 1907. The capital structure was overhauled, £2,500 being cancelled, leaving £475,000. The new cars and trailers delivered in 1906, and the opening on 10 August of the new Snaefell Summit hotel, completed the physical re-equipment of the line, stabilising the capital account. Results for the years 1907-13 are, therefore, presented in the form of a graph. (In 1907, a dividend of 1 per cent was at last paid on the ordinary shares.)

In 1906, the company had bought Laxey Glen and Gardens. First-class military bands were engaged each summer, including the Royal Artillery (Portsmouth) and HM Life Guards, and traffic was further enhanced. The company's involvement in the 'Glen Industry' was considerable, and dated back to an agreement of 28 September 1892 between Saunderson (as trustee for the Howstrake Company) and R. M. Broadbent (the future proprietor of Groudle Glen) whereby the sum of ¾d was payable to the company for each person entering the glen. Although the Howstrake company's

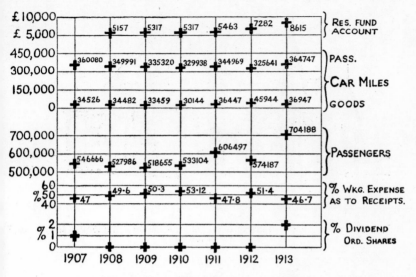

M E R traffic and finance, 1907 to 1913

private road commenced at Derby Castle, the portion to Groudle was free of toll, the toll-house being placed on the corner just beyond the entrance to Groudle Glen; tolls were charged until the late 1920s. Ballaglass Glen was at first rented and later owned by the tramway, and Garwick was the subject of an agreement like that for Groudle, with payments of 1d per head for adults, ½d for children, no fare from Douglas to be higher than sixpence. Its importance merited a station 30 ft 6 in by 14 ft. Dhoon Glen was rented, with a payment of 1¾d per head to the owners.

In July 1907, the M E R instituted a motor charabanc service from the Bungalow to Tholt-y-Will, at the head of Sulby Glen, where they erected a large rustic tea-room. The licensing returns show two Argus vehicles up to 1913, registrations MN 67 and 68, three for 1914 (the addition being a De Dion, MN 479), and two again after 1917. After the First World War a change was made to thirty-seat Caledons (MN 1053 and 1054), with a further change in 1926 to three Model 'T' Ford vehicles, replaced in 1937-9 by two Bedford twenty-seat WLBs, MN 8685 and 8686. For details of these and

The Bungalow hotel, starting-point of the motor charabanc service to Tholt-y-Will

later road vehicles, I am indebted to Mr W. T. Lambden. In 1907, 42,500 people arrived in the island over August bank holiday week-end, and the queue for electric cars stretched to the foot of Summer Hill, forcing the horse cars to stop.

By this time, the company had resumed possession of all its licensed houses, some of which had previously been let out (and which from 1899 were 'tied' to Isle of Man Breweries). A reference to the loss sustained from unsatisfactory tenancies occurs in the liquidator's report of 1901. A hotels manager was appointed for these activities, which at their maximum comprised six licensed houses, plus the refreshment rooms and a café at Laxey. The former were the Strathallan hotel at Douglas, the Laxey Station hotel, and the hotels and refreshment rooms at Bungalow, Snaefell, Tholt-y-Will and Dhoon. The latter, which was of some size, was to be destroyed by fire on 3 April 1932 and was not rebuilt. The Ramsey Palace concert hall, purchased in 1897, was always let out, and was finally sold off about 1938; it was later renamed the Plaza when undergoing a facelift as the town cinema. There was also a refreshment kiosk at Ballaglass Glen, with a lady attendant who also collected the admission fees.

The collector of transport ephemeria is offered a vast field by

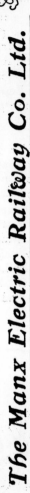

The Manx Electric Railway Co. Ltd.

❧ ❧ Invigorating Trips on the Open Cars ❧ ❧

HEALTH-GIVING SEA AND MOUNTAIN BREEZES.

This Delightful Route

was travelled over by their Majesties the King and Queen in 1902, and no proper idea of the Island's beauties can be formed without a run over it.

The Tour to SNAEFELL SUMMIT and the charming SULBY GLEN takes you right into the heart of the

"MANX SWITZERLAND"

AND

THE LINE TO RAMSEY

in traversing a delightful stretch of country, attains some splendid altitudes where the invigorating air, for which the Island is famous, may be enjoyed to the full amidst the finest Mountain and Marine Scenery.

For further information apply to
F. EDMONDSON, General Manager, 1 Strathallan Crescent, DOUGLAS.

Places to Visit.

From DERBY CASTLE to		Time from Derby Castle	Return Fare
GROUDLE	-	10 mins.	8d.
GARWICK	-	20 „	1/-
LAXEY	-	30 „	1/6
DHOON	-	45 „	1/9
GLEN MONA	-	55 „	2/-
BALLAGLASS GLEN	-		
SNAEFELL SUMMIT	-	60 „	2/6
RAMSEY	-	75 „	2/6

A whole Day's Delightful Outing with break of journey at all points:

No. 2 Tour. To Laxey, Snaefell Summit and Tholt-y-Will, Sulby Glen - - - - - - - 3/-

No. 1 Tour. To Laxey, Snaefell Summit, and Ramsey - 3/6

DON'T WORRY about a Timetable.

During the Season there is almost a constant service of Cars immediately after Breakfast and Lunch.

Edwardian coloured publicity card. The reverse side carried pictorial and advertising matter

the company's excursion publicity and advertising handbills, every possible event in Laxey and Ramsey, and the alluring features of scenes *en route*, being subjects of this form of advertisement. Excellent sepia postcards of the line, the scenery, the glens and Snaefell were sold in their tens of thousands, and a special postbox was installed at Snaefell summit, with its own special franking (the letters being given a second, orthodox, postmark on reaching Douglas). Until 1914, the company had a guide atop Snaefell mountain, and even sold postcards of *him*. In later Edwardian years he acquired a fenced platform for about seventy-five persons from which to deliver his peroration.

During 1906, Frank Edmondson was offered a senior post in Delhi, but stayed with the M E R following a salary increase. Mr E. Barnes, later in life to return to the line as chief assistant engineer, went to Canada, and in 1907 Harold Brown followed him across the Atlantic. Frank Edmonson was promoted to the position of manager and engineer, and there now came to the M E R as chief assistant engineer, Bertram G. Kelly, a young Manxman who had previously studied at the Royal Technical College, Glasgow, and had gained practical engineering experience with Lowdon Bros of Dundee, Cromptons of Chelmsford, the LCC and the Midland Railway. His father, Captain James Kelly, had many

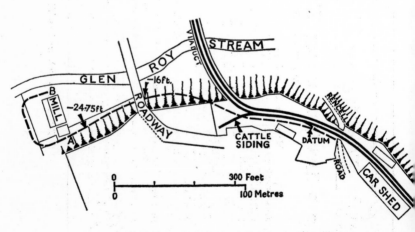

Siding proposed by R. B. Newell in 1911 for Corlett's Mill, Laxey; the gradient was to be 1 in 24. A and B were alternative termini

THE MANX ELECTRIC TAKEOVER

years previously left the island to become piermaster at Southend-on-Sea, whose pioneer electric tramway had its own power station long before there was any public electricity supply in the town.

Attempts to lease and electrify the Douglas horse tramway have already been described (Chapter 3). In 1911, the M E R arranged the electric lighting of the promenade as part of a carnival, and the corporation were so impressed that they placed a contract with the Electric Street Lighting Apparatus Company of London for permanent decorative lighting, for which (until 1923) the M E R supplied the current. This marks the start of the well-known summer and autumn illuminations.

Winding up the Isle of Man Tramways & Electric Power Company was not completed until 1908, when W. H. Walker made a final payment to creditors. Debenture holders were paid off and creditors received 13s 6d in the £, but ordinary shareholders got nothing. The final payment to depositors in Dumbell's Bank had been only 3s 4d in the £. Among those who had lost heavily in the collapse of I O M T & E P and all that it had entailed was

The Laxey refreshment room, destroyed by fire in September 1917

Frederick Saunderson, AICE, who spent his later years as manager of the Douglas Bay Estate and of the Groudle hotel. He died on 9 July 1911, at the age of seventy-one, and lies in the borough cemetery at Douglas.

In the years before 1914 the M E R ratio of costs to receipts reflected credit on its management. Although ordinary shareholders received only two dividends in seven years, three-quarters of the stock was in debentures or preference shares, and the substantial interest payments on these underlines the sustained financial stability. The Blackpool and Fleetwood line showed better financial perform-ance but had an easier route, a more balanced traffic and a much longer visitor season.

The 1914 season, up to 31 July, had been ahead of 1913's record performance, but this ended with the declaration of war, even though there was no sudden panic-exodus from the island. For 1914, passengers carried thus fell to 496,568, and expenses rose to 63.15 per cent of receipts; no dividend was paid on either share category, and an item of £1,000 on further generating plant was to be the last capital expenditure until after the war. Miles run were 305,732 passenger, 35,488 goods. Large internment camps at Douglas and Knockaloe ultimately raised the island's population, but brought little or no traffic. In 1915, passengers carried dropped to 104,224, passenger car miles to 114,373 and goods mileage to 19,346. The Snaefell line was closed, and a debit balance of £9,436 required the issue of second debentures to pay debenture interest for the second half-year. The chairman stated that 'the state of war entirely destroyed the holiday season in the Island. . . .'

The generating equipment referred to in the previous paragraph was a second-hand 750-kW (1,000 hp) Parsons turbo-alternator, No 6999, purchased in October 1914 complete with condensers. It dated from 1906, but had been little used and would offer an output exceeding that of two of the Bellis sets, and a higher efficiency. It got as far as Laxey goods shed, and then the war immobilised the project. The restricted service operated in 1914-18 enabled the water turbine plant to sustain the batteries for much longer periods than hitherto, and the steam plant was virtually needed only at low-water times, when the Laxey Robb-Armstrong engine was used. To provide distilled water for the several battery houses, a water-tower was built in 1916-17 alongside the line between Laxey and South Cape, fed from Laxey power station, where the supply barrels could be filled. It is still *in situ*.

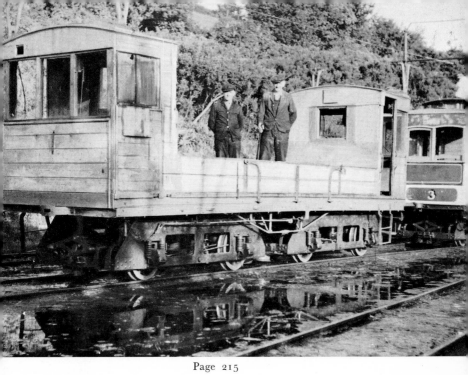

(above) *Snaefell works car* Maria, *formerly used for transporting coal, at Laxey depot,
September* 1954. *The bogies were borrowed from No* 5; (below) MER *staff, about* 1907.
*Manager Harold Brown is fourth from left on second row, with engineer Frank
Edmondson on his left. On extreme right of same row is Robert Newell, the permanent
way superintendent. The two back rows consist of station-masters*

No 2 at the r
Snaefell Sum
hotel, about 1

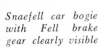

Snaefell car bogie
with Fell brake
gear clearly visible

Conductor San
son collecting
mail at Belle
August 195

In 1916, the loss climbed to £19,171, and second debentures funded the debenture interest for the entire year. Two directors were at the war, so secretary C. A. Huni was elected managing director. In the course of the year, 109,959 passenger miles had been run and 111,982 passengers carried, goods mileage being 19,288. Colonel Boscawen left the board in 1917 to become a member of the British government.

Passengers in 1917 rose to 119,683, with mileages of 111,595 (passenger) and 17,179 (goods), and only £52 was lost on working; the debit balance was now £28,222. On 24 September 1917, fire destroyed the large rustic refreshment room at Laxey, and it was not rebuilt. The year 1918 saw a working profit of £5,812 from 173,000 passengers, 134,315 passenger miles and 22,579 goods miles. Some plant and a charabanc were sold, and the debit balance increased by £3,189 to £31,411.

The bread strike of 4-5 July 1918 saw M E R service halted, in common with all other island transport. The position of the M E R employees had shown a parallel slow improvement to that of the corporation tramwaymen; before 1917 wages had been 30s in summer (for *any* hours) and 24s 6d in winter, but from 1917 they secured a 56-hour week at sixpence an hour. According to Mr Alfred Teare, MBE, a pioneer labour leader, the company were by no means the worst of the island's employers to deal with, although Frank Edmondson was a tough bargainer in the company's interest.

The physical status of the Manx Electric system had remained quite good during the war, but the accrued deficit of £31,411 was a formidable burden for the future, especially in the light of the increased costs of basic commodities such as coal.

GEORGE F. MILNES & Co. LIMITED.
BUILDERS
CASTLE CAR WORKS
HADLEY
NEAR WELLINGTON
SALOP

CHAPTER NINE

Manx Electric, 1919 to 1956

Everyone who has travelled abroad will recognise an old friend in this railway. It is the counterpart of innumerable friendly little continental railways, and shares their complete disregard for speed. It is like stepping back into the days of our forefathers to experience its pleasant, ambling motion, which is calculated to soothe the most impatient passenger to a quiet appreciation of the charm of this way of travel—Miss Maxwell Fraser, *In Praise of Manxland*

With the war ended, visitors were soon coming back to the Isle of Man, and to the Manx Electric. The Snaefell mountain railway, closed since 9 August 1914, reopened on 10 June 1919. No passenger figures are given in the reports for 1919 or 1920, but 295,426 passenger miles were run on the system in 1919, and 26,477 for goods. Earnings amounted to £57,102 with a profit margin of £31,501 that enabled all past debt to be wiped off, though debenture interest was again funded by second debentures.

The modernisation of the power supply was now resumed. After a fruitless attempt in 1919 to sell the unused Parsons turbo-alternator in order to buy a diesel plant, it was decided to carry out the scheme envisaged in 1914. The turbo-alternator was installed in the winter of 1919-20 on a new overhead gantry in the Laxey power station, between the old engine room and a new boiler house, and an overhead crane was installed in the enlarged engine room thus formed. By 1921, a new boiler house, partitioned off from the engine room by a wood-framed partition, contained a new in-

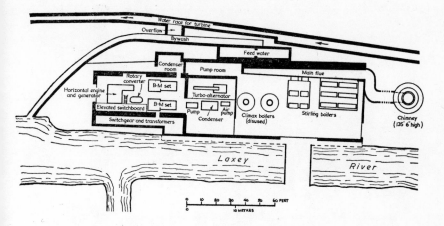

Laxey power station at its maximum extent 1921-35, after the addition of
a turbo-alternator. The river bridge carried both broad and narrow gauge
tracks (for coal and ash?)

stallation by the Stirling Boiler Co Ltd, consisting of two 120 lb/in²
water-tube boilers of 8 ft 6in diameter, one with an evaporative
capacity of 12,000 lb/hr and the other of 4,000 lb/hr. These
replaced the Climax boilers, which were taken out of use as the
new units became serviceable; the three Galloway boilers of 1894-8
had been removed before commencing the new 86 ft by 40 ft
building. The new boiler room was approached by a relocated
bridge across the adjoining river, and the flues were connected
to a steel plate chimney 135 ft 6 in high on an 18 ft 7 in plinth,
tapering from 8 ft diameter at the base to 6 ft at the top. A few
years afterwards the chimney was shortened and given a forced-
draught fan.

The turbo-alternator was a low voltage machine (400 volts 25
cycles three-phase), and thus required a 400/7,000 volt step-up
transformer, which was supplied by the British Electric Transformer Co of Hayes. Other auxiliaries were a 9½-hp 440-volt
three-phase air pump motor by the Mechanical & Electrical Engineering Co of Walsall, and a 50-hp Brook centrifugal pump
motor. In 1924 or 1925, the new installation was provided with
Hodgkinson motor-driven mechanical stokers.

Laxey power station, 1922

In 1920, car miles soared to 394,953 passenger and 34,195 goods, Snaefell passengers totalled 84,956, and the line earned £89,780, with a profit of £40,909. This cleared the interest on second mortgage debentures from 1915 to 1920, and enabled the company to pay preference share dividends for 1914 and 1915. The reserve for special renewals now stood at £13,535, and the company's investment account at £64,505. A three-car lean-to annexe was added to the Derby Castle trailer car shed; a consulting engineers' report on post-war policy had lately recommended four new motor cars and two trailers.

The following year, 1921, saw a more sober passenger figure of 667,178, with earnings of £63,708, but the operating ratio rose to 70.21 per cent and the net profit was more than halved. Preference share dividend was paid for 1916, and interest on the second mortgage debentures, which totalled £40,500 in 1921 but were then redeemed to £36,000. Only £915 was carried on to the 1922 accounts, and the investment account had shrunk by two-thirds. 1922 saw preference share interest paid up to 1918, 1923 paid for 1919, and 1924 paid for 1920; ground was being neither gained nor lost. The second mortgage debentures were now down to £22,500, and in 1925 to £18,000, when arrears of interest were paid up to the start of 1923.

Bertram Kelly, chief assistant engineer, left the M E R in 1922 to take charge of the construction of Douglas Corporation's first electric power station at North Quay. Corporation supply commenced on 18 May 1923, and Mr Kelly was appointed borough electrical engineer. In October 1925 he gave a prophetic address to the I O M Municipal Association which was almost an exact outline of the island-wide public supply system inaugurated by the I O M Electricity Board in 1932-3. Mr Kelly's retirement, in 1947, was no more than a prelude to full-time church work; an honorary diocesan Reader since 1919, his ordination twenty-eight years later was the beginning of an intensive second career, for he served three years as curate and then fourteen years from 1950 as vicar of the large parish of Kirk Braddan, widely known for its open-air services —in his bishop's words, 'a great work splendidly done'.

In 1924, winter service on the M E R gave nine northbound and eight southbound weekday journeys, some starting or finishing at Laxey. Saturdays had four extra services in all, but Sundays saw but two cars each way. One morning weekday journey north from

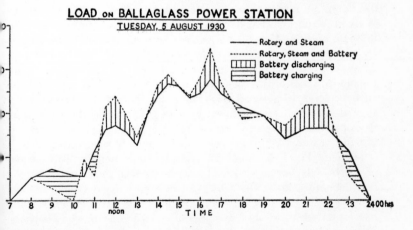

Loading diagram showing how battery equipment absorbed the excess peak demand, in this case at Ballaglass. The peaks occur as visitors leave and return to their hotels and boarding-houses for meals

Laxey was expressly for schoolchildren. Parcels were collected at 10.00 and 3.00 from a *Times* branch office in Victoria Street, from 'Mr Newby's, Buck's Road', and from the Steam Packet Company's goods offices. The timetable's footnotes included 'goods, merchandise, livestock and parcels conveyed between all stations'. From about 1920 to 1939 a once-daily 'Ramsey Express' was run, taking only sixty minutes and carrying a special headboard.

The remaining steam plant at Snaefell was last used on 3 September 1924, and was replaced by a second 1903 rotary converter transferred from Laxey. This in turn was now replaced by a second-hand BTH rotary converter, which differed from its predecessors in being started from the AC side. This left only two steam generating stations, Ballaglass and Laxey. The 1904 AC distribution system continued in use, as did the supply of current to domestic consumers in Onchan and to Derby Castle and Douglas Bay hotel. This, too, was an AC supply, but dual wiring allowed the remaining consumers to use DC in winter and allow the Douglas alternator set to be shut down. It is said that the winter sermons at St Peter's church in Onchan were often punctuated by theatrical dimmings and brightenings as the M E R cars took power!

Sir William Vaudrey, addressing the company meeting of 16 December 1925, saw matters currently as 'very satisfactory'. First debentures had been reduced by a sinking fund to £189,538, and the boom in textiles had been coupled with a fine summer. Sir William Vaudrey, chairman, and director C. A. Huni, both died in 1926, and Sir Arthur Griffith-Boscawen came back to the board. In 1929 he was to serve as chairman of the Royal Commission on Transport, parent of the mainland Road Traffic Act of 1930. Labour troubles on the mainland meant that in 1926 only half the 1926 preference dividend could be paid, though the second mortgage debentures were reduced to £13,500. During the coal strike three-car trains were run, one car being a light 1893 or 1894 trailer, but this ceased when solder ran out of the controller terminals!

In 1927, Frank Edmondson, manager and engineer, was elected to the board. Second debentures were reduced to £8,000, and the first debenture stock, the subject of redemption payments for some years, now stood at £184,500, but there was no preference share interest payment. Motor-bus competition had now appeared between Douglas, Laxey and Ramsey. A plan was drawn up in 1927 to replace the Bellis-Morcom generating sets by diesel units, using 150-kW Crossleys or a 300-kW Maldons, but this was not carried out. The following year, 1928, saw the only serious accident the line has known, when a trailer broke loose near Fairy Cottage and thirty-two passengers were injured (an earlier collision on 17 September 1908 also caused injury). The only fatal accidents to passengers ever to have occurred on the M E R appear to have been one or two cases of inebriates falling from rear platforms into the path of trailer cars.

Mr J. Rowe, later to become company secretary, joined the Douglas office staff during 1929. The Strathallan office staff at this time comprised a traffic superintendent, a clerk for goods, a typist, and two male clerks. All ticketing and cash were handled by this office, including the through tickets to Ramsey and Laxey from mainland railways, which had to be collected. In the economic slump of 1929-30 the M E R was not too badly affected; the second mortgage debentures were completely redeemed, the debenture stock interest paid, and 2 per cent paid on the preference shares for the remaining half-year of 1923.

In the early hours of 5 April 1930, a fire at Laxey depot destroyed the building and eleven cars, and was probably due to a cigarette-end dropped behind the seats of a car igniting the dust and dry waste that tends to accumulate there. The depot was promptly rebuilt, and three replacement trailers obtained from English Electric by midsummer; the fire claim was for £6,140.

On the night of 17-18 September 1930, a rainstorm and ensuing floods in the centre and north-east of the island produced an accumulation of debris behind the weir of the hydro-electric plant at Laxey. Between two and four thousand tons of debris filled the river bed, and the river took to the adjoining road, flooding the power station and other properties as far down as the harbour. The floods submerged the water turbine and much of the steam plant, but the water remained below the turbine's elevated platform and the switchgear. On 18 September only the steam turbine was in commission, exhausting to atmosphere; Ballaglass No 2 set was started up later that day, and ran until 25 October. Water power became available on 25 September, but the other plant had to be stripped and the parts dried in a heated box, larger parts being cleaned and dried *in situ*. No 1 Bellis set came back into use on 22 October, No 2 on 31 October, and the Robb-Armstrong No 3 set on 20 November; the only subsequent failures were of a wattmeter transformer and of an air pump stator coil. The flood repairs cost £3,472, including river clearance and road repairs, for which an ensuing legal judgment placed responsibility on the company.

In charge of the Laxey flood repairs was Mr J. F. Watson, later to become general manager and chief engineer. He had joined the M E R as an apprentice in 1916 (his father had been with the I O M T & E P from 1897), and following war service and a period on the mainland, he returned to the M E R in 1929 and became assistant to the chief engineer in 1936.

From 1930 onwards, the debenture interest payments were a veritable millstone around the M E R's neck. Motor-coach and bus competition was now a serious factor. The year 1931 was materially worse than 1930 and the debenture interest went unpaid, the holders having agreed to a postponement until 1 October 1933

MANX ELECTRIC RAILWAY

Boat Passengers are notified that THE MANX ELEC-TRIC RAILWAY PASSENGER AND MAIL EXPRESS (stopping at Baldrine, Laxey and Ramsey only) and

Due in Ramsey within one hour from time of departure from Douglas

will not leave Derby Castle Station before 3.30 p.m. This is the quickest passenger service in operation be-tween Douglas and Ramsey connecting with this steamer's arrival.

The Manx Electric Railway Company's Motor Lorry which is in attendance on the Pier at the arrival of passenger steamers will convey your luggage to Derby Castle at a nominal charge. Instruct porter on steamer to place your luggage on the Manx Electric Railway Motor Lorry.

F. EDMONDSON, General Manager

MORRIS MODERN PRESS, LTD.

M E R notice displayed in I O M S P steamers, *circa* 1930

of the second half of the year's payment due to them, in view of
the line's recent ordeals. The renewals fund stood at £20,752, and
the debt to the debenture holders was £4,117 10s. In 1932 it grew
to £12,352 10s, but the renewals fund also climbed to £20,854, less
£1,125 written off on further flood repairs.

To eliminate painting and overhaul of Snaefell cars at Laxey,
a three-rail, mixed-guage siding was laid in at Laxey in about
1932, on which Snaefell cars could be transferred by traversing
jacks on to 3-ft gauge bogies and taken down to the main Derby
Castle works. The surviving sector table at the Snaefell depot
appears to have been removed at the same date.

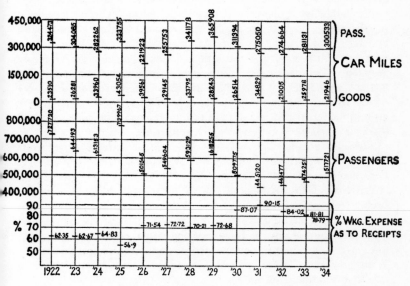

Manx Electric traffic and finance, 1922 to 1934

In 1933, 2½ per cent of the cumulative total of debenture interest
of £20,587 10s was paid off, and the special reserve for renewals
stood at almost £20,000. A further 2½ per cent was paid off in the
year to 30 September 1934. Public electricity supply was now
becoming available throughout the island, and the M E R supply
of AC current to domestic consumers in Onchan and to Derby

Castle and Douglas Bay hotel through the 1894 underground mains came to an end between 1931 and 1933. The last such customer for M E R power was the Howstrake holiday camp, dating from the 1920s. With M E R generation costs at some £5,000 a year and the newest plant some twenty years old, discussions began with a view to taking current for the line from the Isle of Man Electricity Board, through a network of substations.

On 7 November 1934, an agreement was reached with the I O M Electricity Board by which they were given a prior charge on the company's real estate for £15,978, the company being obliged to seek hire-purchase terms for the equipment and transmission lines involved. The new layout consisted of six rectifier substations, at Douglas, Groudle, Laxey, Snaefell, Ballaglass and Bellevue. Of these, Ballaglass, Bellevue and Laxey are fed direct from the public supply at 33,000 volts 50 cycles AC, while Douglas, Groudle and Snaefell are fed at 6,600 volts AC through the 1904 lines from a purpose-built transformer substation at Laxey; an emergency supply at 3,300 volts is obtainable at Douglas. To reinforce the 550-volt DC feeders, an additional overhead line hung from ordinary ears was added from Douglas to Groudle, supplementing the 1894 underground feeder, whilst beyond Groudle it is carried on pole-mounted brackets all the way to Queen's Drive, Ramsey.

The new rectifiers were fan-cooled, mercury-arc, traction units by the Hewittic company, with Hackbridge transformers. At Douglas, one 200-kW unit was placed in the former engine room, and two similar units were put in the existing building at Groudle. Laxey (two units of 200 kW) and Bellevue (one of 150 kW) were new buildings, at Snaefell (two of 150 kW) part of the old engine room was used, whilst at Ballaglass the two 150-kW rectifiers seem lost in the vast emptiness of the original buildings. The 1904 Witting, Eborall DC switchgear was re-used throughout, for white marble insulation does not age!

The steam generating plant at Ballaglass was by this time already idle, No 1 set being last used on 16 August 1934 and No 2 set on 30 August; the plant was dismantled in 1935, including the battery. At Laxey, the steam turbine (No 4 set) ran for the last time on 6 September 1934, followed by No 3 set on 22 September. This left the two Bellis-Morcom sets and the water-turbine plant to maintain the supply during the final winter. By April 1935, all was ready, and the water turbine plant, No 2 set and No 1 set were used for the last time respectively on 28, 29 and 30 April, this marking the

end of all M E R steam generation; the new supply system came into
use on 1 May. A book loss of £53,000 was sustained in disposing of
the old plant but the shell of Laxey power station was eventually
sold in 1944 for nearly £5,000. The new Laxey substation was near
the site of the 1895-6 terminal, beyond the Rencell Bridge.

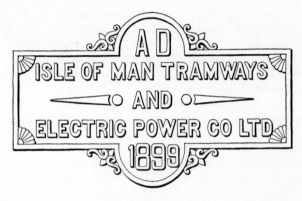

Plate on sluicegate of Laxey turbine headrace, disused since 1935

Increasing national prosperity made 1935 a better year. Passengers reached 543,126, the expenses ratio fell (through power econo-
mies) to 74.35 per cent, and mileages were 308,560 passengers and
39,839 goods. The reserve fund stood untouched at £23,582.
Debenture interest was paid up to 30 September 1933, with two
years of arrears remaining. The debenture holders had agreed to
a postponement of arrears payment until October 1936, for the
board, in a circular letter, held out hope of paying further amounts
in that year. Increasing motor traffic on the island roads made it
necessary to install trolley-actuated traffic lights at three points,
Half-Way House in March 1934, Ballure on 9 June 1936, and
Ballabeg on 25 June 1936.

Although they assembled every three months for a board meeting
at Strathallan Crescent, the board of directors wisely made little
effort to interfere in the working of the line. The operating methods,
were very specialised. Most visitors arrived on Saturday, and their
first exploration on Sunday gave an opportunity to put out advertising literature; the general line in advertising was that of a

'Riviera coast' service, with the palm tree a major motif in design. Buyers of the 5s two-day rover tickets were given a four-page explanatory leaflet, with the leading theme 'If fine, go to Snaefell'. In 1927, rover tickets had allowed any number of Snaefell journeys, but this soon had to be stopped—the cars could not cope! Sunday afternoon, if fine, could be busy, and with Monday the rush was on in earnest; between 9.30 and 10.15 the cars were filled with rover ticket holders, and a similar rush occurred between 1.45 and 2.30 pm. Takings on Tuesdays were lower—the 'rovers' were often on their second day, though Wednesday was an alternative choice. Thursday was bedevilled by a regular long day Fleetwood excursion, whose arrivals congested Laxey, queuing for Snaefell. Friday and Saturday were relatively blank days.

Each week, the Saturday arrival figures were rushed to the office to allow an estimate of the crew requirements for the following week. Tide tables were also consulted, for the tides materially influenced the availability or otherwise of deckchairs on the Douglas beaches, a counter-attraction to MER excursions. The recent widening of the northern end of Douglas promenade had, however, brought business to the MER in the carriage of mines waste from Laxey, used in this and other civil engineering projects associated with public relief employment. Weather forecasts were anxiously studied, and on fine days queues formed from 8 am onwards for the full-day Snaefell—Sulby Glen tours, on which lunch was taken at the Summit hotel, the Bungalow, or Tholt-y-Will. Both tours (Douglas—Laxey—Snaefell—Sulby, tour No 1, and Douglas—Laxey—Snaefell—Ramsey, tour No 2) were offered at 4s 6d.

Staffing in the 'thirties comprised station-masters at Douglas, Groudle, Laxey, Bungalow, Summit and Ramsey, assistant station-masters at Douglas, Laxey and Ramsey, booking-clerks at Douglas (two), Laxey and Summit, kiosk attendants at White City, Sulby Glen, Dhoon and Ballaglass, and five inspectors, one of whom was chief inspector. Until 1930, a station-master was also positioned at Garwick. Platform staff comprised twenty-four double crews, a yard foreman to select cars and issue instructions, with a maintenance staff of a chargehand, two cleaners, an armature winder, two joiners, two painters, a blacksmith, and from four to six labourers; apprentices varied between three and five. On the busiest days, the indoor staff would help out as drivers, a tradition which continues to this day. Each of the six substations was manned, but in winter the reduced load enabled that at Bellevue o be closed from September to May. In summer, it operated from o am to 6 pm.

Mr Edmondson died in January 1936; his assistant, Mr E. Barnes, was appointed manager and engineer in his stead. The year's passengers climbed to 552,815, though the expenses ratio still hovered at 74.93 per cent; car miles were 315,338 and 36,627. The debenture interest debt at 30 September was £24,705, but a further £5,000 was paid off on 6 October. The next year, 1937, was even better; 570,833 rode the line, and the car miles (307,890 and 30,914) showed better loading, and thus an improved profit ratio, the expenses ratio falling to 63.83 per cent. Of the debenture arrears of £20,000, £7,316 was paid off on 1 October, and the capital charges owed to the 10 M Electricity Board had already been reduced by £2,663, roughly one-sixth.

At Groudle, the traction battery continued in use, due to the maximum demand' tariff charged by the 10 M Electricity Board. In 1938, an ingenious form of traffic and traction load control was introduced in an attempt to even out power consumption. Cars were despatched according to the passage of marked counters on an electrically-driven belt representing the line from Douglas to Laxey, timed to carry a car to Laxey in thirty minutes, the intention being to avoid simultaneous uphill starts from different points on the line. The device was disused after the 1939 season, but came back into use from 1954 to 1956. On the hillside above the car sheds, an electric sign proclaimed 'M E R for Scenery'; a gorse fire later damaged it, and when re-erected the wording was changed to Electric Railway'.

In 1938, however, passengers fell to 514,360, the expenses ratio rose to 72.6 per cent, and miles run were only 296,573 passenger and 23,043 goods. By 1 October 1938, the debenture arrears were further brought down to a little over £12,000, and it seemed a fair assumption that the debt might be wiped off by the early 1940s. A little ground was being gained each year, and one-fifth of the debt to the Electricity Board had now been cleared.

With the outbreak of war in 1939, one-third of the summer's traffic vanished, leaving but 489,621 carried, expenses at 78.12 per cent and miles run down to 279,119 and 15,748. The debenture debt climbed back to over £16,000. Sir Bernard Greenwell, chairman since 1926, had died on 28 November 1939, and was replaced by Mr A. W. Bolden, whose major interests were in South American railways. This left only Sir Arthur Boscawen, Ernest Remnant, and

secretary A. D. Foster of the original team of 1902. The debenture
holders, by resolution of 19 December 1940, waived all interest
due to them from 30 September 1939 (leaving arrears frozen at
£16,459), and the War (Local Conditions) Committee similarly
waived repayments to the Electricity Board, to which the company
still owed £10,000.

By March of 1940, M E R staff had fallen to thirty. Already the
Manx government had been obliged to assist distressed hotel and
boarding-house keepers. The M E R staved off their immediate crisis
by selling 1939's remaining stocks of liquid refreshment, and by
selling the Strathallan Brows and the glen below Summer Hill,
now Calvary Glen. Later, they applied to the War (Local Conditions) Committee for a loan of £6,000, estimated to cover the
following year's working. In the event this was never used, for new
wartime traffic arose in the conveyance of interned aliens to farm

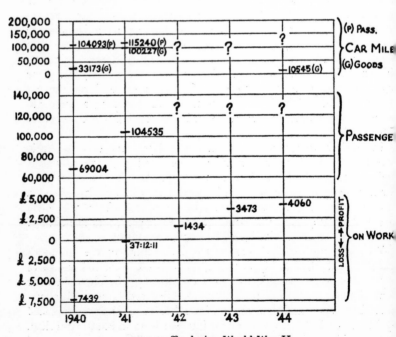

M E R traffic during World War II

work sites, peat-cutting traffic from Snaefell, and the haulage of mine waste from Laxey to Ramsey for runway construction at Jurby air station. A siding was laid at Laxey for this traffic from the northbound track to the mines' deads heap, passing between the Agneash road crossing and the I M R S garage. The Snaefell line closed from 20 September 1939, and did not reopen until 2 June 1946. All the company's investments (chiefly in South American railways) were frozen for the duration, but in any case when ultimately sold were far below their book value.

Mr Remnant died in May 1941 and Mr Bolden the following month, and were replaced as directors by Messrs A. D. Foster and A. G. Hunt; S. A. Young (a business associate of Foster's) became secretary. Under the I O M Defence Regulations, the accounts for 1942 and 1943 were not published, and no figures for passengers and goods appear. In 1944 the maximum-demand electricity tariff ceased to apply, and after August the Groudle traction battery was abandoned. The building still contains the disused Thury booster of 1904, and another (archaic) booster of the 1895-6 era is used in the Snaefell car shed for drying out cars each spring.

By March 1945, Messrs Boscawen, Foster and Hunt were able

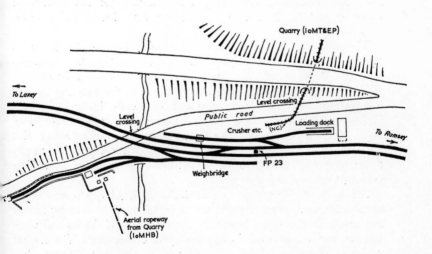

Dhoon quarry sidings in 1946, before removal of associated quarry plant

to resume published accounts. Happily the overall debit balance of 30 September 1941 had been reduced from £17,482 to £8,514, and 1944 had brought a working profit. The debt to the Electricity Board was a little over £5,000, the pre-war debenture arrears about £16,000, and the debt to the I O M government £6,000. In 1945, with a miniature boom of war-weary visitors, 216,080 passenger miles were run, with 12,306 goods; the line made £11,636 working profit, and the overall balance on the year was £3,121. The moratorium on debenture interest continued, and the debt to the Electricity Board fell below £5,000. The report mentions intended renewals to make up wartime leeway.

Next year, 1946, saw even better results with 1½ million passenger journeys. The Snaefell reopened on 2 June, the through return fare from Douglas now being 5s. Miles run climbed to 327,944, with goods at 15,941. Of the profit of £32,699, £15,000 was put aside for 'repairs' and the credit balance carried forward for the year was £9,713. The reserve fund for special renewals still stood at around £24,000, and £12,000 now appeared in the capital account for rectifier equipment, on which the hire-purchase debt had been cleared. Another link with the 1902 board was broken by the death of Sir Arthur Griffith-Boscawen, leaving only ex-secretary A. D. Foster, who became chairman. A. G. Hunt had also died, and new directors Robert Holmes (of the Greenwell concern) and G. B. Parker, a barrister with Manx connections, took their place.

The same year had also seen the resumption of the circular tours to Sulby Glen. Before the war, the No 1 tour was Douglas—Laxey—Snaefell—Sulby and No 2 tour Douglas—Laxey—Snaefell—Ramsey, both offered at 4s 6d. After the war the tour numbering was reversed, with No 1 tour at 7s and No 2 at 6s. The vehicles used for the road journey were the two twenty-seat Bedford WLBs of 1937, MN 8685 and 8686. The tours ran for seven seasons, but with the end of petrol rationing, increasing coach competition began to affect results and operation ceased after the season of 1952. The vehicles were sold off in 1953.

For 1947, the year's profit was £28,858, leaving £10,071 to be carried forward, even though the government loan was repaid in full and half the 1939 debenture arrears paid off. Miles run were 320,400 and 14,398, and £3,037 was spent on renewals. The capital structure of the company was adjusted to clear the £53,000 loss on power plant, leaving the issued capital at £409,826. A com-

(above) Snaefell car No 6 leaving Laxey depot en route for Derby Castle, 1961, being towed by No 30, then in green livery; (below) Ramsey line mail train with van No 3 descending from Ballaragh towards Ballamoar, June 1963

(above) *The long descent from Ballabeg towards Laxey, 2 April 1966. The nearest pole is ex-*DSET*; (below) even finer seascapes are obtained from Bulgham's ledge. No 19 is resplendent in new paint, the date is as above*

mission on public transport reported in July 1947, acknowledged the need to retain the MER and the social value of year-round service. In 1949 the Manx government brought in outside experts; the railway study was made by G. B. Howden of the GNRI, and that of the road services by Messrs Arnold, Robinson and Wright of the Tilling group. Their report foresaw the MER's crisis and raised long-term doubts about Laxey—Ramsey, but the Road Services did not escape criticism, especially on fare levels, The Tilling men were anxious to 'omnibus' the entire island, as might be expected. The chief effect of these surveys was to rationalise the bus service to the detriment of the MER.

The wave of prosperity still rode high in 1948. A working profit of £22,402 (net profit £16,859) made possible the payment of renewed debenture interest, legally due from 20 January 1948, and the final clearance of arrears. Mileage had been 321,243 passenger, 13,971 goods. In his annual statement of March 1949, chairman A. D. Foster explained the intended transfer of the company's direction to Douglas, and proposed a 'scheme of arrangement' to reform the company's financial structure. Mr E. Barnes, general manager and engineer, was brought on to the board, joining Messrs Foster, Holmes and Parker. A set of Ferodo centre-rail brake-shoes was tried on a Snaefell car, without positive results.

In 1949, the MER had to go to court to contest Douglas Corporation's ambitions to run buses beyond the boundary along King Edward Road to Groudle. The threatened Groudle licence was not granted and the buses ran only to White City, with a DCT payment to the MER for traffic thus abstracted. The service ran from 1950 to 1957 (compensation in 1957 was £344), and recommenced in 1959, when the fee payable to the MER was re-negotiated at 0.525 pence per passenger.

From 1 October 1949, the secretary's office, latterly at River Plate House, 10-11 Finsbury Circus, London EC2, was transferred to Douglas and merged with the registered office at 1 Strathallan Crescent. A. D. Foster retired for health reasons, Holmes became chairman, J. Rowe became secretary, and former secretary S. A. Young joined Messrs Holmes, Parker and Barnes on the board. The capital reconstruction scheme approved by the Manx government on 26 November 1949, wrote down the company's issued capital from £403,231 to £310,731, of which £140,200 was in 10s ordinary shares and £170,531 in 4½ per cent first mortgage debentures. Presenting his first report in February 1950, Mr Rowe stated

O

MANX ELECTRIC RAILWAY

DOUGLAS, LAXEY AND RAMSEY

Commencing SATURDAY, 23rd SEPTEMBER, 1950, and until further notice

WEEKDAYS | SUNDAYS

DOUGLAS	a.m.			noon	p.m.							Thursdays only	Saturdays only	p.m.	
(Derby Castle) dep	7 0	8 45	10 0	12 0	2 30		4 0	5 30	7 0	8 45		10 30 T	10 30 S	1 45	5 30
Groudle Glen															
Baldrine															
Garwick Glen															
LAXEY	7.30	9 15	10 30	12 30	3 0		4 30	6 0	7 30	9 15		11 0 Stop	11 0	2 15	6 0
Dhoon															
Glen Mona, B'glass															
RAMSEY (Plaza) arr.	8 15	10 0	11 15	1 15	3 45		5 15	6 45	8 15	10 0			11 45	2 55	6 40

Saturdays only: 2 0 S

RAMSEY (Plaza) dep.	a.m.			p.m.							Thursdays only	Saturdays only	p.m.	
Glen Mona, B'glass	7 0	8 30	10 30	12 15		2 0	4 15	5 30	7 0		8 50	10 20 S	3 0	6 45
Dhoon														
LAXEY	7 40	9 10	11 10	1 0	2 0 S	2 45	5 0	6 15 7 45		9 30	11 5 STOP	3 40	7 25
Garwick Glen													
Baldrine													
Groudle Glen													
DOUGLAS (Derby Castle) arr.	8 10	9 40	11 40	1 30	2 30	3 15	5 30	6 45	8 15	10 0		4 10	7 55

T—Thursdays only   S—Saturdays only

Goods, Merchandise and Parcels conveyed between all stations. Goods and Parcels collected and delivered everywhere within Douglas Town Boundaries. Goods, Merchandise and Parcels conveyed by Motor Road Service to and from Douglas, Onchan, Garwick, Laxey, and intermediate points.

General Offices : 1 Strathallan Crescent, Douglas.

E. BARNES, General Manager and Engineer

Telephones : Douglas 61. Laxey 226. Ramsey 2240

N.M.P.

The last year of winter Sunday service

that the 1949 profit was £14,006, which permitted payment of debenture interest and 2 per cent on the reconstructed ordinary shares. Miles run were 303,403 and 15,278, and £6,176 had been spent on renewals. The reserve fund now stood at £29,122.

In 1950, the island's post-war boom abruptly collapsed, and visitors fell by 75,000. Mileage was but 284,583 (goods 17,147), and profits were £4,732, of which £2,974 was spent on renewals and £2,158 carried forward to 1951. Only the aid of the previous year's net revenue balance enable debenture interest to be paid. The renewals fund still stood at a nominal £29,122, but the grass-grown 1894 trackwork now needed major renewals. Despite this, the 1950 winter timetable (as in other post-war years) showed early and late runs timed for seventy minutes, and the entire timetable for the winter of 1951-2 was so timed. In that year, for the first time, the winter Sunday service was withdrawn, lack of traffic being given as the reason.

In 1950, construction of an Air Ministry radar station on the summit of Snaefell mountain called for winter journeys by a Snaefell car. This meant that the overhead line on the upper section had to be left in position despite the risk of gale damage, whereas normally it is taken down in winter and tied to the Fell rail chairs.

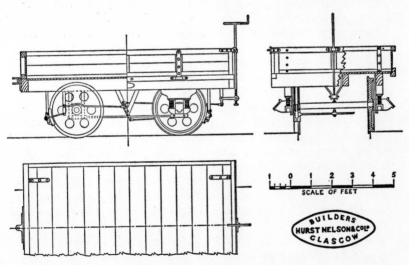

The Snaefell open wagon supplied by Hurst Nelson & Co Ltd in 1896 (still in use) with inset of name plate

To avoid this, the Air Ministry in 1951 supplied a four-wheel Wickham railcar with a Ford V8 petrol engine and with a centre-rail clasp-brake, so that the radar operator could drive to and from the summit station. This vehicle weighs 2½ tons, and was fitted with Fell guide wheels in 1954-5 because of its instability in high winds. In 1957, Wickham's supplied a larger four-wheel car with a Ford 28-hp diesel engine; this vehicle was Fell-equipped from the start and has a one-ton goods portion and detachable snowploughs. Both cars are kept in a separate shed at Laxey (extended in 1957) and both can carry four passengers as well as the driver. Their summer operation is limited to Sunday mornings, when the electric cars do not run. The 1951 car was re-engined in 1964-5. Both cars were in blue livery until 1966, but are now brown and yellow.

During 1951, Mr R. J. Clutton was appointed to the board from Schroeder's Bank, inheritors of the debenture stock trusteeship. Mr Clutton had some (perhaps ominous) prior experience in 'disposing' of several South American railways, bargaining with dictators in their native Spanish! New trustees were appointed, including Mr J. R. Quayle, then chairman of the Isle of Man Bank. Car mileage was much the same as in 1950, at 284,524 passenger and 15,928 goods, but the profit was a mere £2,244, and a £5,000 transfer from general reserve was made to meet debenture interest. The £1,852 spent on deferred renewals was hardly significant.

In 1952, the M E R obtained from the I O M Highways and Transport Board a quantity of rails and overhead poles from the former Douglas Head Marine Drive tramway. Earlier, poles on the Snaefell line's upper portion had been replaced by timber substitutes. During the 'thirties, replacement of the original poles with a Stewarts & Lloyds stepped pole had commenced, but some of the ancient tapered poles of 1893-4 still survive, as do most of the 1898-9 poles on the Ramsey line, now minus their decorative collars. The D H M D poles, although equally old, had lasted well thanks to their galvanised top section and rust-resistant lower parts. The first D H M D rails, when laid in 1955 near Lonan Old Church, were found to be unduly noisy due to head corrosion, and no more were obtained, but further poles followed in the next few years.

Mr Barnes died on 2 November 1952, and 12 November saw the start of joint managership by J. Rowe and J. F. Watson; Mr Watson had been assistant to Mr Barnes since 1936. The 1952 operating profit was £4,318; mileage run was 282,021 passenger and 10,213 goods. Repairs and renewals totalled £1,767, and old stock valued at £942 was written off, which left the renewals fund at £27,274. Material ordered but not yet delivered accounted for a further £1,484. A further £3,000 had been transferred from the general reserve account and, with the holders' agreement, only six months' debenture interest was to be paid. Late in 1952, Mr Barnes' place on the board was taken by the late R. C. Drinkwater, a member of an old Manx family, whose affection for the island's most scenic transport amenity was to be of great help in ensuring its survival.

1953 saw an operating loss of £863, and a further £7,000 transfer exhausted the general reserve. Miles run had totalled 268,806, plus 8,480 for goods, and all repairs had been charged against revenue. The only bright spot was the sale of property amounting to £5,660, which sum went to the trustees for the debenture holders; this included the glens at Dhoon and Ballaglass, whose new owner was the IOM Forestry Board. The newer of the two Dhoon quarries had already passed to the Highways Board, who used it until 1961-3. A total of £2,213 had been spent on track material, principally a new crossover installed in the following winter on the Snaefell line below the Bungalow to make possible normal up and down working during Tourist Trophy race weeks. Prior to 1954, these events (which closed the mountain road crossing) saw a two-car shuttle on the upward track and three cars on the downward, with a single car working to and from the summit.

The company promoted a Bill seeking winter closure at any date between 31 October and 3 May and authorising fares beyond the limits imposed in the original Acts of 1892-7. In the June 1954 debate, Advocate McPherson pointed out for the company that the two-car winter service was costing £3,538; winter passengers were about 37,000 of the 1953 total of 814,357, plus journeys by 200 contract holders and the forty pupils of Dhoon school. Winter receipts were about £2,500, and the service employed twenty men. But although efficient operation of the Douglas—Ramsey bus route by IMRS had robbed the MER of its once-substantial residential traffic, for people in the Maughold peninsula it is still their local transport, and winter closure was defeated 12-10. The fare increases were approved, but too late for the 1954 season to benefit. Mr H. C. Kerruish, speaking in the Keys debate on behalf of his Garff constituents, said that 'they thought there was a greater degree of civility and courtesy from this service than from any other company in the island'.

For 1954, the working loss grew to £2,005. Car miles were cut to 253,503 passenger and 7,026 goods, and the debt on debenture stock had been allowed to grow by further moratoria to £9,145. The debenture holders had it in their power to realise the assets and wind up the concern, but took the opposite course; the chairman pointed out that they were now providing an amenity for the island from their own resources.

The island's loss in popularity after 1950 might form the basis of a whole series of essays, and one is tempted to cite the negative part of the Manx character as in part responsible, for change comes hard to many hoteliers, shop and boarding-house keepers. The change in the island's permanent population over the period from 1951 to 1961 (55,253 down to 28,150) underlined the general exodus of the more ambitious. Recognising that the post-war boom in the holiday industry had evaporated, to be succeeded by a long and painful decline, the island government in 1955 appointed a Commission on the Visiting industry. The commission reported on 13 January 1956, and among its recommendations were the continuance of both the coastal tramway and the Snaefell line, with implied government assistance.

With good weather and higher fares, 1955 saw a working profit of £4,075, though the final result was a debit balance of £10,542. Car miles were 259,693 passenger and 8,744 goods, and debenture interest arrears were now £22,974. Every effort was made to get maximum results for the least expense, and an interesting publicity effort was a leaflet for long day excursion steamer passengers, explaining how to reach Snaefell and return in time for the boat. Maintenance work was limited by lack of funds, but included the cropping of dropped rail ends near Laxey and their thermit welding as shortened on site, and repairs to the timbers on Ballure bridge. This last job required single-line working between Lewaigue and Ramsey, during which a collision occurred on 3 August; four passengers were taken to hospital, but were not detained. The sixtieth anniversary of the Snaefell line on 21 August was marked with special headboards and posters and some useful press and television publicity.

In December of 1955, the M E R directors wrote to the government stating that they could not continue in business beyond 30 September 1956. They were willing to sell the line for £70,000, excluding the Douglas and Laxey hotels, and suggested the formation of a new company with a capital consisting of the sale

price of £70,000, plus working capital of £30,000. The island's
Executive Council appointed a sub-committee of M H K's J. B.
Bolton, J. F. Crellin and H. K. Corlett to look into the whole
question. They, in turn, imported three specialists from the London
Midland Region of British Railways, R. Varley, MIEE, M Inst T
(formerly manager of the Mersey Railway), D. A. Paterson and
J. H. Fowles, who produced an estimate of £674,000 for the complete renewal of cars, track and nearly everything else, to be spread
over sixteen years. They considered that it would be cheaper to
use double-deck buses, and soon afterwards certain other parties
were to be seen lurking at M E R stations and along King Edward
Road taking information for their anticipated replacement bus
services.

Whitsun 1956 saw a well-attended L R T L convention in Laxey,
with an exhibition opened by the lieutenant-governor, and jointly
arranged by the Douglas Society of Model Engineers and the writer.
Speeches at the convention dinner included noteworthy contributions from J. E. Ellison (chairman of the Laxey Commissioners)
and R. C. Drinkwater of the M E R, and much favourable publicity
resulted. Another guest was H. C. Kerruish, MHK, who on 5 June
took eighteen of the twenty-four members of the Keys for a trip
up Snaefell, where they weighed the view against the cost and
affirmed their belief that the island could not afford to let the line
close.

The sub-committee presented its dismal report in the Keys on
Tuesday, 19 June, and recommended that no assistance be given.
After a pungent debate during which the line's chief detractor
was seen to be J. B. Bolton (who wanted a road up Snaefell), the
report was put aside, and the House agreed to a proposal by Mr
Kerruish that a new committee be appointed to investigate the
possibility of continuing the railway at a reasonable cost. Its members were Deemster Sir Percy Cowley, MBE, Sir Ralph Stevenson,
KCMG, H. C. Kerruish, J. B. Bolton and G. Taggart, and they were
to report back in October.

On 10 July the company petitioned Tynwald for leave to introduce an abandonment Bill, which was rejected by a small majority;
the alternative solution (in October) was an indemnity against losses
to 30 September 1957, under which the company agreed to continue for a further twelve months. Track renewal, the last carried
out by the company, was commenced south of Baldromma-Beg.
The direct loss on working in 1956 was £3,169, and car miles

were 253,603 (passenger) and 8,536 (goods). S. A. Young died in February, 1957, and the final directorate consisted of Messrs Holmes, Parker, Clutton and Drinkwater.

The Committee of Tynwald sought a further expert report, this time with two members chosen from tramway rather than mainline railway fields. An inspection followed on 2-3 July 1956 by J. W. Fowler AM Inst BE (chairman of the Light Railway Transport League), C. T. Humpidge, BSc, M Inst T, general manager of Bradford City Transport, and (once more) R. Varley of British Railways, all of whom found that the line could indeed be kept going for far less than the sum previously quoted. They considered that the line could not be constructed today for at least twenty times its sale value, if at all, and that its intrinsic worth was incalculable. A difference of opinion survived between the two new investigators and Mr Varley, who seemed convinced that new rolling stock would be essential.

In August 1956, the Tynwald committee met the directors, and entered into a provisional agreement for the sale of the line to the government for £50,000, ie, about £2,000/mile. The company, influenced by the views of those directors who put the island's interests before their own, made a very real sacrifice in agreeing to this figure, for the reduction of £20,000 brought the price down to about the estimated scrap value of the plant, ignoring the land value.

The committee reported on 6 November 1956 in favour of purchase, recommending a ten-year renewal programme for Douglas—Laxey and Laxey—Snaefell, and the proposals came up for full debate on 12 December. Deemster Sir Percy Cowley put the case for the line's acquisition with great earnestness. His main opponents were J. B. Bolton and a new member, J. M. Cain, a director of the IMR and IMRS. Mr Cain suggested that his own company could carry all the MER traffic with ten extra buses, which could be taken to mean that only one passenger in three would bother to make the journey at all if it were by bus. Telling points in the railway's favour included the fact that 70 per cent of visitors rode it, the degree to which its existence helped Ramsey, and the annual disbursement of £31,000 in wages.

The ensuing vote was 17 to 4 in favour of purchasing the line and commencing the initial ten-year programme of renewals, and by 17 April 1957 the necessary Bill was signed in Tynwald. It was a historic decision, and in this way the Manx Electric system escaped a fate that would have been bitterly regretted ever since, a closure whose moral effect would have been very serious for the whole future of the Isle of Man.

As a parallel, consider the Hill of Howth tramway in Ireland, replaced by buses shortly after its closure. Traffic promptly dropped by about two-thirds, with the result that the buses, although cheaper to run, still lost nearly as much money as the trams.

CHAPTER TEN

Nationalisation and After

Established services and attractions such as the Manx Electric Railway and Snaefell Mountain Railway should be preserved and developed—Commission on the Visiting Industry, January 1956

On Saturday morning, 1 June 1957, the lieutenant-governor, Sir Ambrose Dundas Flux Dundas, drove flag-bedecked M E R No 32 in brilliant sunshine from Derby Castle to Groudle, to mark the transfer of the undertaking to the Manx government. Aboard the car were Deemster Cowley, Mr Kerruish, Tourist Board secretary L. Bond and the joint managers, with Sir Ralph Stevenson, first chairman of the new Manx Electric Railway Board, which was set up in May 1957 to manage the undertaking.

Boards of Tynwald are composite bodies consisting of elected members from the House of Keys and non-Tynwald members appointed by the governor. The new M E R board had three Tynwald and two outside members. Chairman was Sir Ralph Stevenson, GCMG, MLC, the Keys members were R. C. Stephen and A. H. Simcocks, and the nominated members T. W. Kneale, M ENG, and T. W. Billington. Mr Stephen was concerned with traffic operation, Mr Simcocks with publicity, Mr Kneale with permanent way and engineering, and Mr Billington with accountancy. T. W. Kneale was a former divisional executive engineer of the North Western Railway of India, and although professionally retired, in his M E R capacity spared none of his still considerable energies. The board's first term of office extended to 30 November 1961.

The intention was to relay the Douglas—Laxey section in the first seven years, followed by Laxey—Snaefell in the next three, the work to be financed by annual grant. On 18 June 1957, Tynwald voted £40,000 for the first two miles of new track, and orders were placed for 200 tons of 60-lb flat bottom rail, specially rolled at Workington. The new track used 6 ft by 9 in by 4½ in sleepers and such sophisticated devices as elastic rail spikes, rubber pads (on one stretch) and proper transition curves; the noted curve at Groudle lost a 'dog-leg' of particularly vicious character. On 10 October, 3,000 sleepers arrived at Ramsey in the *Ben Ain*, followed a few days later by the 200 tons of rail, delivered to the lineside site at Queen's Drive which Bruce had bought in 1899 during the dispute over the Ramsey terminus. Permanent way foreman Mr Fred Comaish, who had worked on the line since 1899, retired on 15 January 1958, and in view of the heavy work programme (with 110 men at work) the board created a new post of engineering assistant, filled by A. R. Cannell from the Harbour Board, who had previously served an M E R apprenticeship.

Help was also made available to the M E R board between 1961 and 1965 under the winter employment schemes, by which the island government sought to offset the seasonal nature of tourist employment; the amount in each year depending on the level of employment. Under these schemes, the three lines were completely weeded, and the fences and drainage works repaired and cleared. The Ramsey line revealed itself as far from life-expended, thanks to a good original design of rail section and generous ballasting. The line was thereafter treated with a selective weed-killer and in parts with a brushwood killer, applied by a special tank wagon of 1958 with a small petrol engine providing pressure spraying at 5 mph. Other winter work schemes saw Laxey and Ramsey stations resurfaced in tarmac, and the same treatment was later given to Derby Castle yard. The Forestry Board also greatly improved Dhoon and Ballaglass glens.

Passengers in 1957 had shown a drop of some 56,000, and Tynwald on 10 December voted £9,000 to offset this and cover rising costs, plus £3,820 for track. By this time, the board had decided to adopt a new colour scheme of green and white for the cars, and the first of fourteen green cars appeared on 24 December. This unhappy choice is further referred to in the rolling stock chapter, and was abandoned after 1959. Attempts were made to obtain the Laxey—Douglas school contract, and late cars were run to

Douglas and Ramsey for entertainments, but attracted little patronage.

Annual estimates are presented to Tynwald by each board by 31 March. The M E R board in its first year found that adding renewals to operating losses would require an annual £45,000 instead of the intended £25,000, and would mean a 2s 10d subsidy for every 5s fare; so reported Sir Ralph on 18 April 1958. A storm broke over the heads of the board, and proposed remedies included the permanent closure of the Ramsey line. On 22 May, a vote of 11 : 10 resolved (just) to stay in business, but to run purely as a scenic railway, with no early or late cars and with complete closure from 13 September to 16 May of each year. The next stage of relaying would be financed by a loan, and this involved the issue of £20,000 of Manx Electric Railway Board 5 per cent guaranteed stock. This twenty-year loan had been recommended in the second advisory report of 1956, and in July 1958 the board was granted borrowing powers up to £110,000. The completion date for Douglas—Laxey was now extended to 1965.

The M E R duly did as it was told, introducing an eleven-journey 10 am to 6 pm service in June 1958 and, as might be expected, uproar ensued. The unfortunate chairman and three of the four board members resigned on 18 June, and the corporation and Road Services promptly sought licences to run to Groudle and points *en route*, on the grounds of inadequate M E R service.

On 8 July, the courageous survivor, Mr Kneale, found himself joined by a new board comprising H. H. Radcliffe, JP, MHK, W. E. Quayle, JP, MHK, Lieut-Commander J. L. Quine, MHK, and R. Dean, JP. The new board stated that they would try and run the line within its subsidy ceiling of £25,000, and would maintain a winter service. The full twenty-journey timetable was restored from 12 July. In Mr Radcliffe, the new chairman, the M E R had found a vocal champion, and in the ensuing debate the line's chief adversary, Mr Bolton, was told that the railway would last long after he himself had ceased to grace the Tynwald chamber!

In 1957, the board had bought two Leyland 'Cubs' from Douglas Corporation, and experimented with a renewed Sulby service. For 1958, a more grandiose conducted tour was evolved, with I M R co-operation, modelled on one of pre-war years. For 14s, it offered a full day tour, Douglas to Snaefell, a five-course lunch at the summit, bus from Bungalow to Tholt-y-Will and on to Sulby Glen station, train to Ramsey and M E R to Douglas. Participants were

imited to fifty, and bad weather refunds offered. This excellent
:our attracted only moderate support, and was not repeated in
1959, officially due to difficulty in keeping the two buses serviceable owing to their age. The vehicles had a useful last outing on 7
August 1959 when they ran a shuttle service in Ramsey from the
Plaza to the Royal Manx Agricultural Show at Lezayre Road. In
1960 they remained disused, and were sold in 1961. The Post
Office contract, which might have been lost if the line had closed
in winter, was successfully renegotiated in 1959 at improved rates.

The Snaefell Summit hotel was re-equipped and redecorated
or the 1958 tours, to the designs of architect T. H. Kennaugh,
and has maintained a really excellent standard of catering ever
since. Good business is also done in the sale of such items as Snaefell souvenirs, leather goods and headscarves, and the board has
produced an excellent range of colour postcards. The Bungalow
hotel was closed and demolished early in 1958, and was replaced
by a public shelter and conveniences (to whose cost the board con-
ributed) after unsuccessful attempts to obtain tenancy of an RAF
building alongside the mountain road.

Another 200 tons of new rail arrived at Douglas in September
1958, and a further 100 tons a year later. By 1962, the total bought
had reached 600 tons, of which 539 had been laid by 1964. In
January 1960, Tynwald made a special grant of £9,000, and a
urther £3,000 was voted in June 1961 to cover a wage increase,
but good traffic results enabled the board to report back that this
um was no longer needed. In 1959-60, a reduced working deficit
eft £6,000 of the basic £25,000 grant available to finance further
relaying, and when Colonel Robertson of the Ministry of Transport
visited the island in April and May 1960, the M E R track passed
his inspection with flying colours. The year 1959 saw the repainting
of Ballure bridge, which absorbed forty gallons of paint and six
man-months. M E R efforts to obtain the school contract beyond
the Maughold area were still unsuccessful; I M R S opposition was
vehement, and (as contractor for the rest of the island) all too
effective.

1959 and 1960 saw an overhaul of M E R publicity. Press advertising, which had much increased in 1958, now ceased again, and
was replaced by advertising spots in cinema programmes. A twenty-
minutes 16-mm film was made, based on a full-day trip from
Douglas to Snaefell and Ramsey, and has since been shown to the
public on summer evenings at the Sefton booking office, a shop

The new station at Ramsey, 1964

on Douglas promenade. M E R advertising began to appear in corporation buses, and walled panels were used to screen Derby Castle
yard; in 1964, a similar wall was put up to screen Laxey goods
depot. Since 1966, the M E R has sponsored weather forecasts on
Manx Radio. The results of the board's publicity and of the lavish
distribution of timetables for display in hotels, boarding-houses,
offices and shops can be judged by comparing the post-nationalis-
ation Snaefell traffic figures with those for six earlier years :

1948	77,000	1957	92,000
1949	76,000	1958	68,000
1950	60,000	1959	94,000
1951	56,000	1960	96,000
1952	61,000	1961	124,000
1953	48,000	1962	111,000

Renewals were also made from 1958 onwards to the overhead
line, using traditional round-section trolley wire and phosphor-
bronze overhead parts. An arrangement was reached with BICC
and the Colton Electrical Equipment Company for the continued
manufacture of round wire fittings. In 1958-62 the overhead poles
received a very thorough repainting in dark green, as did the lineside buildings, whilst new white paint on accommodation gates
added further to the line's appearance. The overhead line gang has
two tower wagons, normally based at Laxey shed, a convenient

centre from which to reach any failure. In November 1961, Mr Alfred Callister retired from his position in charge of Derby Castle car sheds, after thirty-eight years' service, and was succeeded by Mr Lewis Gale, with Mr Alan McMullen as assistant.

From winter 1959-60 co-ordination of timings at Derby Castle with the promenade buses was arranged, each car being met by a

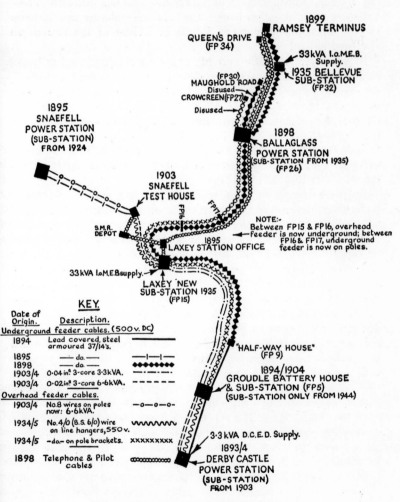

The present MER electrical feeder system

connecting bus. In summer, horse-car timings were also matched to M E R arrivals. To eliminate the costly part-day manning of the substations at Ballaglass, Snaefell, Bellevue and Groudle, automatic switchgear by Bertram Thomas (Engineering) Ltd was ordered in 1962 and installed in 1963-4, together with self-resetting circuit breakers. These units differ in their functions, that at Bellevue having a total operating cycle of ninety-five minutes duration. These automatic time switches have introduced several new and hitherto largely unknown phenomena in the behaviour of the line as an electrical entity!

In 1962 Mr Radcliffe and Mr Quayle were promoted to board chairmanships which carried membership of the Executive Council, the Manx cabinet. Thus on 8 March 1962 a third M E R board came into being, with T. H. Colebourn, MHK, as chairman, Major-General Sir Henry Sugden, MHK, as vice-chairman, and E. R. Moore, MHK, as the third Tynwald member. Mr Kneale and Mr Dean were reappointed by the governor as the non-Tynwald members. Mr Colebourn soon showed himself as staunch an M E R defender as Mr Radcliffe had been.

By 1962, operating and renewing the M E R had cost about £180,000. Meanwhile, reconstruction of the Marine Drive had already cost £216,000, ie, almost as much as the eight-times-as-long M E R/S M R. The withdrawal of the Fleetwood steamers since September 1961 had been keenly felt in afternoon riding. During 1962, the road bridge across Glen Roy at Laxey was reconstructed, and foot passengers were allowed across the M E R viaduct, partially paved up for the occasion. A timed commentary on the scenery on the Snaefell route, with attractive background music, was introduced in the mountain cars, two receiving the equipment in 1962 and the other four in 1963; the tape was recorded by Mr Howard Lay, now Attorney-General, and was played on the uphill journey, with occasional humorous side-effects in case of delay or mist. In 1963, a grandstand was built at the Bungalow for the TT races, with a mobile licensed bar, and a footbridge was erected at the same location in 1965. The short-lived green and white livery finally disappeared late in 1963, and the senior staff were issued with uniforms closer to M E R tradition than those of 1958-9 with their Ruritanian embellishments and exaggerated green lapels.

In 1963 the combined totals of deficiency and winter work grants became subject to a new accountancy practice whereby any unspent amount at the year end was repaid to the government

Late snow in Glen Mona as No 19 pauses at Ballaglass, 2 April 1966, during map surveys for this book

The failed drysto
wall at Bulgham
late May 1967, phot
graphed during r
moval of the loo
stones

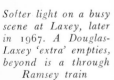

Softer light on a busy
scene at Laxey, later
in 1967. A Douglas-
Laxey 'extra' empties,
beyond is a through
Ramsey train

treasurer. Good seasonal earnings could thus no longer be used to boost the board's civil engineering programme for the ensuing year. The total allocated for 1963-4 was £39,683, to which must be added the cost of a new Snaefell shelter at Laxey (54 ft by 10 ft), and an entirely new 39 ft by 24 ft station building at Ramsey. A scheme for a new Laxey coastal line station, and a chairlift across Douglas harbour (for operation by the M E R) fell victims to a budget deficiency. Poorer weather in 1963 put income £3,000 below the estimates, and rising wages brought the year's operating deficit to £32,682.

The board pressed on with the relaying, duly completing Douglas—Laxey by 1965. Some resleepering was carried out on the Ramsey line, mainly between Dhoon and Ballaglass. The next task was the Snaefell track, whose 24-ft Fell rails had corroded at their fishplates and were heavily worn across their working dimension, especially on curves. The running rail was less worn— the head is quite good—but is a poorly designed section with over-thin foot and web; some was relaid in 1961. The United Steel Companies at Workington were willing to make new Fell rail, but the cost (when known) provoked another sharp debate.

At Derby Castle, Douglas Corporation had bought the former entertainment complex, and the scheme's advocates now mounted a powerful attack on the incongruity of M E R and horse cars passing the planned swimming-pool and solarium. They sought to expel the M E R depot and terminus to the heights of Oncham Head : reputedly, representatives were found surveying the board's yard without permission, and were duly given suggestions as to where they might go instead. At one stage it was suggested that M E R cars might run behind the new centre in tunnel, but final plans published in August 1964 showed the M E R and its depot undisturbed, with the new building cantilevered over the tracks, a footbridge crossing to the seaward footway. The site was cleared in 1966 and construction began in 1967, with the swimming pool scheduled for completion in 1969 and the solarium in 1971. Some rearrangement of the M E R terminal tracks is probable.

Mr J. Rowe retired from the position of secretary and joint manager at the end of 1964, the end of a thirty-five year association with the M E R. Mr Rowe was the patient bearer of many of the author's queries and, with his M E R colleagues, fought the line's case with great zeal during 1955-6. Mr J. F. Watson now became general manager, engineer and secretary, Mr H. Gilmore became

P

chief assistant engineer and traffic manager, Mr E. Halsall accountant and Mr A. R. Cannell engineering and traffic assistant. Sunday,
5 July 1965, saw HRH Princess Margaret and Lord Snowdon make
an evening Snaefell summit trip from the Bungalow by special car,
accompanied by the lieutenant-governor. In April 1965 Onchan
commissioners bought Groudle beach for development, which, if
and when undertaken, should bring traffic to the M E R.

Snow usually treats the island lightly, and blockages have been
chiefly one-day affairs. On 3 March 1965, No 9 on the 2.45 pm
from Ramsey became lodged in a drift at Ballafayle when the
power failed, but the line was open again by next day, and a shuttle
service, Douglas—Laxey and Ballafayle—Ramsey, was maintained
meanwhile. Mr and Mrs H. C. Kerruish (the Speaker of the Keys
and his wife) were among those who accommodated the stranded
passengers. The only regular movement on the Snaefell line in
winter is by the diesel cars used by the staff of the Ministry of
Defence radar station. These have several times found their path
blocked by the snow, and the operator has sometimes been
marooned on the mountain for several days.

The board had up to now maintained the company's goods service, with collection and delivery in their area and in the town of
Douglas by lorries based at Douglas and Ramsey, which transhipped their loads to covered vans (or open wagons) at the termini.
Payment was 'weigh and pay' or by monthly account, and the rates
remained low, for certain categories only 1s 6d a ton. Parcels were
also collected from Mr E. Hudson's shop, King Street, Douglas.
By 1965, the lorries needed replacing, but this was considered un-
economic. Service thus ceased as from 1 April 1966, after the
I M R S had proved unwilling to provide connecting haulage. Goods
brought to the termini are still conveyed (on a 'between stations'
basis), and it is common for Ramsey traders, finding a desired item
out of stock, to have it sent up from Douglas by the next tram.
Isle of Man Road Services now took over the lorry work over the
whole distance, and a bus had to be pressed into service on 4 April
1966 to cope with the parcels traffic.

On 23 March 1966, Tynwald provided a vigorous debate on the
Snaefell relaying, now estimated to cost £145,000. Mr Bolton again
mooted his road-to-the-summit proposal, and sought to delete from
the board's 1966-7 estimates of £106,977 the first £12,500 instalment for the Snaefell task. None the less, the estimates were passed,
and Mr Colebourn emphasised the successful absorption of a

MANX ELECTRIC RAILWAY

Douglas, Laxey, Ramsey & Snaefell

TIME TABLE—Saturday, 21st May, 1966 and until 16th September, 1966

Time from Derby Castle :— THE SNAEFELL MOUNTAIN RAILWAY OPEN from 21st May until 16th September, 1966 CARS AS REQUIRED BY TRAFFIC

Groudle 12 mins.; Garwick 20 mins.; Dhoon 45 mins.; Ballaglass 55 mins. Change at Laxey for the Glorious Trip to the Summit of Snaefell Mountain (2,034 feet above sea level)

The run on the Open Cars by the Direct Route to Ramsey through magnificent Woodland and Marine Scenery is of unrivalled popularity

FROM DOUGLAS

WEEKDAYS

DOUGLAS (Derby Castle) dep.	a.m. 7 0	8 30	10 0	10 30	11 0	noon 12 0	p.m. 1 0	2 0	2 30	3 15	4 0	5 0	5 30	6 30	8 0	9 0	10 30
W. City, Majestic, Howstrake																	
GROUDLE GLEN															boat car		
BALDRINE																	
GARWICK GLEN	7 30	9 15	10 30	11 0	11 30	12 30	1 30	2 30	3 0	3 45	4 30	5 30	6 0	7 0	8 30	9 30	11 0
LAXEY																	
DHOON GLEN																	
GLEN MONA																	
BALLAGLASS GLEN																	
BALLAJORA, LEWAIGUE																	
RAMSEY (Plaza) arr.	8 15	10 0	11 15	11 45	12 15	1 15	2 15	3 15	3 45	4 30	5 15	6 15	6 45	7 45	9 15	10 15	11 45

Extra Cars will also be run between the advertised times as required by the Traffic

FROM RAMSEY

RAMSEY (Plaza) dep.	a.m. 7 15	8 30	10 30	11 30	noon 12 0	p.m. 12 30	1 45	2 30	3 30	4 0	4 30	5 30	6 30	7 15	8 30	9 30	10 30
LEWAIGUE, BALLAJORA																	
BALLAGLASS GLEN							boat car										
GLEN MONA																	
DHOON GLEN	8 0	9 0	10 15	11 15	12 45		1 15	2 30	3 15	4 15	4 45	5 15	6 15	8 0	9 15	10 15	11 15 stop
LAXEY																	
GARWICK GLEN																	
BALDRINE																	
GROUDLE GLEN																	
Howstrake, Majestic, W. City																	
DOUGLAS (Derby Castle) arr.	8 30	9 30	10 45	11 45	12 45	1 15	1 45	3 0	3 45	4 45	5 15	5 45	6 45	7 45	8 30	9 45	10 45

SUNDAYS

a.m. 7 0 boat car	8 30	10 0	11 0	p.m. 1 0	2 0	2 30	3 15	4 0	5 30	6 30	7 30	9 0	10 30
7 30	9 15	10 30	11 30	1 30	2 30	3 0	3 45	4 30	6 0	7 0	8 0	9 30	11 0 stop
8 15	10 0	11 15	12 15	2 15	3 15	3 45	4 30	5 15	6 45	7 45	8 45	10 15	

a.m. 8 20	9 0	10 15	12 15	p.m. 1 45	2 30	3 15	4 15	4 30	5 30	7 15	8 30	9 30
9 0	10 15	12 15	1 15	2 30	3 15	4 15	5 15	6 15	8 0	9 15	10 15	
9 30	10 45	12 45	1 45	3 0	3 45	4 45	5 45	6 45	8 30	9 45	10 45	

RETURN TICKETS ARE AVAILABLE FOR BREAK OF JOURNEY AT ALL THE CHARMING GLENS EN ROUTE BOTH GOING AND RETURNING

1, Strathallan Crescent, Douglas. Phone Nos.: Douglas 61 : Laxey 226 : Ramsey 2249   Telegrams : Electric Douglas

J. F. WATSON, M.I.E.E.
General Manager

Manx Electric Railway Board summer timetable. In some years (1967 included) a separate timetable applies from Whitsun to early July

£4,000 wage increase and £3,000 under-spending on the deficiency grant. He saw an increased role for the line as the island's roads grew more crowded. However, by his casting vote the M E R board had decided to seek Tynwald permission to close in winter, since a mere 550 patrons used the line each week and the winter loss was now £5,200. This would require a winter Maughold service by I M R S, which they were ready to provide. The court's remarks caused Mr Colebourn to refer this back to his board, and no further action was taken.

M E R fares, which had remained low for many years, were increased to perhaps more harshly realistic levels in 1964, when Douglas—Snaefell return became 12s and Laxey—Snaefell 8s 6d. Reductions were granted on production of vouchers distributed by hotels and boarding-houses, but from 1965 these were replaced by privilege rates made available on specific days (Tuesday, Friday and Saturday). An innovation of August 1964 was a railways interchange tour between Douglas and Ramsey for 6s, one way by I M R and the other by M E R, but this was not repeated. A further 5 per cent fare increase occurred in 1968, without adverse effect on traffic, and the best bargain is still the two-day rover ticket (now 16s) which allows unlimited travel on the coastal line and one trip up Snaefell. Fares are differentiated in favour of the longer-distance traveller, and books of residents' tickets (known as name tickets) are sold at a substantial discount. In winter, lower ordinary fares apply, and the Ramsey return at 4s is surely the cheapest 34-mile ticket anywhere; it is only sixpence more than the summer fare of 1899.

In April 1965, the I O M government set up a commission to investigate public transport to and within the island. It comprised two members of Tynwald who had formerly sat on the M E R board (Mr Radcliffe and Mr Quayle), together with D. R. Hunter (shipping manager of ICI, Liverpool), G. E. Lambert (transport consultant) and Captain J. C. Kelly Rogers of Aerlinte Eireann, Dublin; Mr Radcliffe was chairman. Mr Colebourn gave evidence on 31 January 1966, and said that the M E R board planned to retain all its lines, but to run them as a scenic railway. He also remarked on the punitive effect of breakfast-table tour soliciting by coach proprietors, and revealed a $3\frac{1}{2}$ per cent rise in passengers for 1965, which looked good against the reduced patronage reported by the steam railway and the buses, the former then on the verge of closure. The examination of coach operation was one of the com-

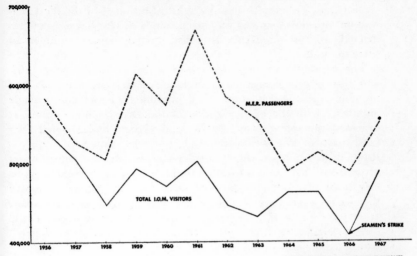

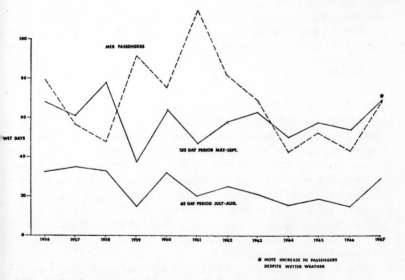

Graph showing M E R passengers in relation to island visitors and island
summer climate (The 1968 passenger figure was 551,000)

mission's chief functions, and the major coach proprietors were to some extent brought to heel by the institution of a Traffic Commission and licensing system. Coach stands in Douglas are now restricted, and stopping time at other loading points is limited to three minutes.

The commission's 125-page report appeared on 31 May 1966, and was largely concerned with island access (sea and air), but proposed the amalgamation of all internal transport into a single authority, with the sole exception of the Douglas horse trams. It proposed the retention of the Douglas—Laxey and Snaefell lines (and part of the steam railway), but the closure of Laxey—Ramsey. Much space was devoted to hovercraft, and the prospect of renewed day excursion traffic from the Lancashire coast by some new form of rapid cross-channel service would certainly improve the M E R's position, especially if fed from its mid-point at Laxey. It is the perfect day-tripper ride, and a Laxey terminal would spread delighted patrons both north and south (and up to Snaefell) within the confines of a short visit.

The commission's proposal to close Laxey—Ramsey was not adopted, and events in 1967 seem to confirm the line's continuance, but some remarks thereon may not be out of place. The commission considered the M E R's function to be the provision of a service calculated to attract visitors to the island, and implied that this could be achieved wholly by keeping Douglas—Laxey and Laxey—Snaefell, but they overlooked the fact that Snaefell's seasonal capacity is limited to about 120,000, that of its six cars. The M E R attracts about 500,000 riders every year, and in 1965 one in six rode to Ramsey, or bought two-day rover tickets which entitled them to do so, and which would not have been bought had their only objective been Snaefell. Instead of taking two M E R rides, they would take only one, and the effect of closing Laxey—Ramsey would be a reduction of perhaps one-third in the traffic between Douglas and Laxey, the reverse of the commission's aim. A better way to increase the traffic figures is surely to revive visitor interest north of Laxey, providing some new attraction in the Bulgham-Dhoon area, which has no equal scenically. A cliffside restaurant and viewing terrace would be a possibility here where the scenery fully equates with that on the Marine Drive.

Mr T. W. Kneale died on 12 January 1966, and after the 1966 elections a new board was appointed in October. Major-General Sir Henry Sugden, KBE, CB, DSO, MHK, returned as chairman, with

Miss J. C. C. Thornton-Duesbery, JP, MHK, as vice-chairman. The number of non-Tynwald members was increased to three, Mr J. R. Gelling, Mr E. R. Moore and Mr M. F. Strickett. That year, 1966, saw the island disaster of the seamen's strike, during which two late cars were deleted on the Ramsey line, and little use was therefore made of a revived facility—a ticket allowing travel between Douglas and Ramsey one way by MER and the other by the Ardrossan or Belfast steamers of the IOMSP Co. Further losses by the Road Services brought a cut in the winter Ramsey bus service and some extra winter business for the MER.

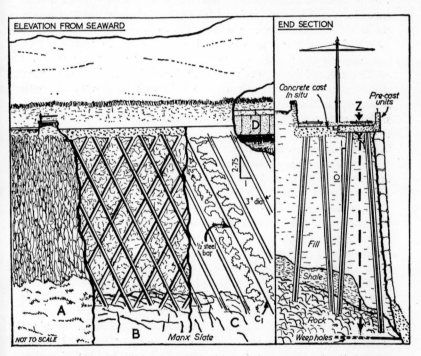

The Bulgham reconstruction, 1967. A shows the appearance of the original dry stone wall, B is a part section showing the lattice effect of the piles (116 in all) and C shows the detail of one row, with C1 representing penetration by the liquid grout poured down the bores. D shows the interlocking pre-cast units inserted where the parapet wall was removed; 40 were used, of which 24 spanned the failure. The end section shows how 16 extra vertical piles Z were sunk to a greater depth. Zone Y was filled with concrete after the pre-cast units were erected

The following year, 1967, was to provide a prime example of the M E R's resilience under stress. At Bulgham Bay, the seaward embankment wall at its southern end crosses a deep natural cleft in the 600-ft cliff, this cleft containing a mass of material lying largely on shale. Since 1965, a bulge in the masonry at its base had caused concern, and in mid-afternoon of 20 January 1967 it failed, shortly after the 1.25 pm Ramsey—Douglas and 1.15 Douglas—Ramsey (car No 21) had passed. Services were maintained to each side of the failure, and passengers walked the track for the intervening distance. Parcels traffic was next diverted to road van, with a rail van serving as transhipment warehouse at Derby Castle. Motor cars Nos 7 and 21 were isolated north of the failure. By 27 January the M E R had built steps into the dividing wall to allow passengers to transfer along the parallel road, closed since the previous day, but renewed structural movement caused further anxiety, and that evening a hired Road Services bus replaced the cars between Laxey and Dhoon Glen, using the top road through Ballaragh. The wall above the initial fall collapsed next day, but things now stabilised, and all-tram shuttle service recommenced on 1 February. A newly-printed timetable added five minutes to journey times and modified five departures to synchronise the Bulgham connections.

Repairs were the joint concern of the Highway and Transport and M E R boards, and C. S. Allot & Sons of Manchester were brought in as consultants early in February. Meanwhile, No 20 ran the gauntlet and replaced No 21, and by 30 March Nos 6 and 9 had gone north and several trailers were brought back from Ramsey for summer requirements. The M E R prepared to build up a northern section summer operating fleet, and to provide transfer station facilities on a scale commensurate with summer traffic.

On 22 March Highway Board chairman R. E. S. Kerruish announced that quotations for repair were awaited and that this would include the restoration of the tramway. The repair employed a method known as 'Reticulated Pali-Radice', an Italian technique carried out in Britain by Fondedile Foundations Ltd of London. As can be seen from the drawing, the effect may be likened to that of burying a net in a mess of otherwise unstable material, and in this case 116 three-inch diameter concrete piles were used in four parallel double rows, with some later extras to give additional assurance. The contractors began work on 1 May, and with one-third of the job complete by 18 May, grout had already appeared on the face of the wall. Night work commenced in mid-May,

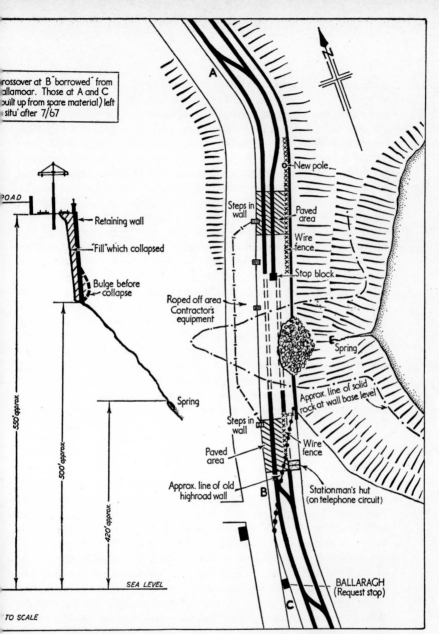

rossover at B "borrowed" from
allamoar. Those at A and C
built up from spare material) left
n situ' after 7/67

OAD

Retaining wall

"Fill" which collapsed

Bulge before
collapse

550' approx.

500' approx.

420' approx.

Spring

SEA LEVEL

TO SCALE

New pole

Steps in
wall

Paved
area

Wire
fence

Stop block

Roped off area
Contractor's
equipment

Spring

Approx. line of solid
rock at wall base level

Steps in
wall

Paved
area

Wire
fence

Approx. line of old
highroad wall

B

Stationman's hut
(on telephone circuit)

BALLARAGH
(Request stop)

C

Traffic working at the Bulgham slip, 1967, with cars reversing on either
side of the gap. When regular trailer operation commenced on May 20,
north-side cars used the seaward track south of A for both arrival and
departure, and their empty trailers were gravity-shunted into the terminal
track while their motors withdrew to north of A. On the southern side,
conventional run-around shunting was used, with the inner track serving
as the terminal. Through running was resumed on July 10

with completion scheduled for 15 June. The M E R built the stations shown on the plan by 20 May, when the special summer service came into operation, so arranged that an empty car always awaited an arrival at Bulgham between 10.00 and 18.00 hrs, thus avoiding conflicting flows of passengers. These special arrangements were to see 66,000 transfers by 10 July, more than the whole year's passenger total on the reopened steam line. Further car moves had been made on 23 April before the contractors lifted the tracks, motor cars Nos 16, 19 and 27 and trailers Nos 36, 41, 43, 44 and 48 being sent north, and No 20 coming south with a trailer and three vans; the trailers were hauled past the work site on the end of a rope. Mid-June saw the work nearing completion, and on 29 June prefabricated track was positioned by a Highway Board crane working from the adjacent roadway. The overhead lines followed, and at 7.00 am on Monday, 10 July, the first through car (No 21) left Douglas for Ramsey, complete with van, and the 7.15 am (car No 22) left Ramsey for Douglas. There was no special ceremony—the M E R was simply 'back to normal'.

For 1967 island visitors rose to 489,000, and the M E R's new full-scale timetable (10 July to 18 September) was fully justified. It provided 17½ daily journeys in each direction, and gained good traffic in spite of renewed I M R competition. The rise was greatest in longer distance journeys; queues for Ramsey cars were seen at Laxey for the first time for some years, and Ramsey station ran 'specials' to the Dhoon at 9.45 on weekdays and 12.45 on Sundays.

In the legislature, another battle had been fought. The Isle of Man government estimates for 1966-7 had included provision for the first instalment of Snaefell track repairs, but in the final estimates of May this had been deleted. Following a Tynwald excursion to the summit on 6 June 1967, attended by the governor and Lady Stallard, Sir Henry Sugden brought the issue to the fore by a motion in Tynwald asking for a Finance Board vote to carry out essential maintenance on the Snaefell line, and in the debate of 20 June Sir Henry carried the day. Progressive renewal of the downhill braking rail was authorised, a typical Manx compromise, being a slower execution of the original project. M E R technical skills saw the prompt production of a rail-bending rig carried on spare bogies, and 100 tons of centre rail were produced at Workington in 1967; work commenced on the Summit—Bungalow section in October, 1968.

The board's senior officer, Mr J. F. Watson, C ENG, FIEE, retired on 31 December 1967 after thirty-eight years' service; he had held the posts of rolling-stock superintendent (1930), chief assistant engineer (1936), chief engineer and joint manager (1952) and since 1963 general manager, engineer and secretary. His successor was Mr Harold Gilmore, with Mr A. R. Cannell as chief assistant engineer and Mr J. R. Gordon as traffic superintendent; Mr Watson's brother, Douglas, became ways and works superintendent. Mr J. F. Watson now became inspector of seasonal railways to the Isle of Man government in place of Mr H. Maxwell Rostron; previous holders of this post had been Mr R. Varley (1963-5) and, earlier, Mr T. W. Kneale.

The operating year is today divided into summer and winter timetable periods, changing in mid-May and mid-September, and occasionally with separate early and main summer timetables. The winter service (weekdays only since 1951) requires four two-man crews. In 1959, for example, No 1 Douglas crew booked on at 6.40 am to work the 7 am to Ramsey, and finished at 2.40 pm. The corresponding times for No 2 Douglas crew were 2.15, 2.45 and 9.40 pm. No 1 Ramsey crew booked on at 6.30 am to work the 6.55 to Douglas, finishing at 2.30 pm, and No 2 Ramsey crew took over the 2.55 pm (booking on at 2.30) and finished with the 8.45 pm from Douglas. Each turn included one changeover duty in which cars exchanged crews as they passed (normally between Bulgham and Ballaglass), the 11.45 am from Douglas changing with the 11.55 am from Ramsey, and the 2.25 pm from Douglas with the 2.55 pm from Ramsey, to ensure that crews finished at their home stations.

In summer, Douglas provides three regular sets of men to Ramsey's two, and two sets of men work from Laxey. In 1964, changeover duties were the 1.0 pm, 5.0 pm and 8.0 pm from Douglas, and the 1.45 pm, 5.30 pm and 8.30 pm from Ramsey. Sundays require five crews, two each from Douglas and Laxey and one from Ramsey. Crews for the numerous extra cars are held on call according to estimated requirements, and these special cars are inserted at intervals determined by demand. Traffic control is by telephone between station-masters, and the double track makes any more complex arrangements such as signalling unnecessary. On blind corners there are pole-mounted boards, red at entry and white for exit, and should a car stop there the conductor must be sent back as lookout. Single-line working during winter track renewals is catered for by staff and ticket, a red, a white and a blue staff covering the three sections Douglas—Garwick, Garwick—Dhoon Quarry and Dhoon Quarry—Ramsey. The 64-page rulebook had its last major revision in 1926; as well as general instructions, it has sections for station-masters, inspectors, motormen, conductors, linesmen, permanent-way staff, and those working the Snaefell line. The sheer physical extent of the M E R sees the inclusion of some orthodox railway practices, and another reflection of the 'distance' element is in the comprehensive spares allocated to each motor car and those held in the linesmen's emergency boxes at Douglas, Laxey and Ramsey. M E R cars carry external oil-lamps in case a power failure should see them marooned without lights, though the former internal oil-lamps are now incomplete, at least on summer-only cars.

On the Snaefell line, the first car at about 8.45 am is reserved for hotel staff and supplies, and stops at the mountain substation while its crew switch on the upper section current. The first service car on fine days leaves Laxey at about 10.30 am, the subsequent frequency being determined by the weather and the loading reports telephoned from Douglas. On Sundays, first departure from Laxey is normally at 2 pm. The last departure from the summit is at about 6.00 pm, and again is partly filled by catering and station staff. Bungalow station has become important again, as in the Sulby Glen era, but now with road-borne visitors who leave their cars there and take the mountain line to the summit; special cars are sometimes sent up from Laxey to pick up coach parties, those on certain tours taking their lunch or tea at the Summit hotel. Surprisingly, Snaefell crews take only about a week to learn the road and the various lineside 'marks' where brakes are applied or released. The maximum service frequently is ten minutes, with six cars.

The mail contract covers both lineside collection and bulk loading. The box locations are shown on the route maps, and are listed by the Post Office as follows:

Location	Type	Monogram
Onchan Harbour	Wall, type B	VR
Groudle	Wall, type C	VR
Half-Way House	Wall, type C	VR
Baldrine	Wall, type B	G VI R
Laxey Station	Pillar, type B	G VI R
Glen Mona	Wall, type C	E VII R
Ballajora	Wall, type C	VR
Bellevue	Wall, type C	E VII R

For the summer of 1965, the collections were by the conductors of the 7.15 am and 2.55 pm cars from Ramsey, for the following winter those of the 7.20 am and 11.55 am. The Snaefell summit box is a private one, and is cleared before the last car; the mail is transferred in a locked bag at Laxey for transmission to Douglas.

At the same dates, bagged mail travelled in summer by the 12.00 noon, 1.45 pm and 7.15 pm from Ramsey to Douglas, the 7.00 am and the 5.30 pm from Douglas to Ramsey, the 7.00 am Douglas—Laxey, and the 6.15 pm Laxey—Douglas. In winter, the runs were 7.25 am Monday to Friday and 4.25 pm Saturday Ramsey—Douglas, 6.35 pm Laxey—Douglas, 7.00 am and 5.45 pm Douglas—Ramsey and 7.00 am Douglas—Laxey. The mail travels in locked four-wheel vans and is transhipped at Derby Castle to or from Post Office motor vans.

Ten supervisory and engineering staff were added in 1958 to the Derby Castle shed team, including three apprentices, giving the line a much changed air from its crisis days. The company's rather venerable selection of motormen (one ex-D H M D) have been joined by several younger men, aided as usual in summer by student conductors, while older and more senior staff still attend to station matters. Conductors' duties include gravity-and-push shunting of trailers at Douglas, Laxey and Ramsey, aided by slight gradients. Outside work on track and overhead is the responsibility of two specialist gangs, who, in the lack of a special works car, have the use of Nos 1, 2 and 9, which run in this capacity (minus seats) each winter; in 1959-60 Nos 5 and 7 were also used, and an ECC-class car is commonly on overhead line duty, with ladders on the footboards.

At Derby Castle, all classes of repair are undertaken, and many parts are made on the spot. Periodic inspection by long-experienced staff allows faults to be rectified in good time, and averages include wheel profiling at 60,000 miles and new armature bearings (on 1903 motors) at like intervals. Brake-shoes last for about two months in winter, trolley wheels one month. Axles are tested ultrasonically, using equipment installed by the company. Car painting, to the traditional high standard, takes place in the rearmost portion of depot No 2, where internal doors and a heating boiler and radiators are provided. The permanent winter staff now numbers ten, and the more settled staffing makes possible the retention of men with special skills who might otherwise, if only employed seasonally, tend

to drift away. Political crises, however, do still tend to cause
occasional resignations.

Imagine now that you are aboard a Manx Electric car at Derby
Castle, with a ticket for Ramsey. The car starts away easily at the
imperceptible foot of Saunderson's embankment, going into parallel
at the second crossover and climbing vigorously past the depot, now
on 1 in 23.6. Looking back, the builders are hard at work on
Derby Castle's site, where the writer well remembers the sound of

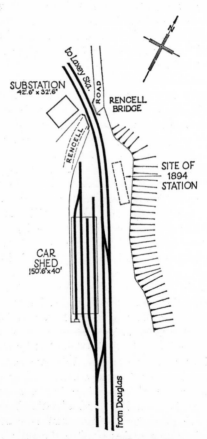

Present layout at Laxey depot

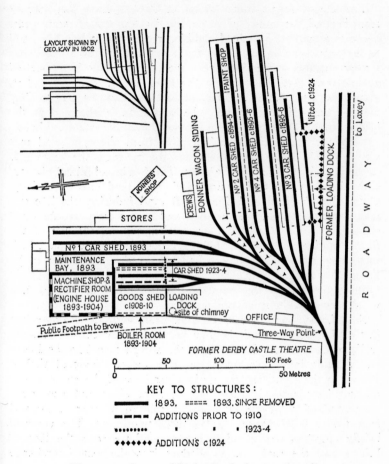

The present layout of Derby Castle depot and works

passing trams during variety performances. There is now no regular uphill stop at Port Jack, and the line swings in a broad sweep round the Douglas Bay hotel, giving a glimpse back across Douglas Bay, the track still at 1 in 23.6, as the long straight vista of King Edward Road opens up ahead. With the rather wearied buildings of White City on the right, Onchan Head station is approached, and the gradient temporarily eases.

The site of 1894's trailer siding at Onchan Lane can here be seen; beyond, the bungalow residential development of recent years becomes apparent. Sustained climbing recurs before Far End, and as the open headland with the gaunt remains of Howstrake Park's former entrance comes into view, the overhead line is silhouetted against open sky. On reaching the level summit track at 258 ft, a splendid view of the rocky coast north of Groudle Bay to Clay Head opens out. At Groudle, the substation is glimpsed at the bridge curve, to the rear of the former Howstrake estate toll-house.

After the viaduct, virtually invisible from above, a good rear view of Banks Howe is obtained, and the car starts the long climb to the Half-Way House traffic lights. This is a broad inland plateau, with ahead Lonan Old Church and the inland hills of Mullagh Ouyr, Claugh Ouyr and Snaefell. Beyond Baldrine, the line forsakes its hitherto roadside location and curves on a tree-shrouded embankment into Garwick Glen station, passing the site of the former station and siding. At Ballagawne, the line runs on a high shelf above the road, leading to Ballabeg crossing, again with traffic lights. An ancient graveyard, Kist Vaens, was cut through in forming the line at this point, and was marked in 1894 with a wooden cross, white stones and a notice.

Now Laxey harbour and Head appear, with the Ramsey line just distinguishable, and the line begins its long cliff-top descent to Fairy Cottage. At South Cape, the abrupt turn into the Laxey valley leads into a secluded run through tall ivy-clad timber. Below, to the right, are the various survivals of the steam power and turbine plants. On these long descents, 28-30 mph running is commonplace, with the close-spaced rhythm of rear motor and lead trailer bogies as a staccato accompaniment. The car-shed briefly amplifies our sound to a roar, and we cross the Rencell bridge and the main Laxey viaduct into the SMR interchange station.

Leaving Laxey, the retaining wall and adjacent site of the 1897 Snaefell station are briefly glimpsed before the car crosses the former washing floors, curves to the right, and soon begins to climb the shelf leading to Minorca and over Laxey Head. Minorca's high road bridge and stream follow the ivy-clad ruin of the test house, and with increasingly wild vegetation on either hand, the harbour and Old Laxey are now seen spread out below, with Clay Head beyond. Curving north-west, and still climbing, the steep slope to the cliff-edge frames a splendid view out to sea, the view

(above) *Directors' Special at Douglas Head terminus, Douglas Southern Electric Tramways, 16 July 1896; (below) the Douglas entrance to the Marine Drive, with entrance gate and lodge, about 1908. Note the half-bridge just beyond the car, and the lightweight trailer No 16*

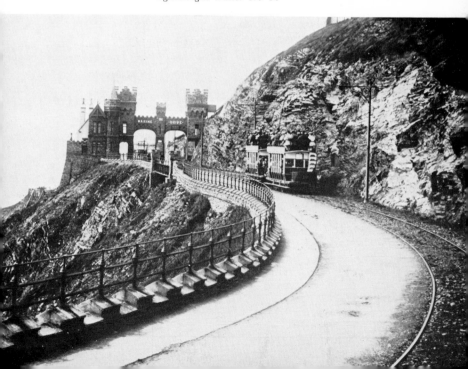

(above) *Trailer No 13 and motor car 8 at Little Ness, 30 May 1939; (below) Mr W. E. Vick and the author (at right) discuss the imminent removal of No 1 from Little Ness, 23 June 1951*

often including the Cumbrian coast and hills. Approaching Skinscoe, the line turns a little inland and parallels Strooan ny Grogee (Bobby's River) until this is crossed beyond Ballamoar. The fields on either hand, although more intensely farmed, are still full of coarse vegetation and reeds.

At Ballaragh, the high overall level of approach to Bulgham's cliff-edge viewpoint disguises its true nature. Only as the car runs on to the shelf does the line's real situation become apparent. Suddenly the most splendid tramway spectacle in these islands comes into view, with the line approaching the 600-ft contour—higher than Blackpool tower—and the visitor interested in civil engineering will be looking out for the site of 1967's slip, now neatly repaired.

Beyond the Bulgham summit, the scene changes abruptly. The tramway now runs into the first of a succession of heavily timbered valleys nestling below North Barrule. A multitude of stopping places serves the farming community, and the gradients between Dhoon Glen and Dreemskerry are so varied that reference to the gradient profile is essential. When opened, the Ramsey extension had gradient posts throughout, and some survive here and there. The wider expanse of Glen Mona, leading away inland, is best seen by glancing back when entering the Corony stream's Ballaglass ravine, immediately after Ballagorry cutting. The heavily wooded country masks the sharply curved track at Cornaa station, where the line commences the wide southward detour which separates it from the road as far as Lewaigue. To seaward, on most days, the Calder Hall power station is clearly visible.

After Ballafayle's two farms, the scenery is more open, with Port Mooar visible to the north east and, beyond, the green massif of Maughold Head and its white lighthouse. Inland, the little domed hills about Ballajora and Dreemskerry afford equal pleasure. Beyond Dreemskerry, the long straight run to Lewaigue affords views across the sheltered inland valley in which nestles the Crowville farm. Now the eye is drawn ahead by the returning seascape, with all Ramsey Bay, and the Point of Ayre beyond, coming into view.

From Bellevue to Ballure, the cliff-edge location almost rivals that approaching Laxey, with the added interest of Ramsey pier and its miniature tram, and often yachts in the bay. Plunging among ancient trees, Ballure viaduct is crossed, with a brief glimpse of the stream in the green depths. Until the grooved rails and unique scroll-ornamented bracket arms of Walpole Drive are

Q

reached, the line winds its way across open fields, but as suddenly becomes a roadside tramway once more, until at Queen's Drive it begins its final back-garden approach to the Plaza terminal.

No parallel scenic ride now exists in Britain, and few anywhere in the world—yet it is still the object of periodic political attack. When contemplating that glorious stretch of country north from Laxey, one surely cannot believe that a legislature that sinks well over £200,000 in a project like the Marine Drive will lightly cast aside such a superb, underexploited asset.

M E R Board—*Government grants representing subsidy,* 1959-67 (from annual reports)

Year ending 31 March	Deficiency grant (£)	Rail and sleeper purchase grants (£)	Weed clearance schemes (£) (a)	Other items (£)	Annual totals including winter work schemes (£)
1958(b)	40,000(c)	—	3,820	9,000(d)	52,820
1959	25,000	—	5,225	—	30,225
1960	25,000	9,000	6,000	—	40,000
1961	25,000	—	6,978	—	31,978
1962	25,000	—	6,000	—	31,000
1963(e)	25,000	—	6,800	—	31,800
1964	32,683	—	7,000	—	39,683(e)
1965	35,238	(f)	6,322	11,492(g)	53,052(e)
1966(k)	37,784(h)	13,220	(j)	—	51,004
1967(k)	42,677(h)	16,500	(j)	—	59,177

Notes

(a) Grants for winter work schemes were not always spent in the year of allocation. See also Note (e)

(b) Figures shown for 1958 cover the period from October 1956 to March 1958

(c) Includes payment to former company under 1956 indemnity and for track renewal

(d) Board expenses

(e) From 1963 the government accounting system was changed. Any surplus earned on revenue account was now repaid to the government instead of being carried forward. In 1964 £6,000 was paid back, in 1965 almost £2,000. Deducting these repayments, the true subsidy for 1964 was £33,683 and for 1965 £59,000. The process is understood to continue, but figures are not available for later years (see Note [k])

(f) £7,950 was voted for 1965 but was not spent until 1966, owing to delay in delivery of sleepers. This amount is included in the £13,220 for 1966

(g) For new Laxey and Ramsey stations

(h) Includes major track renewal on Snaefell line and cost of inserting new sleepers on Ramsey line. The latter purchase accounts for £5,500 of the £16,500 purchase grant for 1967 and is the only major expense envisaged for the Ramsey line for some years

(j) Not claimed

(k) After 1966, the board's accounts and the report of the public auditors (W. H. Walker & Co) no longer appear in the annual report. Accounts were thereafter in the hands of the government treasurer, to whom the board submit monthly analyses. The figures given here for 1966 and 1967 are taken from the board's published estimates.

In all these figures, due account should be taken of the 65 per cent rise in labour costs over the decade 1956-66.

CHAPTER ELEVEN

Manx Electric Rolling Stock

In 1893 electric traction was in its infancy and no clear tradition had been established in the design of its cars. Two-axle electric cars still tended to follow horse-car practice, but the Manx line required long bogie vehicles, and the nearest equivalents at that date were the large trailer cars used on steam tramways. Contemporary steam tramway trailers were of both top-covered and single-deck types and of considerable length, using a channel-steel underframe with oak cross-members, plate-frame bogies placed at the extreme ends, and (in consequence of this) a high-level platform with corner access, usually closed off by a gate.

For the new line from Douglas to Groudle, cars were again ordered from G. F. Milnes of Birkenhead. The first two batches of electric cars (three in 1893, six in 1894) were virtually elongated Milnes single-deck steam tramway trailer cars, with deepened plate-frame bogies of otherwise typical design into which the two electric motors could conveniently be fitted, one in each bogie. The internal body styling was the same as that of horse cars 27, 28 and 29 of the Bay line, and the oddly-shaped five-arc roof sticks provided the otherwise traditional turtleback construction with good water-shedding properties. Dr John Hopkinson's patent bow collectors were mounted rigidly on the roof close to each bulkhead.

With these electric cars came some open trailers which were in effect lengthened open horse cars on light plate-frame bogies. The corner entrances of the motor cars allowed the conductor to pass to and from the trailer footboard, and this layout was retained in subsequent deliveries. The first trailers were open 'toastrack' vehicles, but they were soon fitted with roofs—perhaps reflecting the fear of broken overhead lines—and all subsequent open trailers had roofs as delivered. By 1895 the company, in collaboration with G. F. Milnes, had evolved its own design of saloon motor tram, with a wider underframe and straight sides to permit cross-seats for better viewing. The popularity of the open trailers made it advisable to add some cross-bench motor cars to the fleet, and several batches were brought from 1898 to 1906.

By 1900, the rapid adoption of electric tramways elsewhere had brought on to the British market more sophisticated types of electric car truck; these were featured in the new cars of 1903-6 and also replaced the older plate-frame type under some earlier cars. Similarly, new motors and control equipments replaced the original (largely experimental) types. The original car bodies, however, continued in use, and the fleet has survived the ensuing half century with surprisingly little change, apart from the rebuilding of six trailers. Seven trailers and four motor cars were destroyed in the Laxey depot fire of 5 April 1930, and four new trailers of traditional open design were ordered to replace them. Modifications have been carried out in recent years to the control equipments and to the springing of some of the trucks, and the opportunity was taken to buy modern air-brake equipment from Sheffield and Glasgow when those tramways closed in 1960 and 1962.

Little provision was made for goods at first, but after 1903 goods traffic became much more important, requiring new vehicles and the adaptation of some obsolescent passenger vehicles. With the growth of motor traffic this business declined again, and the surviving goods vehicles are now used for mail and between-stations parcels traffic, some of it quite bulky. The goods stock has always been numbered separately from the passenger cars, which are here dealt with first. For details of the Snaefell cars, the reader is referred to Chapter 6, though for completeness these vehicles are included in the tables.

The cars are listed in the order of their present-day (or final) numbers, which are not in all cases those they bore when delivered.

Motor Cars
Nos 1 to 3 G. F. Milnes & Co Ltd 1893

These were the original electric cars supplied for the line from Douglas to Groudle, and were built as unvestibuled single-deck saloons with longitudinal seats for thirty-eight (later rerated thirty-four). They were 34 ft 9 in long and 6 ft 6 in wide, and ran on two Milnes plate-frame bogies set at 23 ft 8 in between centres. Each bogie had one Mather & Platt 25-hp 250-volt series motor, giving a total tractive effort of 3,000 lb. The motors were nose and centre-of-gravity suspended, and drove the outer axle only, via unshrouded double helical gears, a very unusual type for so early a date. A Hughes patent coupler was fitted at each end of the car, and these are still the M E R's standard. Internally the cars were attractively detailed; each window head had a mirror panel above it, and the bulkhead panelling resembled that of the 1893 bay tramway saloon horse cars, save for the external lamp-box. The traditional eye-window flap of the bulkhead carried a Milnes builder's plate of the early type.

Service braking was by hand, the brakestaff being placed outside the dash and applied by a wheel. For emergency use the cars had a Milnes patent auxiliary 'scotch' brake, applied through a second brakestaff to the left of the platform door, close to the bulkhead; this applied a triangular scotch to the inner pair of the leading bogie's wheels, against the possibility of a runback. In the opposite corner stood the Mather & Platt controller, whose handle's swing required the cutting of an aperture in the side weatherboard, now partly obscured.

The control equipment was frankly experimental. It appears that the cars had a form of mechanical remote control; twin resistance frames hung from the underframe at the car's centre, and across them passed inclined rods carrying bevel gears, so that the resistance connections were made beneath the car by a rod linkage from the platforms. The platform controllers would thus make only the on-off and reversing connections, and had simple copper segmented wooden drums. A brass plate on the underframe above the resistance grids proclaimed 'Mather & Platt Limited, Engineers, Manchester'. No further cars had this primitive type of control.

In 1903, these and other early cars were retrucked and re-equipped by the new M E R company, using Brush type 'D' equal-wheel bogies of 5 ft 0 in wheelbase; No 1 was completed on 4 July 1903, No 2 on 20 July and No 3 on 2 August. Each new bogie had two 25-hp motors made by the Société l'Électricité et l'Hydraulique of Charleroi, Belgium, supplied by their agents, Witting, Eborall & Co. New American-built controllers of General Electric's type 'K 11' were fitted, with matching resistors, and the cars were given air brakes made by the Christensen Engineering Co of Milwaukee, and supplied by R. W. Blackwell & Co. Each equipment consisted of a type 'A 5' motor-driven compressor set operating at 200 rpm, with three-way valves, gauges, and a single reservoir; the working pressure was 90 lb/in².

The original axlebox springing of the Brush trucks comprised small semi-elliptical springs whose ends supported round suspension links going direct into the solid bosses on the frame. By 1906 these links had been fitted with coil springs, much softening the ride, and earlier (in 1904) the design of motor suspension had also been altered. The maker's plates showed the works numbers, the batch being Nos 974 to 999.

No 3 was destroyed in the Laxey fire of 5 April 1930, and was not replaced, but Nos 1 and 2 still exist and are possibly the oldest electric cars at work anywhere in the world. They return to passenger service for the peak period of each summer, and spend the rest of the year on maintenance duties. No 1 now has removable windscreens for use in winter, first fitted in 1963-4. The Brush bogies (Nos 979 and 980) under No 2 were fitted with new axlebox coil springing in 1962, those under No 1 (Nos 984 and 991) remain as modified in 1906. By 1964, both cars had received ex-Sheffield Maley & Taunton compressor sets. In October 1947 the K 11 controllers of both cars were rewired to the K 12 control system, giving reduced sensitivity to maximum loading and less critical motor balance requirements; with the K 11 type, even wheel diameter relationships were important.

Nos 4 to 9 G. F. Milnes & Co Ltd 1894

With the coming of all-the-year service in 1894, six more cars (Nos 4-9) were bought, with vestibuled ends more suited to winter service. Vestibuled variants of Nos 1-3, they had offset saloon doors that required a shortening of the adjacent longitudinal seat, reducing the capacity by two to thirty-six (later rerated to thirty-two). An iron gate again hung from the cab-front corner pillar, and half-doors were now provided on each side of the entrance. Internal detail was as before, but the finish of the bulkheads was especially fine, with panelling in oak and ash. As built, these cars had a double guard rail outside their full-drop windows, and similar rails were fitted to Nos 1-3. In recent years the windows have been altered and only lower partly, thus obviating the need for guard rails.

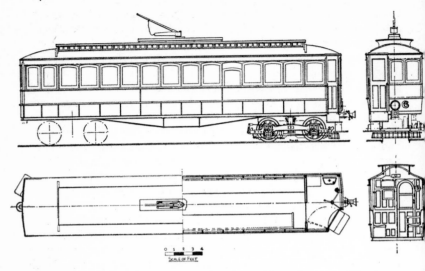

M E R 5-9 class car as now running, but without bogie modifications

The bogies were like those of 1893, but the resistance grids were now hung transversely below the underframe, without the visible mechanical actuation of the 1893 cars. Again, no details survive of the controllers, though they were still admitted to be 'experimental'. The two motors were Mather & Platt 25 hp as on Nos 1-3. Dimensions were 34 ft 8 in long, 6 ft 3 in wide, and 23 ft 8 in between bogie centres. The long, narrow interior gave rise to the name 'tunnel cars'.

In 1899 car No 4 exchanged trucks and equipments with open car No 16 receiving a later type of Milnes plate-frame bogie with four 20-hp motors by the Electric Construction Company of Wolverhampton. The other cars received Brush type 'D' bogies in July and August 1903, and were re-equipped in similar fashion to Nos 1-3, with four 25-hp Belgian motors, K 11 controllers, and Christensen air brakes. Nos 4 and 8 were lost in the Laxey depot fire of 5 April 1930, and were not replaced. In 1932, the longitudinal seats of No 5 were replaced by new cast framed reversible upholstered seats for thirty-two by W. S. Laycock of Sheffield, forming eight rows of two-and-one seats and eight bulkhead seats. The moquette used in No 5's last reupholstering is particularly pleasing. A centre partition was added at the same time.

Nos 5, 6, 7 and 9 still exist; 5 and 6 have a centre partition, 7 and 9 are structurally unaltered. All four received ex-Sheffield Maley & Taunton compressors by 1964. No 5 received K 12 controllers from No 14 in 1963, Nos 6 and 7 were changed to K 12 in January 1946, but No 9 still has K 11. Nos 5-7 have trailer air-cocks. Brush bogies 977 and 978 under No 6 have been given modified axlebox coil springs, bogies 974 and 976 under No 7 have shock absorbers, and bogies 982 and 997 under No 5 have both these modifications, whilst bogies 987 and 993 under No 9 are un-altered. No 9 has served at various dates as the snowplough car.

Nos 10-13 G. F. Milnes & Co Ltd 1895

Nos 10-13 were essentially similar cars to those for the Snaefell Mountain Tramway described in Chapter 6. Both types were basically derived from Nos 4-9, but a major step forward was that instead of facing inward on longitudinal seats, passengers could now view the scenery from transverse seats, with double reversible seats for forty and a triple fixed seat at each bulkhead. A proto-type drawing by Milnes survives and shows the sides canted to give maximum width at the waist-rail, but in the event the cars had straight sides built out to a width of 6 ft 9 in; overall length was 37 ft 3 in, height 10 ft 0 in, and the cars weighed about $5\frac{1}{2}$ tons without the motors.

Nos 10-13 were less expensively finished, and cost only £260 without equipments; the interiors were of pitchpine. They had plain shallow-arched roofs, and were glazed only in the vestibules, the six side windows having only striped linen roller blinds. The metalwork was of 'Best Staffordshire Bright' iron, and again included steam-tramway type platform gates. The bogies were of the standard Milnes plate-frame type, with two 25-hp Mather & Platt motors as before; brake equipment was as on the earlier cars, but they had a newer type of Mather & Platt controller, with a pedestal-type cast-iron case. The electrical equipments and the improved spring bow collectors of the 1894 type were installed by the I O M T & E P at Derby Castle. On these cars and those of 1894, straight spur gears were probably used from the start.

Nos 10-13 remained unaltered until 1902, but were then effect-ively withdrawn from passenger service; two were stored (perhaps as potential extra vehicles for the Snaefell line?) and two were used to augment the goods fleet. No 12 reappeared in March 1903 as a cattle car, and another became a 'goods motor' in 1904, though a tentative drawing was prepared in 1904 showing one in a hybrid mixed traffic form, with sixteen removable seats in a centre compartment. The two stored cars languished in Laxey depot until 1918, officially withdrawn, and then became frieght trailers.

Nos 14 to 18 G. F. Milnes & Co Ltd 1898

The initial requirement for the Ramsey extension was apparently assessed at nine motor cars and some additional trailers. The attraction of open cars was now evident, and an order was placed with G. F. Milnes for nine American-style cross-bench cars with glazed bulkheads and a clerestory roof. Each car was 35 ft 5 in long, and 6 ft 3 in wide over the grab-rails, with projecting footboards. Seating was for fifty-six on fourteen cross-benches, including a fixed bench on each platform. A note on a later Milnes specification reveals that the numbers allocated to these cars were 14 to 22, but initially only Nos 14 to 18 were to be placed in service as motor cars.

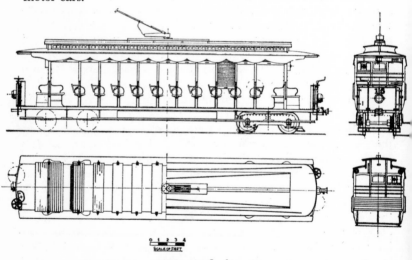

SCALE OF FEET

MER 14-18 class car

It was decided to use four-motor equipments of increased output, and nine sets of four totally-enclosed 20-hp motors (Nos 4389 to 4424) were obtained from the Electric Construction Company of Wolverhampton, together with General Electric K 11 controllers. The Milnes plate-frame bogies were of a more fully developed type to take two motors each, having an odd centre-of-gravity motor suspension and open spur gears. The Milnes auxiliary brake and the wheel brakes were both operated from hand-wheels, and involved a special drilling in the plate frame of the bogie; they are known as 'ECC bogies' from the type of motor. When intensively used on the Groudle shuttle, an oiler tended the gears at each return to Derby Castle!

In 1899, No 16 exchanged trucks and equipments with 1894 saloon car No 4, probably because a higher-powered enclosed car was needed on the Ramsey service. After 1903, Nos 14-18 were fitted with side roller shutters for use in bad weather. When the 1893-4 trucks and equipments on other cars were replaced by the new company, No 16 received Brush type 'D' bogies (now Nos 990 and 992), running on these from 11 July 1903. The footboards of all cars in this class were lengthened about 1906-8. No 15 received K 12 controllers from No 25 in 1936, and Nos 16, 17 and 18 were converted to K 12 from 1939; No 14 still has K 11. No 17 has a non-standard scotch brake mounting with a sub-frame, as on the Brill-type trucks. All five cars still exist.

Nos 19 to 22 G. F. Milnes & Co Ltd 1899

The last four sets of 1898 ECC equipments had been held back for use under these new and luxuriously finished cars, which thus received ECC 20-hp motors (four per car) and K 11 controllers. The bogies and brake equipment were as for Nos 14-22 (i) but with an elegant brass handle to the brakestaff instead of a wheel. Earlier cars were so modified later.

Nos 19 to 22, known as the 'winter saloons', were delivered in the summer of 1899 as fully glazed vestibuled eight-window saloons, having transverse slatted seats for forty-eight in pitchpine and sequoia. They are 37 ft 6 in long and 7 ft 4 in wide, and seat forty on double seats, with a triple and single seat at each end bulkhead. The centre partitions now fitted may not be original; the style is in keeping, but the construction is different. Body weight is about 6½ tons. They were given oak and ash lining timbers and a generally de-luxe finish throughout, though the ceilings were unlined.

The new company found after 1903 that the winter service cars needed better running gear, and in September 1904 No 21 received Brill type '27' trucks from new open car No 30. Nos 19 and 22 followed suit in October, taking the trucks of Nos 29 and 31, and

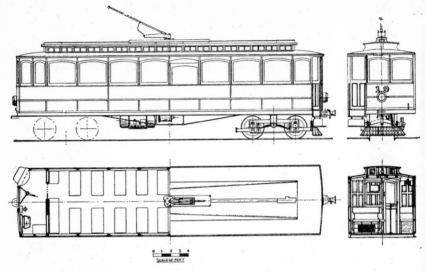

MER 19-22 class winter saloon, as now running

No 20 exchanged trucks with No 28 in November. These were a narrow-gauge variant of the Brill No 27 truck, in which the bolster embraces the side frames. They had the same four 25-hp Belgian motors as the contemporarily re-equipped older saloons, and as a result of this changeover 19-22 received Christensen air brakes, again taken from Nos 28-31. Four Westinghouse compressors were obtained and fitted to these cars in 1947-51, and four Maley & Taunton compressors bought in 1962 from Glasgow are held as spares.

At a later date, probably about 1932, 19 to 22 were given upholstered seating, with moquette covering. Three cars received new cast framed reversible seats by W. S. Laycock of Sheffield, but No 20 retains its original seat frames. All four cars have trailer air-cocks, and each car has at least ten makers' plates! Nos 19 to 22 are still hard at work throughout the year, and are the mainstay of the MER service, covering between 30,000 and 35,000 miles every year. Their cumulative mileage is about 800,000 per car.

No 23 Isle of Man Tramways & Electric Power Co Ltd 1900
No 23, built at Derby Castle sheds to the design of Mr Frank

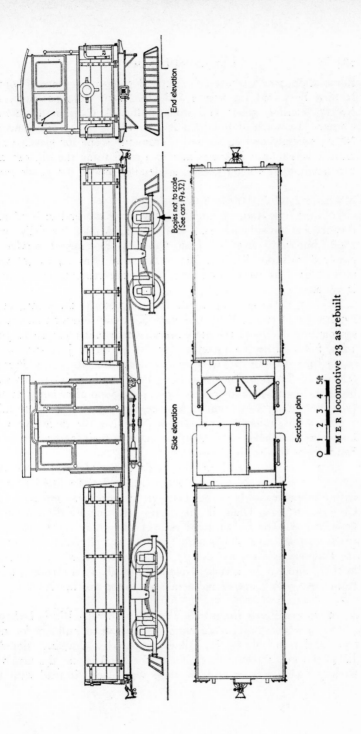

End elevation

Side elevation

Bogies not to scale
(See cars 19.32)

Sectional plan

O 1 2 3 4 5ft

M E R locomotive 23 as rebuilt

Edmondson, was a centre-cab electric locomotive for use in winter. It then borrowed the bogies and equipment from passenger car No 17, hauling goods and stone traffic. A collision at 'Bonner Corner' just north of Bulgham Bay on 24 January 1914 damaged No 23 severely and eliminated it from the scene for eleven years, until it was rebuilt in the winter of 1925-6 using the old cab and two newly-built wagon bodies, as detailed under the goods stock.

Nos 24 to 27 G. F. Milnes & Co Ltd 1898

To work the Ramsey extension, the company had ordered nine fifty-six-seat cross-bench cars from G. F. Milnes for delivery in 1898, but only five of these (Nos 14-18) entered service as powered cars on delivery. The other four (Nos 19 to 22) were instead used as motorless trailers and were renumbered as 40-43 in 1899.

In 1903, the new company decided to motorise these cars, using Brush type 'D' trucks, Belgian motors, K 11 controllers and Christensen air brakes. No 42 re-entered service as a motor car on 19 June 1903, followed by No 43 on 9 July, No 41 on 18 July and No 40 on 27 July. All four cars were given roller shutters by Clark, Burnett & Sons of 'London, Paris and New York', and similar blinds were fitted to Nos 14-18 and trailers Nos 44-48. Soon after being motorised, Nos 40-43 were renumbered respectively as 24-27, forming a class with similarly-equipped open car No 16; these five were known as 'paddlebox cars', from the shape of their footboards, modified to clear the Brush bogies.

No 24 was destroyed in the Laxey depot fire of 5 April 1930, and was not replaced. Nos 25-27 still exist, and were fitted in 1964 with ex-Sheffield Maley & Taunton compressors, replacing the Christensen sets. Their Brush bogies were modified in 1906 as described elsewhere, but have escaped the more recent changes; truck numbers are 988/989 for car No 25, 981/995 for car No 26, and 985/986 for car No 27. No 27 received K 12 controllers in 1939, and No 26 in 1948; No 25 still has K 11 controllers, taken from car No 15. Dimensional details are as for Nos 14-18.

Nos 28 to 31 Electric Railway & Tramway Carriage Works Ltd 1904

The new company made enquiries of several builders for new cars, and although G. F. Milnes prepared a drawing (dated 7 January 1904) showing cars akin to the 1898 batch, the firm was already facing closure and an order was placed instead with the

Electric Railway & Tramway Carriage Works Ltd at Preston, for
four motor cars and four trailers. The motor cars, Nos 28 to 31,
were fifty-six-seat cross-bench vehicles owing much to the earlier
Milnes designs, and were 35 ft long over dash plates, 6 ft 3 in
wide over grab-rails, and 10 ft 6 in high from rail to clerestory.
Each car had two Brill type '27' bogies set at 23 ft 6 in centres,
and each bogie was fitted with two Belgian 25-hp motors by the
Société l'Électricité et l'Hydraulique. These were the first M E R cars
to use the Brill type of truck, with its outside-hung motors. It
retained the Milnes 'scotch' brake, in suitably modified form.

Nos 28 to 31 arrived in July 1904, and later that year exchanged
trucks with winter saloons Nos 19-22, as already described, receiving
Milnes 1898 trucks and ECC 20 hp motors. That also lost their
Christensen air brakes, being now referred to by the staff as 'ratchet
cars'. Roller shutters were fitted from the start. All four cars still
exist, the only recorded modification of recent years being the
conversion of No 28's controllers to type K 12 in 1954. The other
three still nominally have K 11 control, but it is doubtful how many
K 11 circuits now remain, if any; recording of rolling-stock changes
has not always been fully maintained.

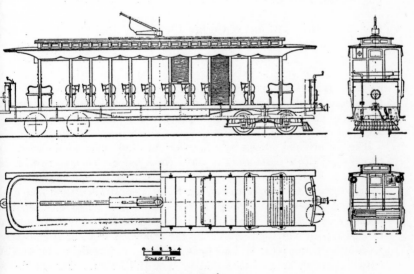

M E R 32-33 class car

Nos 32 and 33 *United Electric Car Company Ltd* 1906

Motor cars Nos 32 and 33 were built by the UEC Company at Preston who were successors to the Electric Railway & Tramway Carriage Works Ltd. They were fourteen-bench fifty-six-seat cross-bench cars built to the same style as Nos 28-31, with roller shutters. The dimensions given for Nos 28-31 apply also to Nos 32 and 33.

These two cars each received four 27½-hp GE 60 motors, thus having 110 horsepower available. From 1928 to 1939, the bogies of No 33 were used in winter under the rebuilt locomotive, No 23. As built, the two cars had K 11 controllers, but No 32 was changed to type K 12 in February 1948. Their Christensen air brakes were replaced by ex-Sheffield Maley & Taunton sets by 1964, and there are now no Christensen sets in use.

Passenger Trailers

The motor trams are numbered approximately in order of building but this does not apply to the trailers. These have always followed on from the highest-numbered motor tram, and as the fleet expanded the trailers were several times renumbered. The present numbers are those carried from 1906, when the fleet reached its maximum, with Nos 1-33 for the motor cars and Nos 34-62 for the trailers. The classes are listed here in order of delivery.

Nos 49 to 54 *G. F. Milnes & Co Ltd* 1893

Although the first three power cars each had only 50 horsepower, their designers may have thought that they could haul two loaded trailers up the 1 in 24 gradients; hence the initial order for three motor cars and six trailers? Experience doubtless showed quickly that the available power would only suffice to haul one trailer, and after the first year deliveries of power cars and trailers were in approximately equal numbers.

The six original trailers of 1893 were virtually elongated eleven-bench open horse cars on light plate-frame bogies. They were 28 ft 9 in long, 6 ft 3 in wide over grab-rails, 6 ft 9 in wide over foot-boards (this is a standard dimension for all open trailers) and seated forty-four persons. As delivered, the end benches had elongated pillars carrying iron lamphouse arches, though lamps were not carried during the 1893 season. By the following year, light canvas roofs on wooden frames had been added, supported by the two (now occupied) lamp arches and by new full height pillars at the fourth and eighth positions.

(above) *The Browside Tramway at Laxey, with a car just arriving;* (below) *sparse traffic on the Douglas Head Incline Railway, 9 August 1953.* SS *Viking lies at the breakwater in her penultimate year of service*

Isle of Man tramway tickets described in Appendix 5

An ingenious (and effective) emergency brake was adopted for the trailers. Each trailer had hand wheel brakes and the Milnes patent auxiliary scotch brake, giving two wheel-operated brake-staffs within each dash, plus a further safety feature—a chain attached to the scotch brake linkage with a ratchet action on the pull rod. This chain is secured to an anchor point on the motor car, and contains a weakened link, so that in the event of a breakaway the trailer would be automatically braked and its rigging remain undamaged in the process.

It seems that these 1893 trailers were at first numbered from 11 to 16, though only Nos 15 and 16 are known from photographs. When motor cars Nos 10-13 arrived in 1895, trailers Nos 11-13 are thought to have become Nos 23-25; in 1898, the class apparently became Nos 28-33 (views exist of Nos 32 and 33), and in 1903 or 1904 they were moved up to occupy Nos 49 to 54, leaving Nos 28-33 free for new motor cars. At about the same time, their 1894 canvas roofs were replaced by light wooden roofs, still without end bulkheads. Later rebuilding included the addition of panelled bulkheads, and detail differences exist in the class, Nos 49, 51, 53 and 54 having six posts while No 50 has only four; the extra posts were fitted in 1947-8. No 52 was less favoured, and became a rail carrier, mounted on ECC bogies for added strength. The other five are still used in mid-summer, Nos 50, 51 and 53 having lost their scotch brake and its staffs, the emergency brake chain being now connected directly to the wheel brakes.

Nos 34 to 39 G. F. Milnes & Co Ltd 1894

These trailers had fixed roofs, horizontally boarded end bulkheads with a centre drop-light, and canvas side curtains. They were thus able to offer considererably wider scope for year-round use. These cars again had eleven four-seat benches, and were 29 ft 0 in long, and 6 ft 1 in wide over the grab-rails. Metal 'safety rail' hooks were fitted to the pillars, as on the 1893 batch. The running gear and brake gear were as in 1893.

As delivered, these cars were very probably numbered from 17 to 22; photographs exist of Nos 17 and 19. In the 1898 renumbering they became (permanently) Nos 34 to 39. Four of the class, Nos 34, 35, 38 and 39, perished in the Laxey depot fire of 5 April 1930 and were not replaced. The other two, Nos 36 and 37, still exist, and are used in mid-summer; they retain their scotch brakes as originally fitted.

R

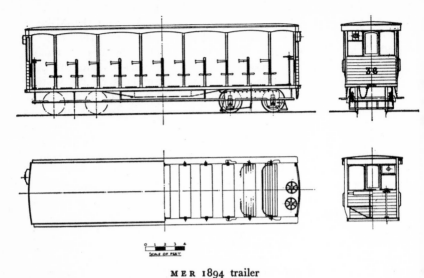

MER 1894 trailer

No 59 G. F. Milnes & Co Ltd 1895

This was a special saloon car to be used by the directors and their guests. As built, it was a four-wheel car with Milnes trunnion running gear and 28 in wheels; the $3\frac{1}{4}$ in axles turned in gunmetal bushes. It was 22 ft 2 in long and 6 ft 9 in wide (see drawing), and seated eighteen on red Utrecht velvet reversible seats with armrests. A carpet by Spence of Douglas was fitted over the linoleum floor, the bulkheads carried mirrors and the ceiling G. B. Cowen photographs of local scenes. As delivered, the car weighed 60 cwt.

The original Milnes specification for this car survives in the MER records (blueprint 3374 of 29 January 1895). The body length was to be 16 ft 6 in inside, 17 ft 2 in outside, plus two platforms of 2 ft 6 in each; width was 6 ft 3 in over side pillars and 6 ft 9 in over steps, platform height above rail 2 ft 4 in, wheelbase 6 ft. The underframe was to be of thoroughly seasoned pitchpine of suitable strength put together with knees and framing bolts and strongly trussed, the floor of Baltic pine boards tongued and grooved and properly secured to the side sills and cross rails. The end platforms were supported by strong arms hung from the headstocks and rails and had a railing, a dash plate, a step with grab handles, two brake spindles for ordinary and auxiliary brake, a hinged gate to close the platform on one side, and an ornamental iron railing to enclose it on the other. A strong wrought-iron jaw with pin was provided for coupling up to the motor car. The side, corner and door pillars, panel backers, and car frame were to be of white States ash, side panels from floor to waist of teak, roof similar to motor cars with swinging ventilator frames glazed with ornamental glass, and inside walls panelled with fancy woods. The price quoted was £150, with delivery in three months.

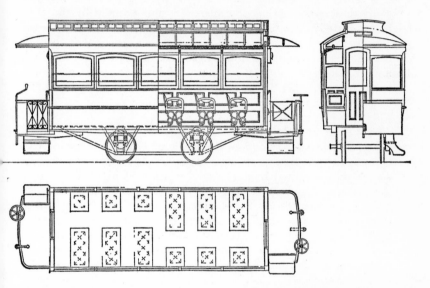

Builder's drawing of M E R saloon trailer 59. To scale this drawing, wheel-base=6 ft

A possible number allocation was 26, but no definite evidence exists and the records refer only to 'Mr Bruce's Special Trailer'. In 1903 this number was required for a motor car and the saloon trailer may have become No 32, but by 1906 it had become No 59. In August 1902 it served as the royal saloon for the journey of King Edward and Queen Alexandra. Previously, in 1900, it had been remounted on spare lightweight plate-frame bogies, though the bolt holes for the original wheel trunnions still show on the sills. No 59 still exists, with its original seats and interior fittings, and has only been used in regular service since 1933, when the platform entrances were transposed to coincide with those of the adjacent motor car.

No 60 G. F. Milnes & Co Ltd 1896

In 1896 a fourteenth trailer arrived, basically of the 1894 type but with teak-and-white horizontally divided end panelling; its drawing of 8 June 1896 survives in the M E R records. Seating was for forty-four on eleven benches, length 28 ft 9 in, width over posts 5 ft 9 in. Its original number may well have been 27, since the conjectural renumbering of trailers Nos 11-13 would by this time have created a continuous series from 1 to 25, or 26 with the 1895 saloon. Finally, at some date between 1903 and 1906, it became No 60. Damaged in the Laxey fire of 1930, it was repaired, and still has the distinctive feature of brass seat end grab-rails, as on contemporary Douglas horse and cable cars. Its bogies and brake gear are unaltered.

Nos 44 to 48 G. F. Milnes & Co Ltd 1899

For the Ramsey extension, the last four cross-bench motor cars ordered as Nos 14-22 had entered service as trailers and become 40-43; they acquired their electrical equipment in 1903. In 1899, the remaining unbalance was redressed by five new cross-bench trailers, Nos 44 to 48. These were of a more substantial design than those of 1893-6, with a clerestory roof, and were mounted on the standard type of Milnes plate-frame bogie with the usual combination of wheel brake, auxiliary scotch brake, and emergency brake linkage. Seating was again for forty-four on eleven benches, and dimensions were 28 ft 8 in long, and 6 ft 5 in wide over grab-rails. The clerestory ends were unglazed, and the centre bulkhead windows had a drop-light as on the 1894 and 1896 cars.

Nos 44-48 were never renumbered. They were fitted with side roller shutters after 1903, and then remained intact as a class until 1930, when No 44 was destroyed in the Laxey depot fire. Nos 45 to 48 still exist, and amass a considerable mileage. No 45 has lost its scotch brakes and staffs, being re-equipped in the same way as Nos 50, 51 and 53.

Nos 40 to 43 G. F. Milnes & Co Ltd 1903

The new Manx Electric Railway Company ordered four cross-bench trailers for delivery late in 1903 from the Hadley Castle

Car Works of G. F. Milnes. Almost identical with the five built by the same company's former Birkenhead works in 1899, they were 28 ft 6 in long, 6 ft 5 in over grab-rails, and seated forty-four on eleven cross-benches. These cars took the Nos 40-43 which had just been vacated by the 1899 cars, lately motorised and re-numbered 24-27. They were mounted on the heavier 'motor' type of Milnes plate-frame bogie, presumably from the four 1898 cars which were then being motorised.

Nos 40-43 (11) were among the first M E R cars to be fitted as new with the familiar roller shutters, which work on the principle of a roll-top desk. A letter of 17 December 1903 from Edmondson of the M E R to H. D. Eshelby, receiver and manager of Milnes, reveals that the M E R had undertaken to fit these shutters to the cars on Milnes' behalf. One had been done, but the acute 'S' bend at the bottom of the pillars, peculiar to these cars, had caused great difficulty, whereas the company's staff had successfully fitted many such shutters to earlier cars. Nos 40 and 41 were destroyed by fire at Laxey depot on 5 April 1930, but Nos 42 and 43 still exist, except that No 42 has lost its scotch brake and staffs, and has the emergency linkage connected to the wheel brakes.

Nos 55 and 56 *Electric Railway & Tramway Carriage Works Ltd* 1904

Two more open trailers were obtained in 1904, under the same order as motor cars Nos 28-31; Milnes was on the point of closure, and the order went to the E R & T C W at Preston. Although the new forty-four-seat trailers (Nos 55 and 56) owed much to earlier Milnes cars, they showed several refinements, such as glazed clerestory ends and wood panelled sills. They are 29 ft 4 in long, 6 ft 5 in wide over grab-rails, and 10 ft 6 in high over clerestory. Roller shutters were fitted as built. Designed to match Nos 28-31, they were mounted on the same Brill type '27' trucks, and shared their high floor level. Both cars still exist; the scotch brakes have been removed in recent years, and one brake-staff at each end is thus disconnected, pending removal, the emergency brake being connected to the wheel brakes.

Nos 57 and 58 *Electric Railway & Tramway Carriage Works Ltd* 1904

A letter of 28 January 1904 from Edmondson reveals that two saloon cars had been in use as winter trailers, with their air brakes removed. To avoid this, an order was placed with the Preston works for two eight-wheel saloon trailers, Nos 57 and 58. With their high clerestory and rattan seating, they were completely unlike any Milnes product. They seated thirty-two on transverse seats, and were 32 ft 9 in long and 6 ft 9 in wide. The bogies were again of the Brill '27' type, fitted with the scotch brake; this was removed in 1943 but later reinstated.

In addition to the hand wheel brake, scotch brake and emergency brake linkage, Nos 57 and 58 were fitted with air wheel brakes operated from the motor car, and thought was concurrently being given to extending this to other passenger trailer cars. This was not carried out, although all the surviving closed motor cars except No 9 have air-cocks. The original rattan seating served for nearly sixty years, and was then replaced by blue plush; No 57 was reseated in 1960-61 and No 58 a year later.

Nos 61 and 62 *United Electric Car Company Ltd* 1906

In 1906 two more trailers were bought from the Preston works under the same order as motor cars Nos 32 and 33, the total outlay being £2,843 15s 4d. They were identical with Nos 55 and 56 save that they had rod-operated instead of rope bells. Dimensions, capacity (44) and trucks (Brill type '27') are as for Nos 55 and 56; the scotch brakes are now removed, but the twin brakestaffs remain, both connected to the wheel brakes. These cars normally run paired with the 1906 motor cars, No 61 with No 33 and No 62 with No 32.

With the delivery of Nos 32-33 and 61-62 the fleet attained its maximum of thirty motor cars (fifteen open, fifteen saloon) and twenty-nine trailers (twenty-six open, three saloon), plus the locomotive and two goods motor cars. This total applied from 1906 to 1920.

Nos 40, 41 and 44 (11) *English Electric Co Ltd* 1930

The fire at Laxey on 5 April 1930 destroyed seven trailers (Nos 34, 35, 38, 39, 40, 41 and 44) and four motors (Nos 3, 4, 8, and 24). Three new cross-bench trailers were at once ordered from English Electric at Preston and became Nos 40, 41 and 44. They were put on the lightweight type of 4 ft 9 in wheelbase bogie salvaged from the burned trailers of 1894. These cars have strap bells, but are otherwise broadly identical with those of 1899 and 1903 which they effectively replaced; dimensions are 28 ft 8 in long and 6 ft

5 in wide over grab-rails, and seating is for forty-four. No 41 has lost its scotch brakes and staffs and has the correspondingly modified runback provision.

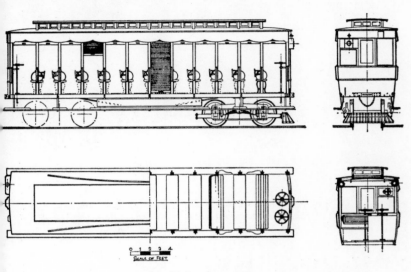

M E R 61-62 class trailer

Certain general features of the M E R passenger fleet require to be described before passing to the goods stock. The two types of Hopkinson bow collector originally fitted to cars 1-10 are described in Chapter 5; these were replaced about 1897 by fixed-head trolley poles with $4\frac{1}{4}$-in wheels. The trolley base used is the Boston Pivotal, marketed by the Anderson Co, and is noted for its compensated springing which gives virtually constant line pressure; despite the many sharp curves, dewirements are quite rare. All cars except Nos 32 and 33 are wired trolley to south end breaker.

Interior lighting on the motor cars has always been electric, but the head and tail lights were at first oil-lamps in bulkhead lampboxes; the original red leading and green rear lights were replaced by orthodox white leading and red tail lights during the 1939-45 war (the same change was made on the horse tramway, from which by legislation the earlier practice came). Some of the older cars rarely used at night still have the pre-1939 red and green bulkhead lenses. Most lamp-boxes have lost their oil-lamps, but separate

Summary of M E R passenger fleet, 1968

Motor Cars

Nos	Type	Seats	Date	Builder	Trucks	Motors	HP
1, 2	Unvestibuled saloon	34	1893	Milnes	Brush	S E H	25
5, 6, 7, 9	Vestibuled saloon	32	1894	Milnes	Brush	S E H	25
14, 15, 17, 18	Cross-bench	56	1898	Milnes	Milnes	E C C	20
16	Cross-bench	56	1898	Milnes	Brush	S E H	25
19-22	Cross-bench	48	1899	Milnes	Brill 27	S E H	25
23	Winter saloons	–	1925	M E R	–	–	–
25-27	Locomotive (body only)	56	1898	Milnes	Brush	S E H	25
28-31	Cross-bench	56	1904	E R & T C W	Milnes	E C C	20
32, 33	Cross-bench	56	1906	U E C	Brill 27	G E 60	27½

Air brakes are fitted to Nos 1, 2, 5, 6, 7, 9, 16, 19-22, 32, 33, 40-48, 55, 56, 57 and 58.
Roller shutters are fitted to Nos 14-18, 25-33, 40-48, 55, 56, 61 and 62.

Trailer Cars

Nos	Type	Seats	Date	Builder	Trucks	Motors	HP
36, 37	Cross-bench	44	1894	Milnes	Milnes (B)	–	–
40, 41, 44	Cross-bench	44	1930	E E	Milnes (A)	–	–
42, 43	Cross-bench	44	1903	Milnes	Milnes (C)	–	–
45, 48	Cross-bench	44	1899	Milnes	Milnes (B)	–	–
46, 47	Cross-bench	44	1899	Milnes	Milnes (A)	–	–
49-51, 53, 54	Cross-bench	44	1893	Milnes	Milnes (A)	–	–
55, 56	Cross-bench	44	1904	E R & T C W	Brill 27	–	–
57, 58	Saloon	32	1904	E R & T C W	Brill 27	–	–
59	Short saloon	18	1895	Milnes	Milnes (B)	–	–
60	Cross-bench	44	1896	Milnes	Milnes (A)	–	–
61, 62	Cross-bench	44	1906	U E C	Brill 27	–	–

Snaefell Cars

Nos	Type	Seats	Date	Builder	Trucks	Motors	HP
1-6	Vestibuled saloon	48	1895	Milnes	Milnes	M & P	25

Key to Manufacturers and Builders

Brill — J. G. Brill Co, Philadelphia, USA
Brush — Brush Electrical Engineering Co Ltd, Loughborough
E C C — The Electric Construction Co Ltd, Wolverhampton
E E — English Electric Co Ltd, Preston
E R & T C W — The Electric Railway and Tramway Carriage Works Ltd, Preston

G E C — General Electric Company, Schenectady, USA
M & P — Mather & Platt, Manchester
M E R — Manx Electric Railway Co Ltd
Milnes — G. F. Milnes & Co Ltd, Birkenhead (later at Hadley, Shropshire)
S E H — Société l'Electricité et l'Hydraulique, Charleroi, Belgium (later A C E C)
U E C — United Electric Car Company Ltd, Preston

Key to Milnes bogie types

Three types of plate-frame trailer bogie exist and are here designated by letters. Type A appeared with the 1893 and 1894 cars and have five rivets securing the bolster to the side plates, later variants used four rivets and are shown as type B. These two types are interchangeable; allocations are those of 1967. Type C are motorless E C C 1898 bogies, with deeper side frames than those

railway-type bracket mounted lamps are carried at night for emergency use. All motor cars have jumper sockets for trailer lighting, but not all trailers have full ceiling lights; those of 1893-4 only have bulkhead lamp-box lighting. Electric headlamps were fitted to all earlier cars by about 1903, and in pre-war years an extra spotlight was mounted on cars used in winter; this was reintroduced in 1966-7.

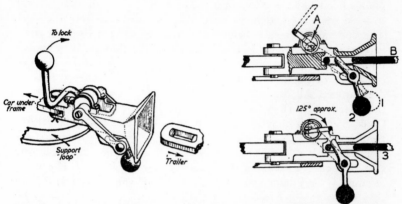

The Hughes' patent coupler, as fitted to MER motor cars. This combined buffer/coupling was devised for use on steam tramways by Albert Hughes, a partner in G. F. Milnes & Co. The trailer coupling bar B is locked in position by the action of a swinging catch and by rotating the control lever. When uncoupling, the control lever is raised to position A and the catch weight then moved manually from position 2 to position 1

In summer, cars run with their brush access covers removed so that atmospheric moisture taken up by the windings during the winter can be freely driven off, and before any car is used a lengthy drying-out on a booster is necessary. Troubles with armature failures can be expected to diminish as the benefits of new non-hygroscopic insulation materials make themselves felt; an MER car is, in fact a vehicle of literally indefinite life.

Car wheels are generally reprofiled at 60,000 miles. Motor cars have 32-in spoked steel wheels with separate tyres, and are sent in batches to a Sheffield firm for retyring when due. Trailers until recently had chilled iron wheels, but these are now being replaced by cast steel wheels, the first cars to be completely changed being Nos 36, 48 and 56 in 1965. Axles are tested ultrasonically at intervals, as are replacement 4 ft 8½ in axles bought from British Railways and turned down for M E R use. Warning of approach is by a foot gong, and internal car signalling is by G. F. Milnes' rather archaic rod-operated bells. Bell connections on trailers are now out of use.

Until 1957, the electric line's cars had always been turned out in various combinations of red, cream and teak. The first closed cars had varnished teak upper side panels, with light cream rocker panels lined out in yellow and red, but Nos 10-13 of 1895 appear to have been finished in teak from sill to waist rail from the start. The company's crest, a beautifully coloured 'Three Legs of Man', was transferred on to each side panel of the saloons. The trailers had the brown posts of the bay tramway cars, with the boarded bulkheads of the 1894 series probably in dark red, relieved only by the number. All dashes of the 1893 trailer cars were in the traditional red. The 1893 motor cars bore the title 'Douglas & Laxey Coast Electric Tramway', those of 1894 'Douglas and Laxey Electric Tramway'.

The winter saloons of 1899 bore on the rocker panel the new title 'Douglas, Laxey and Ramsey Electric Tramway'. The word 'Tramway' was later replaced by 'Railway', and this transitional title seems to have bridged the liquidation; it had appeared by 1904 on Nos 4, 9 and 19-22. The new company's paint style was much like that of I O M T & E P save for the rocker panel being painted red and lettered with the company title in full ('The Manx Electric Railway Company Ltd') and for rather more elaborate painting of the window trim. The wooden drop-frames continued in a grained finish, as before. On the new cross-bench trailers, the lower external panel was red, below teak. In the post-1939 period the title was gradually replaced by the initials M E R.

After nationalisation, the first board adopted a 'new look' colour scheme of green and white externally, grey and white inside. By 1958, fourteen cars had been so treated; these were motor cars Nos 1, 20, 21, 22, 25, 27, 29, 32 and 33, trailers Nos 50, 61 and 62, and Snaefell Nos 2 and 4. The practice thereafter lapsed, the last green car being Snaefell No 4 (until September 1963), and the traditional red, cream and teak being fully restored. The only surviving part of the 1957 livery is in the cream ceilings of some Snaefell cars, a definite improvement on the rather dark traditional finish.

The best-riding cars are, of course, those on type '27' Brill trucks, to which no substantial modification has ever had to be made. The motor sound on both these cars and the Brush-bogied cars is relatively unobtrusive. The Brush bogie as supplied had a characteristic roll, due to the generous lateral limits inherent in its bolster design, but when resprung and given shock absorbers as on No 5 it offers a superb ride. The ECC bogies provide a much more solid ride, and with their open gearing produce a strident tramcar gear sound; the body (due to lack of a sprung bolster) constantly adapts itself to track contours, the front visibly responding to super-elevation before the rear! Since this has continued for seventy years, the process appears to be harmless.

Trailer noise varies with the type of bogie frame and wheels fitted; those using steel wheels and plate frames give a particularly ringing note, the others less so. The M E R's most characteristic 'personal' sounds are the rapid rail beats of fast-running cars on the long down grades, the swish of the trolley wheel, and the musical ring of flanges on reverse curves.

GOODS ROLLING STOCK

In 1894, the legislature imposed on the company the duty to carry goods, mails, merchandise and parcels. Two six-ton open wagons were ordered from G. F. Milnes & Co, and arrived in the island on 30 November 1894, followed soon afterwards by two six-ton closed vans with end platforms. A separate series of numbers was adopted for goods stock, the wagons becoming Nos 1 and 2, the vans 3 and 4. Another six-ton open wagon (No 5) had arrived by February 1896, again from G. F. Milnes.

The extension to Ramsey resulted in the addition of five more six-ton open wagons (Nos 6 to 10). which probably arrived during the construction period of 1897-8, and two six-ton vans with end platforms (Nos 11 and 12) for the Ramsey parcels traffic which began in 1899. All these probably came from G. F. Milnes & Co, of which Bruce was then a director. There were also the three Bonner wagons, which were apparently regarded as road vehicles and were thus not numbered in the goods stock. By 1900, there were thus four railborne vans and eight wagons, plus the engineering vehicles, which at that time comprised twelve platelayer's bogies, three tower wagons, one wire bogie and one cable bogie. The steam locomotive, later named *Injebreck*, had been sold to Douglas Corporation Water Dept, and the contractors' wagons

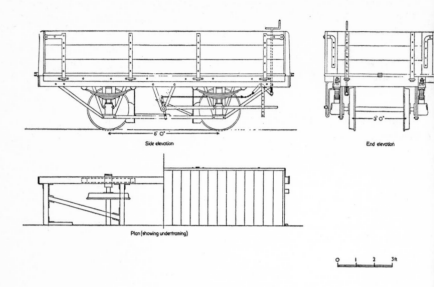

Side elevation

End elevation

Plan (showing underframing)

Drop-side M E R open wagon of about 1897

from the Ramsey extension accompanied her to West Baldwin; during the sale negotiations, the water committee were given a steam-hauled trip from Derby Castle to Laxey and back, perhaps the only steam passenger train ever to run on the line.

Four pre-1900 drawings of goods stock survive in M E R records. They comprise a G. F. Milnes side-door wagon with drop-type door, one by I O M T & E P dated 10 December 1895 of a similar wagon with lifting door, another of a wagon with removable sides, internal screw brake column and lever brake (as always, on the seaward side only), and finally a motor goods wagon similar to the 1898 ECC motor cars but with plain arch roof, two intermediate posts each side, and drop sides to the three sections thus formed. This last vehicle was never built.

In 1900, Derby Castle built an electric locomotive which was numbered 23 in the passenger stock list and has already been described. Passenger car No 12 of 1895 retained its number when rebuilt to a motor cattle car early in 1903, as did the further car of this class (No 11 or 13) which was rebuilt as a freight motor

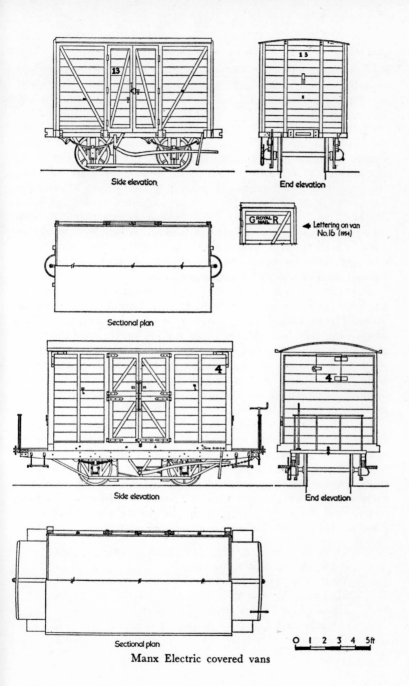

Side elevation

End elevation

◄ Lettering on van
No. 16 (1954)

G ROYAL MAIL R

Sectional plan

Side elevation

End elevation

Sectional plan

O 1 2 3 4 5ft

Manx Electric covered vans

in July 1904. In September 1904 the new company commenced an office record book which, together with the balance sheets and a list printed in a 'weekly returns' book, has formed the basis of this account.

On 16 March 1903, F. Hughes Caley of Milnes quoted for 'light parcels or luggage vans' at £55 each, with detachable bodies; open wagon bodies could be substituted when required. If supplied without wheels and axles, the price dropped to £45 10s. Two new vans, Nos 13 and 14, arrived during 1903-4, possibly from Milnes; No 13 was a 'small mail van' and No 14 was listed as 'luggage van'. Neither had end platforms. The September 1904 returns also showed two un-numbered 'freight trailers', which are thought to have been high slatted-side bogie wagons built at Derby Castle and mounted on de-motored 1893-4 bogies displaced in the 1903 re-equipment. The staff called these 'sheep trucks'.

The next additions were two 'large mail vans' in 1908, Nos 15 and 16, built by the M E R at Derby Castle, originally with end platforms. The fleet then stood at eight four-wheel wagons, eight four-wheel vans, two un-numbered bogie trailers, one motor freight van and one motor cattle van. In the year ended September 1911, the goods motor disappears from the record book and re-emerges as a third bogie trailer; in fact, it was simply de-motored. Only the original purpose-built wagons and vans (Nos 1-16) are shown with numbers in the weekly returns book.

In 1912, the motor cattle car was converted to a trailer, and four more open wagons were placed in service. Of these, Nos 17 and 18 were standard six-ton open wagons built by G. C. Milnes, Voss & Co in March 1912, whilst Nos 19 and 20 were twelve-ton stone wagons on 1893-4 ex-motor bogies, built by the M E R and known to the staff as 'dreadnoughts'. No 19 entered service in February 1912, No 20 in March. This brought the goods stock to its pre-1914 maximum of twenty-five vehicles, as follows :

Open wagons, 1, 2, 5, 6, 7, 8, 9, 10, 17, 18	10
Bogie stone wagons, 19 and 20	2
Vans, 3, 4, 11, 12, and parcels vans, 13, 14	6
Mail vans, 15 and 16	2
Un-numbered bogie trailers (two slatted-side trucks and two ex-passenger vehicles)	4
Locomotive (No 23)	1
	25

The Bonner road-rail wagons are never mentioned in the office records, but were certainly purchased by the M E R and used for at least a few years.

The crash of 24 January 1914 eliminated the locomotive from the scene for eleven years, and probably accounted for two of the three Bonner wagons as well. The next changes occur in 1918, when the other two withdrawn passenger cars of the 10-13 class (still then languishing in Laxey depot) were transferred to the freight stock as trailers. The numbers 21-26 were allotted to these and the four un-numbered bogie vehicles, probably as follows:

No 21 (?)   Freight motor rebuilt July 1904 from passenger car No 11 or 13 and de-motored since 1911.

No 22   Motor cattle car rebuilt early 1903 from passenger car No 12 and de-motored 1912.

No 23 (?)   Freight trailer rebuilt from passenger car No 13 or 11 in 1918, retaining scotch brake and two brakestaffs.

Nos 24, 25   Bogie trailers built by M E R in 1904.

No 26   Freight trailer rebuilt from passenger car No 10 in 1918, and given air brakes in January 1920.

By 1924, cattle and sheep traffic by rail had largely ceased, and sheep trucks Nos 24 and 25 were rebuilt in March and April 1924 as twelve-ton 'dreadnought' stone wagons. The locomotive was

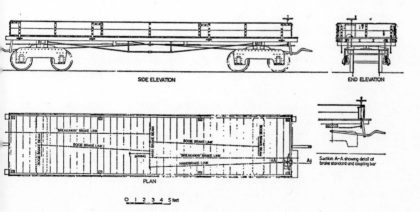

M E R Dreadnought stone wagon No 24

brought back to life late in 1925, using the cab of the original 1900 locomotive (No 23) and two new wagon bodies; when in use, it borrowed the trucks of passenger car No 33. In February 1926 freight trailer No 21 re-emerged as a fifth 'dreadnought' stone wagon, distinguished by a steel underframe, and in March 1927 the ex-motor cattle car No 22 (ex 12) was scrapped; trailer No 23 of 1918 now became No 22 and allowed the locomotive to regain its former number. In 1926, the company bought its first motor lorry.

One open wagon disappeared in 1930, reducing the goods fleet to twenty-five vehicles, but much of the fleet now stood semi-derelict at the Dhoon, where by the mid-'thirties railborne quarry traffic had finally ceased. All twenty-five vehicles survived on the books until 1941, after which regular annual reporting of stock temporarily ceased. The war years saw all serviceable goods stock in use again, particularly on airport construction; stone waste traffic from Laxey reached such a level that on 9 September 1941 the late W. E. Kerruish was able to book 291 tons in a single day. In 1944 van No 15 was wrecked in a run-back at Ballaglass, and freight trailers 22 and 26 were also written off; No 22 remained derelict for some years at Dhoon, and No 26 (ex 10) still exists as a store in Laxey depot, in quite good condition. Perhaps it may one day be restored to its 1895 state . . .

Ownership of road vehicles had risen to two in 1930, three in 1948 and four in 1949, but railborne goods traffic fell again after the war to 'one van load' level, and in 1952 ten open wagons were written off, including (nominally) all five 'dreadnoughts'. 'Dreadnought' 21, which had been retrucked in April 1942 with Brush bogies, was kept for engineering purposes, and is still in good order; it was further altered in 1958-9. Official wagon stock was now down to four, but the remains of the others stood at Dhoon quarry sidings until after 1957. No 10 still existed, derelict, at Derby Castle in 1965.

Following nationalisation, the M E R board refurbished the remaining goods stock (open wagons Nos 1, 5, 7 and 8, and vans Nos 3, 4, 11, 12, 13, 14 and 16), later adopting a pleasing olive green livery. The board's parcels traffic continued to be well supported, and the mail contract assured full van loads to and from Ramsey several times daily. However, life expiry of road vehicles caused collection and delivery of M E R-hauled goods to cease from 31 March 1966, though mail traffic continues, as does a substantial parcels traffic between stations. The surviving vehicles, although few in number, are a representative collection of all periods, and are listed below.

M E R Goods Stock, 1968

No	Description	Tare Weight			Built
1	Six-ton open wagon	2	8	33	1894
3	Six-ton van with platforms	2	10	3	1894-5
4	Six-ton van with platforms	2	10	3	1894-5
5	Six-ton open wagon	not stated			1895-6
7	Six-ton open wagon	2	7	0	1897-8
8	Six-ton open wagon	2	8	3	1897-8
11	Six-ton van with platforms removed	not stated			1898-9
12	Six-ton van with platforms	2	11	0	1898-9
13, 14	Small vans, no platforms	not stated			1904
16	Large mail van, platforms removed	not stated			1908
21	Bogie engineers wagon	4	16	0	1926
26	Large freight trailer used as store, ex-passenger car 10	not stated			1895

All wagons and vans (except Nos 21 and 26) have side lever brakes on the seaward side only, plus screw brakes. Livery was originally bodies and ironwork grey, numbers white.

There are also two rail tower wagons on the coastal tramway, and one on the Snaefell line. The other two non-passenger vehicles on the Snaefell line (coal car 7 and the 1895 open wagon) are described in Chapter 6.

MADE FOR DICK KERR & Cº Lᴰ, LONDON BY THE ELECTRIC RAILWAY & TRAMWAY CARRIAGE WORKS Lᴰ PRESTON, LANCS.

CHAPTER TWELVE

The Douglas Southern

'The situation of this Tramway is in some respects unique . . .'
—D H M D advertisement, 1935

Douglas Head, the southern boundary of Douglas Bay, marks the beginning of a dramatic section of contorted Manx slate coastline that stretches south for some miles before the gentler limestone southern part of the island is reached. In the early nineteenth century, that portion of the Head directly across the harbour from the old town was much favoured as a place of residence, but the old stone bridge at the inner end of the harbour was an obstruction to further development, and when by the 'eighties the Head became a place of resort and entertainment there were several successive schemes to bridge the harbour at or near the site of the present swing-bridge. Most were for ambitious high-level bridges, but one undated scheme by Manx engineer Daniel Cregeen, CE, was for a pedestrian tunnel with spiral stair-way access. In July 1889, engineers Cregeen and Jerram submitted plans for a harbour suspension bridge, and in November Thomas Floyd, CE, presented a similar plan. In May 1890 a practical joker sent out invitations to an inaugural celebration of the works of the 'Douglas Suspension Bridge and Eiffel Tower'; local supporters of the scheme turned up, and, not to be outdone, held their own impromptu celebration. The lower part of the tower was to bring a spiral approach road to bridge level.

The capital of the Tower concern (Douglas Head Suspension Bridge Ltd) was to be £100,000, and the promoters included Major

J. S. Goldie-Taubman, JP, Speaker of the House of Keys. Land was purchased, and the subscription list opened on 22 April 1890. In October 1890 the Earl of Lathom laid the foundation stone of the bridge tower (now to be a rectangular building with hydraulic lifts), but by December 1891 the scheme had collapsed for lack of finance. The site was later used for Hengler's Circus, a wooden structure, and is now largely occupied by the steam packet company's goods department.

At the same time, a project emerged for a coastal Marine Drive, engineered by Messrs Jerram and Livingstone, with a capital of £40,000. Its income was to be derived from pedestrian and vehicle tolls, from which the company (Douglas Head Marine Drive Ltd) would pay 5 per cent of receipts to the landowner, Major J. S. Goldie-Taubman. The subscription list opened on 8 July 1890, and by November parts of the course had been staked out. The new road reached the northern end of Wallberry in 1891, but there the scheme ground to a halt, with the undertaking in the hands of the Chancery Court. It had built an ornate entrance gate, duly dated 1891, and one and a half miles of Drive, including an elaborate timber bridge across Pigeon Stream. Both the Tower company and the Marine Drive company were creations of the Standard Contract and Debenture Corporation, a highly speculative venture.

The Marine Drive company was rescued by a group of Lancashire business men, who took over on 12 March 1892. Work was resumed, and summer 1893 saw the construction of massive timber bridges across the two enormous clefts at Wallberry and Horse Leap, and a turning place at Little Ness. The extended drive from Wallberry to the Whing consisted of shelf cut in the slate cliffs; the new engineers were Messrs Maxwell and Tuke, with one, Nowell, as contractor. The opening of this portion on 7 August 1893 saw a marquee luncheon at Little Ness, and the speeches revealed that a concession had now been granted for an electric tramway along the drive. By November 1893 the Marine Drive was complete to Keristal, but the company was again short of money, and both Maxwell and Tuke had died.

Among the advocates of the tramway were two major D H M D shareholders, George William Lowcock and George Hill, partners in Lowcock, Hill & Co, electrical engineers, of Old Trafford. The unidentified concessionaire of 1893 having evidently withdrawn, Lowcock & Hill secured a new tramway concession in their own names from the D H M D company on 6 November 1894, and sought a contractor who would build their line and accept payment largely in shares. The successful candidate was the Electric & General Contract Corporation of 35 Parliament Street, Westminster, registered on 25 November 1892 to take over the electrical contracting business of William Sebastian Graff Baker, M INST E E. Graff

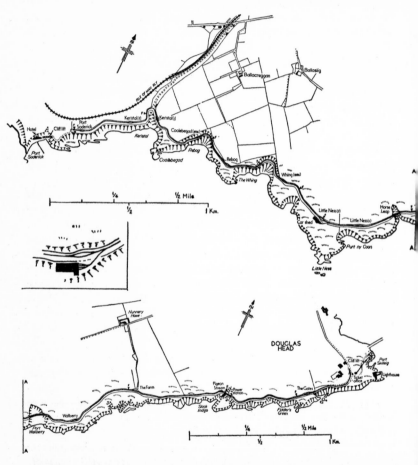

The Marine Drive and its tramway. The passing loops at The Whing and Coolebegad were removed in 1908, and those at Little Ness and Keristal relocated from (1) to (2). F denotes feeder points. The depot fan was made up in 1909 from spare material, to replace the original traverser. Inset shows the depot layout from that date

Baker, an American citizen, was agent for the Thomson-Houston International Electrical Company of Boston, Massachusetts and, in addition to operating the pioneer Roundhay Park electric tramway at Leeds, had secured a concession to electrify the tramways at Coventry. On 10 December 1894, Lowcock and Hill made a private agreement with Graff Baker's E & G C C granting the latter the benefit of the concession which they held from the D H M D, and which was defined on 2 April 1895 as being for ten years, after which the Marine Drive company could purchase the line or extend the lease for twenty-one years. No legislative powers were needed to build the line, as all the land was privately owned.

Meanwhile, the Marine Drive company had come to deal with the E & G C C direct. They were if anything more urgently concerned with improving access to the Drive as it then stood, and on 27 March 1895 obtained permission from Sir John Goldie-Taubman (now knighted) to build a 35-foot roadway down from Douglas Head (from point B to point A on the accompanying plan), and build a tramway on it, the road to remain Sir John's property. Almost as an afterthought, the agreement allowed D H M D to build tramways on the Drive itself, south of the Toll Gates, if they wished. D H M D had given the task of building the proposed access tramway to Graff Baker as early as 25 March 1895, and the latter thereafter dealt direct with Sir John. By February 1896 the agreement was enlarged to permit a link tramway from point B to the Toll Gates (this was ultimately built as an integral part of the Marine Drive tramway) and another extension from point A down to the south side of the new harbour swing bridge. This was to be a 'mechanical tramway, railway or lift' and the gradients imply a cliff-lift type of installation.

It is convenient to deal here with the fate of the access tramway and road after mid-1896. In the winter of 1896-7, the New General Traction Company (to be described later) proposed a totally different tramway extension of a most ambitious character. The Marine Drive adhesion tramway would have been extended down to the harbour, crossing the old stone bridge and continuing to the Victoria pier (see plan); this line was not built, and with its 1 in 12 gradients and reverse curves would have been a hard line to work. The tramway terminus, in fact, remained on Douglas Head, 184 ft above sea level, and an orthdox cliff lift was ultimately built by a private investor as described in Appendix 4.

On 10 April 1895 Lowcock and Hill sold their newly-defined

concession to the Electric & General Contract Corporation, but twelve days later the E & G C C sold its tramway interests and concessions for £39,000 to a new company, the General Traction Company, registered by Graff Baker on 20 March. The E & G C C

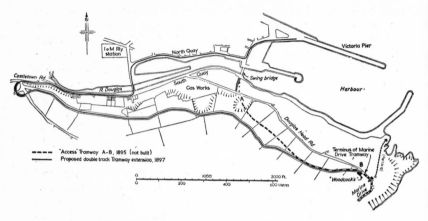

D S E T extension proposals at Douglas, 1895-7

retained only the Roundhay tramway, then about to close, and was finally wound up in 1904. The General Traction Company thus acquired the concession for the Marine Drive line, and proceeded to draw up plans and place orders with suppliers, mainly USA-based. The tramway was now intended to run from the entrance gates to the proposed 'pavilion and gardens' at Little Ness, and was to be completed and opened by 1 June 1896. Later extension to Port Soderick or to the Castletown Road was allowed for.

A separate company, Douglas Southern Electric Tramways Ltd, was incorporated on 21 October 1895 to own and operate the new tramway when built. Its capital was £50,000, divided into 30,000 7 per cent preference and 20,000 ordinary shares, and the registered office was at 17 King Street, Manchester (transferred in 1897 to Atlantic Chambers, Brazennose Street). Share allotment took place on 6 November 1895. Sir John Goldie-Taubman was chairman, and Dr Edward Hopkinson was consulting engineer. D S E T were to pay the General Traction Co £29,000 for building the line, £17,070 in cash and £11,930 in shares (7,834 preference, 4,096 ordinary), this to cover a tramway from the entrance gates to Little

Ness, a car shed and power station, cars and equipment, and three new bridges which, when erected, would become Marine Drive porperty. The General Traction Co could also contract for any extensions, at the rate of £9,500/mile. The D S E T's first managing director was G. W. Lowcock; other early directors were W. P. J. Fawcus and J. S. Goldie-Taubman. T. J. Hutchinson and W. Davenport joined the company later, the latter remaining a director until his death in 1907.

In February 1896, the tramway concession was transferred to D S E T and finalised at thirty years, with a payment to the Marine Drive company of one penny for each passenger (since each tramway ticket would also give access to the Drive) plus 5 per cent of the gross receipts. The 1d per passenger was in turn subject to the 5 per cent D H M D payment to Sir John Goldie-Taubman, and was always separately accounted for. Construction of the Marine Drive tramway had meanwhile commenced (on 30 December 1895 or 13 January 1896—sources differ), and by late February the chairman was able to report completion of roadbed and arrival of rails. By April, the depot had been built, the wooden bridges were being replaced by steel (Horse Leap had been done) and the power station was well ahead. W. Lavington Fletcher was resident engineer, assisted by G. C. Pritt, with J. T. and J. MacMahon for overhead, and Morris Owen of Heenan & Froude, the bridge contractors. Construction was supervised at first by W. S. Graff Baker.

A change of control now occurred in the contracting group. In February 1896, Graff Baker sold his General Traction Company shareholding to a New York bank, and retired from the business shortly afterwards; he died a year later. The purchasers formed an alliance with a syndicate about to build electric tramways at Norwich, and brought in two projected Philadelphia surburban tramways, later to form the Darby, Media & Chester Street Railway. To manage this international tramway empire, a new company, New General Traction Co Ltd, was registered in London on 24 March 1896 with a nominal capital of £140,000 to take over the General Traction Co's interests, contracts and concessions; a major UK shareholder was Baron d'Erlanger, but the enterprise was American-inspired, and both the managing director (Edmund A. Hopkins) and the chief engineer (I. Everson Winslow, formerly the G T Co's secretary) were American citizens. Hopkins and Winslow joined the D S E T board, and Winslow took charge of construction at both Douglas Head and Norwich; he later invented the internal spring trolley standard, which was used almost universally on open-top cars in this country.

One of the last acts of the General Traction Company before selling out to N G T was to obtain an agreement for extending the tramway to Port Soderick. The concession allowed for both this and a line inland along the Drive to the Castletown Road gates, but on 8 March 1896 Graff Baker wrote to Sir John Goldie-Taubman recommending that the line should go on to Port Soderick, the other branch being deferred. His advice was accepted, and the inland line was never built. The extension required an increase of £10,000 in the issued capital of D S E T, and the final cost was £11,145, provided wholly by New General Traction through their nominee Alfred de Turckheim. The N G T holding in D S E T was thus increased in 1897 by £5,573 in preference shares and £5,572 in ordinary shares, which gave them a controlling interest and made the D S E T virtually an N G T subsidiary.

What of the line actually built? The single track, of 4 ft 8½ in gauge, was laid on the landward side of the existing water-bound macadam carriage drive, which was widened where necessary, especially at the passing places. Leaving the loop at the Douglas terminus, the line curved round the Head, and almost at once the Drive assumed the form of a ledge cut in the cliff face; in the middle of this section was a small 'half bridge', later narrowed by removing the outermost girder (the parapet walls still betray this change). Immediately beyond stood the ornamental Drive entrance and toll-gate, prominently lettered 'Marine Drive 1891'. The line passed through the landward arch, and beyond was the second loop. About half a mile further the line reached the first major engineering feature, a three-span lattice-girder bridge 117 ft long, carried on lattice piers and at first paralleled by the wooden bridge of 1891; this was dismantled about 1909 and its timbers used as additional supports for the newer bridge. This spot was known as Pigeon Stream, though the car notices showed it as Pigeon's Stream.

Immediately beyond the bridge was the power station, on the seaward side, and here also was the third loop. The small stream, of exceptionally good water, was contained within tanks and used to supply the boilers—indeed, the power station had to be situated here, because at no other point could the necessary water be obtained. The power station was a building of brick and stone roofed with corrugated iron; a date stone on the west gable was inscribed

Douglas Southern Electric Tramways' power station at Pigeon Stream, showing the original 1891 wooden bridge in front of the 1896 tramway bridge. The lower view shows the dynamos and switchgear, looking east

'General Traction Company 1896' and surmounted by a clock. The octagonal chimney stack was of Peel bricks with a cast-iron top, and stood some 60 ft high, about 27 ft from the south-east end of the building. The engine room formed the basement, and the upper floor the boiler room, plus a workshop with its own engine and vertical boiler, a wheel lathe, and a small rest room; a hydraulic wheel press was placed parallel with the boilers. Outside lay a blacksmith's shop and coal storage sheds, coal being brought during the winter by horse and cart, an extra horse being needed up the steep slope from Douglas harbour. A refreshment room was added after 1900 at the rear of the power station.

From this point, after a short downhill stretch, the line rose considerably, reaching 267 ft above the sea. Beyond this first summit were the two greatest engineering features of the line, first Wallberry bridge and next the bridge at Horse Leap. Wallberry bridge had two spans, total length 256 ft, and was on a down gradient of 1 in 16.01, with the two spans at an angle of $10\frac{1}{2}$ degrees to each other; the steelwork weighed about 102 tons. Drawings published in the *Engineer* for October 1896 showed the track

Horse Leap bridge, Douglas Head Marine Drive

offset to landward, but in the event it was laid centrally; the designed static load was 100 lb/ft². Horse Leap bridge had one span, 120 ft in length, on a down gradient of 1 in 59.6 (drawings show 1 in 42). The two bridges were situated close together about one and a half miles from Douglas Head, and both crossed deep gullies in the cliff face. In 1909 and again in 1919-20 the bridge-work was strengthened, with considerable stiffening of the corner pillars of Wallberry's central support tower.

At Little Ness, about 1¾ miles from the Douglas terminus, a broad shelf of land lay to seaward. Here was constructed the car shed, a wood and corrugated iron building 93 ft long and 40 ft wide; by January 1897 it had been lengthened to 110 ft. It had four tracks, two with pits for three-quarters of their final length, and access was at first by a traverser; a workshop and staff annexe 15 ft square was provided at the north-east corner. Originally there was no loop at this point, the shed being half way along a single line section, with the depot branch crossing the drive. A more isolated position for a car shed can hardly be imagined, and the company's Victorian letterhead betrayed nothing of the real location of 'Tramway Depot, Marine Drive.'

The downhill section from Wallberry ended before the car shed, and then began the climb to the highest point of the line. Beyond the original seventh loop (at the Whing) it included the steepest gradient yet—142 ft at 1 in 11.36—which came just before the summit, where the line reached a height of 280 ft above the sea, 13 ft higher than at Wallberry. The ensuing descent included even steeper grades, with 130 ft at 1 in 10.43, easing to 152 ft at 1 in 12.66, but half way down, beyond the eighth loop at Rebog, there was a short uphill portion, followed by the ninth loop (at Coole-begad) and further downhill sections, partly at 1 in 16.44 and 1 in 18.66. Both Whing and Rebog included 45-ft radius curves. In this way the line wound around several bluffs, and about 2¾ miles from the Douglas Head terminus reached Keristal, the tenth loop, where for the 1896 season it ended.

The Drive now turned inland to end at gates on the Castletown road, where an imposing entrance like that at Douglas Head had been planned, but where in the event only a bungalow and a corru-gated-iron office were built. This later became the registered office of the Marine Drive company. A footpath led along the coast to Port Soderick, which was otherwise accessible only by a glen wind-ing down from Port Soderick station on the Isle of Man Railway.

Development here was by M. Forrester and family (former tenants of Laxey Glen) and a promenade was built in 1897, with a date stone inscribed 'Erected by M. & T. Forrester, 1897.'

With the line complete to Keristal, an opening ceremony was held on Thursday, 16 July 1896, though the line had not yet been inspected or passed. Three special motor cars carried an official party including Dr Edward Hopkinson and Marine Drive directors on a full inspection, following a luncheon at the Villiers hotel at which Advocate Kneen spoke of the possibility of a Spring Valley extension by an inland route back to Douglas. Refreshments at the power station and a speech by managing director G. W. Lowcock concluded the afternoon's events. Next day, 17 July, Major Cardew of the Board of Trade inspected the line for the governor, followed by Colonel Rich on 23 July, accompanied by the New General Traction Company's engineer, Mr Winslow.

Rich reported on the 24 July. He found the curvature (the worst radius was 46 feet) and the gradients (to 1 in 9.1) severe. The bridges were of adequate strength, but he sought more fencing along the Drive generally 'to prevent persons, while looking at passing objects, from falling over the cliff'. He wanted the bridge decking covered with asphalt. Various special checks and fenders were suggested for the curve at the centre of Wallberry bridge, as were red and white signal posts at either end and at the termini, to assist the drivers in darkness or fog. His suggested speed limit was 8 mph. Pending the improvements his approbation was withheld.

Cardew had already reported on the 22nd. He found the American trolley collection system and the motor and control gear satisfactory, other than in the complex manoeuvres needed to apply the electric brake (three handles had to be operated in turn, including the canopy switch) and sought a compulsory application before descending from the Whing in either direction. The proximity of the overhead to the cliff face, which he seemed to imagine as populous, was dwelt upon. He sought (and obtained) warning notices at the Toll-Gates arch and insulation of upper-deck rails near the trolley standard. The bonding he approved.

These inspections, which were carried out under the Railway Regulation Amendment Act of that year, were preceded and followed by some hilarious correspondence between Rich, Lowcock and the governor's secretary, Storey. The season was already advanced, and after further work had been done, the line was allowed to open for public service on 7 August 1896 as far as 'the crossing place north of Whing Hill'. Press advertisements appeared from 10 August, and the fare of 1s return included either harbour steam ferry or swing-bridge toll at Douglas. On 5 September the modifications were complete and engineer James Walker of the Harbour Board made his final inspection for the governor, the line being now acceptable. The season ended on 26 September, 53,536 passengers to the good. For this shortened season, D H M D accepted a reduced toll of ½d per passenger.

Meanwhile, in 1895, the Marine Drive company had issued debentures to the value of £20,000 to finance the completion of the Drive to Keristal and Port Soderick, on which the tramway would be built. This outlay proved to be beyond the company's earning power (the tramway, when completed, took the lion's share of patronage), and by January 1899 the Drive concern was in receivership, a state of affairs which lasted until 1909. The receiver and manager was Thomas J. Hutchinson, FIC, of Bury, and under his receivership a substantial surplus was accumulated.

During the winter of 1896-7, the tramway was extended by three-quarters of a mile to the headland overlooking Port Soderick, involving the embanking of the deep Keristal valley. One new and one relocated loop were involved, and reconstruction elsewhere reduced the maximum gradient; accounts differ as to details. From the terminus, a pathway led to the Port Soderick beach, some 180 ft below; a separately-owned cliff lift was completed later in 1897. The other lift at Douglas was added in 1900, and is described in Appendix 4. The tramway was opened to Port Soderick on 1 April 1897, the start of the 1897 season. The D S E T was always a seasonal operation, paralleled in Britain only by Snaefell and the Giant's Causeway line in Ulster.

The tramway staff consisted of a general manager, a car-shed foreman, and a traffic superintendent, all permanently employed, whilst engaged on a seasonal basis were an assistant car-shed foreman, three office workers (average), three inspectors, and (after about 1909) nine double car crews. On the generating side, there were permanently an engineer and assistant engineer, plus seasonal workers made up of two greasers, one foreman and a night watchman. The first manager was a Mr J. H. Lynn of Bradford, with USA experience, followed in apparently quick succession by a Mr Lynch. About 1899 there came another former G T Co secretary, F. W. Ketley, destined to stay until 1909. At the power station, the first engineer was a Mr Boulter, followed by Mr T. Ellison, then just before the turn of the century by Mr A Randle, whose term of service lasted until 1930.

The single tramway track was laid with 65-lb rails, 30 feet in length, on steel sleepers at 3 ft 6 in centres placed on concrete 'cushions'; 100lb/yard rail was used on the bridges. Rail bonding was with 'Chicago' copper bonds. Points were of Marshall's patent spring type, both these and the rails being supplied by Alexander Penney & Co of London; the points and crossovers are unique in being guarded in street tramway style whilst being designed to mate with open Vignoles track. Some now survive as car shed track at the Crich Tramway Museum. The overhead was supplied by R. W. Blackwell & Sons Ltd, the poles (of bracket arm type throughout) being imported by them from the Morris Tasker Co of Philadelphia, USA. There were two types, of respectively 6 in and 7 in diameter. Double trolley wires were provided all along the line, the poles being placed on the landward side of both the Drive and the bridges. The No 0000 braided copper overhead feeder was carried on the rear of the poles, and section gaps were spaced at about one-third of a mile. Major renewals were made to the overhead line poles in 1907 after trouble from corrosion, and the original ornamental brackets disappeared; the new galvanised top sections proved very durable and some of the poles have enjoyed a second life on the M E R. The poles at Pigeon Stream, Wallberry, Horse Leap, Little Ness, Whing, Rebog and Keristal carried wood-mounted cast-iron nameplates, identical with those used for the majority of Douglas street names, those for Wallberry and Horse Leap being at the bridge approaches.

The generating equipment in the power station at Pigeon Stream comprised two boilers, two engines and generators, and originally one condenser. In the 50 ft by 31 ft boiler room on the upper floor, steam was produced in two Babcock & Wilcox horizontal water-tube boilers of 4 ft 5 in diameter and 120lb/in² working pressure, with a heating surface of 1,426 ft². They were fired by Bennis mechanical stokers of the natural draught sprinkler type and were coupled to a Green's 96-tube economiser working at 100 lb/in². In the basement engine room, which was 50 ft by 24 ft and 22 ft high, were two Browett-Lindley 240-rpm horizontal engines with steam-jacketed cylinders of 14 in diameter and 14 in stroke. These drove through 17-in Eureka belts two Westinghouse six-pole 100-kW 550 volt generators, running at 650 rpm, the current from which passed to the feeders through Westinghouse switchgear on white marble boards. In the separate pump room, 12 ft below the engine-room floor, were two Worthington boiler feed pumps, a Ledward circulating/air pump, and a Ledward evaporative condenser cooled by seawater brought up by a third Worthington pump. In 1898, the feed pumps and pump-room condenser were replaced by two Ledward & Beckett condensing units with electrically-operated valves and motor-driven centrifugal pumps, and in 1906 the plant was augmented by an additional 72-tube Green's economiser unit.

The Whing

The line settled down to normal routine after 1897. The overall atmosphere was unique—the sound of the sea on the rocks far below, the warm sun on this south-east facing coast, the scent of heather and gorse and the ever-present cries of seabirds, heard against a somehow immense silence. The line's regular staff knew all the favourite haunts of the seals—and the crab fishing sites!

The greenish-brown of the contorted slate rock seems kindlier here than on the island's central massif, whilst the water-bound macadam of the original drive and the stone-ballasted tramway track, even when new, were unobtrusive additions to the scene. By the post-1918 era, weathering and a green carpet of tiny plants and grasses were further to mellow all this.

The business office of the tramway, originally at the depot, was later combined with the ticket office at Douglas Head. Here, tickets could be bought at the rate of 1s return, 7d single, or about two-pence per mile. Tickets were checked on the car and at Port Soderick, and break of journey was allowed, a notice on the car bulkheads (from about 1906) suggesting places of particular interest. Another office existed at Port Soderick and, by 1910, to encourage pre-booking, a surcharge was levied on the cars, the single fare being 7d if paid at the ticket office but 9d if paid on the car. This move may have been coupled with a probable reduction from three-man to two-man crews for car and trailer. In 1900, a telephone line was installed from the Douglas Head office to the power station and to Little Ness car shed. There was also a permanent-way work-shop at Keristal junction.

Two further improvements prior to 1908 were the replacing of wooden fencing—which frequently blew away in winter—by iron, and the laying down of a proper car-shed fan at Little Ness, re-placing the traverser. This probably used the points from Whing and Coolebegad loops, which were taken out, leaving nine loops. Seven of these were just long enough to take a two-car set, and were used as passing loops; the other, longer loops were at Port Soderick terminus and just inside the entrance gates on Douglas Head, the latter being used to store trailer cars on its seaward track, ready for use as traffic required. Operation of the line evolved to a pattern using fixed basic services of either four, five or seven cars, according to traffic requirements; these gave head-ways of 12-13 minutes, $10\frac{1}{2}$ minutes or $7\frac{1}{2}$ minutes respectively. Later, a six-car variant was introduced, and a system of oval head-code discs numbered 4, 5, 6 and 7 was adopted. Matching numbers were painted on poles at loops correspondingly scheduled as passing places, thus the maximum service was worked by seven cars, each showing a '7' disc and passing at those loops which bore a figure 7. The chief remaining problem was to inform staff of a change in service frequency with sufficient speed to avoid confusion, and there were some special variants of various shapes, including a

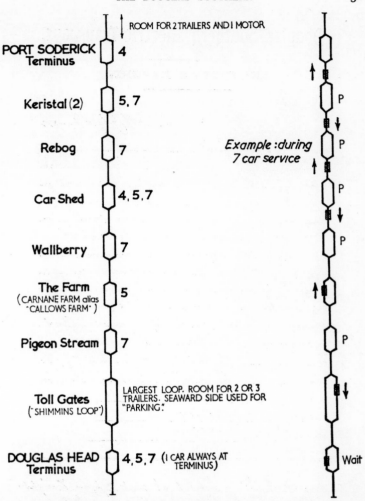

ROOM FOR 2 TRAILERS AND I MOTOR

PORT SODERICK Terminus — 4

Keristal (2) — 5, 7

Rebog — 7

Car Shed — 4, 5, 7

Wallberry — 7

The Farm (CARNANE FARM alias "CALLOWS FARM") — 5

Pigeon Stream — 7

Toll Gates ("SHIMMINS LOOP") — LARGEST LOOP. ROOM FOR 2 OR 3 TRAILERS. SEAWARD SIDE USED FOR "PARKING".

DOUGLAS HEAD Terminus — 4, 5, 7 (I CAR ALWAYS AT TERMINUS)

Example: during 7 car service

P
P
P
P
P
Wait

Operating system diagram for Douglas Southern tramway, using four, five or seven cars. The loops are numbered according to which service frequency used them. In the diagram on the right, P represents a passing place then used. The loop here named 'Car Shed' is that shown as Little Ness (2) on p 308

number flanked by Maltese Cross symbols that may have been used when changing frequencies, and an 'LC' disc to denote the last car of the day.

T

Douglas Southern Electric Tramways.

ENGINEER'S REPORT.

Date...*Sund, July 4th*...1909.

General condition of Station ...*Good*...

Started No. 1 Engine............ ....a.m.   Voltage.............   Shut down.............p.m.

Started No. 2 Engine...*9~20*....a.m.   Voltage.*500*......   Shut down.*8~45*..p.m.

No. of Boilers.*N~1*.........   Line test.*Nil*....AMPS.

Opened, current on line.......*9~30*........a.m.   Shut down.......*8~45*.........p.m.

Average steam...*100*....lbs.   Vacuum...*26*.......inches.

Temp. of feed water.*170°*.   Temp. of feed tank. *120°*.   Temp. of engine room...*74°*.

No. of Cars on line...*2*...   Trailers..............   Miles run.*269*....   State of rails................
-*3712*

Engine oil used...*6*......pints   Cylinder oil used...*3*.....pints   Dynamo oil used.......----pints

Coal consumed.*3¼*....cwts.   Ashes drawn........----.lbs.   Clinkers drawn.*192*.lbs.

Appearance of smoke emitted from chimney *Light*...   Condition of fires.*Good*...

Engineman on watch ....   *C Killey*........8.........a.m........*9*...p.m.

Greaser   „   ....*R Kardan*........----...a.m........----...p.m.

Fireman   „   ....*R Kneik*........----...a.m........----...p.m.

Watt Meter reading _____   *522352*.   _____

Brought Forward ___ __   *51916*

Kilo Watt Out-put To-day _____   *.319*

REMARKS...*A Collision occured at about 7 p.m. to-night
at the point where little one Loop used to be
through J Cain Driver running to Shut Instead of
stopping at Farm Loop and the Jail Car But one
turning to Douglas Head with passengers The passengers
were Shook J Harrison Conductor who was driving the Car from
port S derich got His ankle*   *A Kenelle*...Engineer
Proper Driver A Skimmin   *Broken Both Cars Badly Smashed*

This system of numbered discs may have been introduced as a result of a collision on Sunday, 4 July 1909, the only one known during forty-three years of operation. It was due to an unofficial motorman (actually a conductor) proceeding on to a single line section near Little Ness and meeting another car head-on. It occurred at 7 pm, one of the cars involved being the last on service. The conductor received a broken ankle and his dismissal, and the proper driver was also discharged. Both cars were badly knocked about, but no one else was seriously hurt. In the same year, 1909, Mr F. W. Ketley took up the managership of the Norwich tramways (another N G T subsidiary) and was replaced on 31 March 1909 by Mr R. Orton, hitherto with the N G T-owned Coventry tramways. Mr Orton had already spent some time on the D S E T in 1897, and was destined to retain the managership throughout the tramway's life; his recollections, in retirement, were of great value in preparing this account.

Douglas Southern Electric Tramways Ltd—Traffic Results

Year	Number of days' running	Mileage	Passengers carried	Gross Receipts	Receipts per car mile	Average cost per car mile
1898	132	40,963	94,173	not given	not given	not given
1899	133	37,593	100,769	not given	not given	not given
1902	137	32,505	192,031	£3,944	29.12d	14.84d
1903	123	32,344	201,280	4,135	30.68	16.23
1904	134	35,076	192,075	3,989	27.28	15.75
1905	114	33,313	210,298	4,055	30.66	16.52
1906	121	34,133	229,316	5,542	30.52	15.57
1907	125	36,666	231,664	5,613	36.74	17.69
1908	115	34,050	206,994	5,012	35.32	17.22
1909	125	36,570	194,826	4,790	31.43	14.67
1910	133	36,739	196,088	4,812	31.43	14.99
1911	118	34,578	230,653	4,422	30.69	15.97
1912	124	34,647	212,528	4,076	28.23	16.27

Year	Number of days' running	Mileage	Passengers carried	Traffic Receipts	Total Expenses	
1919	103	?	156,714	£7,714	£2,689	
1920	130	32,421	267,671	13,539	5,738	
1921	96	25,240	181,242	9,121	5,637	

(*Courtesy: W. T. Lambden*)

An additional 5 per cent of the gross receipts became payable to the Marine Drive company from 1 November 1905; the D S E T took this in its stride and by 1913 was paying the full 7 per cent dividend on its preference shares and $3\frac{1}{4}$ per cent on the ordinary shares. But with the outbreak of war in August 1914 the summer season was quickly brought to an end (with only 112 days' operation) and for four anxious years the Marine Drive knew no tramway service. Only $1\frac{1}{2}$ per cent was paid on the preference shares for 1914, and in June 1916 the company was obliged to issue a mortgage debenture for £3,000 on its property. The Drive itself remained open, taking £50 in tolls in 1916-17.

The directors of the D S E T throughout this period were T. J. Hutchinson (chairman), I. E. Winslow and E. A. Hopkins; the place left vacant by Davenport's death in 1907 was not filled. In 1919, Winslow moved to Barcelona, and J. G. Mills was appointed to serve while he was abroad. Mills resigned later in the year and was replaced by William Hart, succeeded in 1923 by W. F. Yaxley.

With the coming of 1919 work went ahead with preparations for reopening. Some strengthening was undertaken to the bridges, an additional Worthington boiler feed pump was installed, and the overhead wiring was renewed. A new workshop was built and equipped at a cost of £547 at the south-west corner of the boiler room, and the total cost of renewals in 1919-20 was £4,000. Thanks to the exceptionally good 1920 season, this was paid for out of revenue, the company's issued capital remaining at £41,445. Profits earned in subsequent years were £3,104 in 1922, £2,494 in 1923 and £2,089 in 1924, the company's financial year ending on 31 October.

Early in 1919, a serious breakdown occurred when condensate water forced off the cylinder head of one of the Browett-Lindley engines. The remaining undamaged unit had to maintain the power supply throughout the 1919 and 1920 seasons. A Bellis-Morcom 250-kW compound set was then purchased and arrived in July 1921, being placed in service (after overhaul) in September. This engine and generator (Bellis & Morcom Ltd No 1466) was built originally in 1902 for Farnworth Corporation Tramways; its two totally enclosed vertical cylinders were of $15\frac{1}{2}$ in and 24 in diameter, the stroke in each case being 12 in. It was placed in a lean-to at the front of the power station, and took over the normal working, the Browett-Lindley engines (repairs having now been completed to the damaged unit) being kept as standby machines.

The new set had a nominal output of 250 kW at 550 volts, working at 350 rpm, but at Farnworth it had been regularly worked at 300 kW. The only major later modification to the steam generating plant occurred in 1926, when the Bennis stoking installation was converted to forced draught operation; new condensers were installed in 1929-30.

In 1921, an agreement was made with Douglas Head Marine Drive Co that, at the end of the concession in 1926, the two companies would be combined, the Drive company taking over the tramways. The amount paid to New General Traction for their interest has not been ascertained, but was clearly well below their original investment. In 1928, the N G T reduced its then capital by one-third and changed its name to the General Consolidated Investment Trust Ltd, in which form it still exists.

Thomas J. Hutchinson, chairman of D S E T for most of its life, now headed the combined undertaking. He had been responsible for the rescue of the Marine Drive company from insolvency to its 1909 reconstruction, and looked on the Drive as a family concern just as the M E R had been the Greenwell's. The Douglas Southern's concession ended on 3 April 1926 and cars Nos 1-12 acquired the new lettering 'Douglas Head Marine Drive Ltd'. The old D S E T was not wound up until 15 April 1929, the delay being due to litigation arising from the death of a workman who fell from Wallberry

---

DOUGLAS HEAD MARINE DRIVE ELECTRIC TRAMWAYS

Passengers may, on request to Conductor, alight from and rejoin a Car at any stage en route which may be of interest to themselves.

PLACES OF PARTICULAR INTEREST.

PIGEON'S STREAM (View of NUN'S CHAIR) . **REBOG**
WALLBERRY . The **WHING** . **KERISTAL**.

D H M D car bulkhead notice (20 in by 10 in)

bridge while engaged on bridge maintenance. Each winter, well-greased workmen (on danger money) clambered about daubing the bridge structures with tar hot from a wagon, leaving a still visible coating of tar drippings across the rock far below. This apart, no incidents involving injury to passengers or staff are known, other than the 1909 collision already mentioned, and despite its gradients, curves and cliff-edge location the tramway had an excellent safety record, though the Board of Trade would have frowned on the practice of greasing the curves around the Whing and Rebog.

The tramway take-over introduced an unusual complication to the D H M D accounts, arising from the need to account separately for that part of the tram fare which represented the Marine Drive toll and for the percentage of gross tramway receipts paid over in return for the concession. To avoid undue disruption to the accounting system, D H M D each year produced separate 'tramways department' accounts as part of their balance sheet, the 'tramway commission' and tolls being shown as though the line was still under separate management. By 1929, the D H M D had a debenture debt of £4,500, part representing a payment of 1926 to D S E T for half the post-1918 bridge improvements and the rest arising from the take-over.

Results after 1929 were less good, and in February 1931 a second debenture issue of £6,500 to T. J. Hutchinson became necessary. Competition began to make itself felt; this competition was indirect, for motor coaches were not allowed on the Marine Drive, only private motor vehicles being given this privilege. The annual general meeting in 1930 heard of a profit of only £596; tramway earnings had been £5,084, with wages at £750 and car repairs at £55. The sum of £210 had been spent on engines and boilers and £254 on condensers, with the result that the tramway had lost £94 on the year despite a passenger figure of around 101,600. Mr Randle left in 1930, his place as engineer being taken by a Mr Foxon, engaged seasonally.

In May 1932, the D H M D tried hard to obtain permission to run charabancs into Douglas and compete for traffic there, but narrowly failed to obtain the town council's approval. Instead, a ticket office was opened on the Victoria pier, Douglas, and a ticket introduced giving travel to Port Soderick via the harbour ferry boat, Douglas Head Incline Rly, Marine Drive tramway and Port Soderick cliff lift, at an inclusive charge. In about 1936 the ordinary fares were dropped to 1s 6d return, 10d single, with an evening excursion at 1s after 6 pm. The cars received electric headlights, to allow for later running in the evenings.

Because the depot was so isolated, a car was left overnight at Toll Gates loop, minus controller keys, for staff transport next morning; this car always carried a barrel of fresh water to Little Ness depot. When the service commenced, two cars went together straight through to the Head, and another followed, waiting at Wallberry for the first service car. Thereafter, a car was always standing at Douglas Head loop to tempt potential riders. Two-car sets were slow and the speedier single cars frequently had to wait at the loops when both were running.

In 1935 a public supply at 3,300 volts three-phase AC, 50 cycles, was brought to two 125-kW Hewittic Electric Co Ltd rectifiers installed in the power station, with separate 196-kVA oil-immersed rectifier transformers by the Hackbridge Cable Co. Maximum demand was about 160 kW. Operating from May 1937, the season's consumption was 43,405 units. The cars were now noticeably more lively when running.

In the now-silent power station, the small workshop which originally had a small engine and vertical boiler now relied on an electric motor for power, while downstairs the 1896 switchgear passed the supply from the nearby rectifiers to the overhead. The steam plant was broken up during the winter of 1936-7, though the boilers and stokers remained in position until 1938, when they were sold and removed to Greece for further service. In 1938 and 1939 the power station served as a garage for two blue-painted 15/16-seater Morris charabancs which were hired to collect late passengers after the cars had stopped running. At Keristal, the café proprietor would ring a handbell five minutes before the last car left for Douglas.

The annual general meeting in June 1938 covered the first year of operation from rectified public supply. Tramway earnings had been £4,609, wages £1,741 (Drive and trams) and passengers 92,174, but the profit at £722 was again disappointing. Abandonment of the power plant wrote off £4,705 (against £409 from sales) and the company's indebtedness had again risen. The book value of the line remained high (£19,369), reflecting D S E T auditors' criticisms over the years of inadequate provision for depreciation. No dividend was paid, and the concern was in fact 'just holding its head above water'. Efforts to improve appearances had seen £55 spent on new uniforms.

Rebog, summer 1939

Power consumed in 1938 was 40,275 units, whilst in 1939 it amounted to 37,130. The line ran for the last time on Wednesday, 15 September 1939, the power being disconnected next day. The final year of operation (to 31 March 1940) saw the gate takings and 1d toll per tramway passenger total £470 as against 1938's £581. The company's wage bill had been £1,645—the actual tramway passenger figure and earnings are unknown. The directors were W. Townley Cottam (secretary), Percy Hutchinson and James Downs Hutchinson, in place of the lately deceased T. J. Hutchinson. On 23 May 1940, Cottam wrote to the Nunnery agent stating 'We have decided not to run the Tramway during the War, and I regret the inability to anticipate any future situation. If there are any passengers, however, the customary toll will be due and payable . . .'

Little remains to be added. The Royal Navy, taking possession of Douglas Head, sealed off that end of the Drive and ultimately demolished the ticket office, whilst Port Soderick fell into a decaying slumber from which it did not recover until 1963-4. On 12 September 1942 the rectifier installation was removed, leaving only the 3,300-volt line to show the source of power supply. In 1946 the Marine Drive company disposed of the whole property to the Isle of Man Highways and Transport Board, who found that the bridges would require complete reconstruction. Meanwhile the Marine Drive company was finally dissolved on 12 January 1948, and the site of the Drive, stripped in 1946-7 of track and overhead, then relapsed into the solitude it knew prior to its opening in 1891. Between 1948 and 1956 the Drive was variously 'closed' and 'open' to pedestrians.

The purely road scheme ultimately evolved was to cut back into the rock at Wallberry and Horse Leap, thus by-passing these two bridges, whilst at Pigeon Stream an embankment took the place of the bridge and obliterated the remains of the power station. A new approach road was built right down to Port Soderick. The task took from 1956 to 1963, and cost £240,000 (£60,000 a mile). Some geological instability and erosion still continue to give occasional trouble. In 1963 battery-electric passenger vehicles operated by the M E R board were proposed (together with a chairlift across Douglas harbour) and vehicle trials were held, but the final result was an orthodox service by small motor buses subject to a weight limit.

Had but a part of the money swallowed up in ultimate reconstruction been spent on the bridgework and tramway during 1945-6, this electric traction wonder might have been with us yet, and would have once again offered a ride unique in the entire world.

ROLLING STOCK

The original fleet consisted of twelve double-deck cars, Nos 1-6 being motor cars and Nos 7-12 trailers. A prototype drawing was prepared by the Brush Electrical Engineering Co of Loughborough in October 1895, showing an unusual car on a Peckham truck. A more accurate general-arrangement drawing bears the General Traction Co title and is dated 2 May 1896. Apart from their equipment, all twelve cars were of identical design. They were

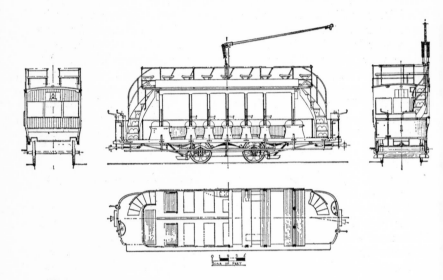

Douglas Southern Electric Tramways motor car No 1, as now preserved

double-deck, open-top, open-ended cars, with cross-bench seating and open sides to the lower deck, including seats on the outward sides of the bulkheads, under the short canopies. Seating was for seventy-five persons, thirty-nine on the upper deck and thirty-six on the lower. On each car both stairways faced the same side, as the roadway was always on the seaward side of the line; the trolley standard was on the landward side of the top deck, instead of in the centre. Similar but diametrically opposite situations applied at Guernsey, Swansea and Mumbles.

The dimensions of the cars were: wheel base, 6 ft 6 in, length, 28 ft 4 in (29 ft 5 in with couplings), maximum width, 7 ft 4 in, and height to top of trolley standard, 14 ft 4 in. Built by the

Brush Electrical Engineering Co Ltd, Loughborough (the enamel builders' plates showed the former title of Falcon Engine & Car Works), the trucks were imported from the USA. These were of the then new 'Lord Baltimore' type, designed by the father of W. S. Graff Baker and made by the Baltimore Car Wheel Company of Baltimore, Maryland. The two motors in cars Nos 1-6 were of the Westinghouse 12A type, of 25 horsepower, and the controllers were Westinghouse type 28A. The motor cars weighed about 6 tons 6 cwt, the trailers 3 tons 13 cwt.

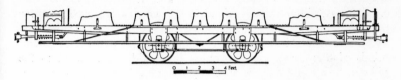

Underframe and running gear of D S E T lightweight trailer

In 1897, four trailers, Nos 13-16, were delivered by the Brush Co, generally similar to the 1896 cars but mounted on lightweight horse-car type trunnion running gear, again of 6 ft 6 in wheelbase. The weight was only 2 tons 12 cwt, and seating was for seventy-six, the extra seat occupying the space which on the 1896 trailers had a platform base for a trolley standard, so allowing the latter cars to be converted to motor cars if desired. Accordingly, two, Nos 7 and 8, were thus converted in 1897 (G E records state 1898); two General Electric 800B 27-hp motors were fitted in their 'Lord Baltimore' trucks, and General Electric K 2 nine-notch controllers were added. Any of the Nos 9-12 batch could have been so motored, and after the 1909 collision Nos 3 and 11 exchanged identities, the motor truck and equipment from No 3 going to the erstwhile No 11, which was renumbered 3 (except for its internal bulkhead numbers, by now hidden behind route notices!)

The livery was crimson and white, lined out in gold and white, with trucks in black and rails etc in brown. This continued until about 1933, except for the post 1926 change in the title carried on the upper deck sides of cars Nos 1-12 (on Nos 13-16 the D S E T title was simply painted out). In 1933-4, the paint style was simplified to yellow lining on crimson, but the more elaborate gold with white paralleling line survived on several trailers. End decency panels lettered 'Port Soderick' were added to the motor cars and some trailers in the 'twenties.

Other modifications over the years concerned the side blinds and the lighting. As delivered, the cars had simple canvas blinds with equal red-and-white vertical stripes and leather retaining straps to secure them when fully rolled or lowered. On the landward side, whose boarding step was in fact never used, the cars had a waist-level barrier rail on vertical guide irons, as on Blackpool and Fleetwood car No 2 at the Crich Tramway Museum. After 1909, cars Nos 1, 2, 3 and later 6 were given a waist panel on the landward side, with the footstep removed, and these cars then received on that side differentially-striped draw curtains arranged in three parts, fastening back to the first, third and fifth pillars and supported by the brass rails. The seaward side openings received Peters' patent blinds of 'Pantasote' cloth, running in mouldings attached to the pillars; these could only be lowered to seat level. In the late 'thirties, these 'Pantasote' blinds were replaced by full-length canvas rolled blinds much as of 1896 design, with a leather strap and brass buckle fastening them to the car sill; possibly they were taken from trailers Nos 13-16.

The electric lighting consisted initially of three roof lights downstairs and two tall standard lights upstairs, one at each stairhead. There were no headlights, but oil-lamps were carried in the lower-deck bulkheads; the trailers had oil lighting only. When electric headlights were fitted, about 1936, the stairhead lights were suppressed, so keeping the car lamp total to five as hitherto. The motor cars originally had internally-sprung trolley masts, but after 1900 these were replaced by outside sprung standards by R. W. Blackwell & Co. Plug and socket centre couplings were fitted to all the cars.

Although there was a hydraulic wheel press and a lathe in the power station, the occasional flat wheels were usually dealt with by fitting carborundum-faced brake shoes to the car affected. All cars ran with chilled iron wheels throughout their lives, with large flange profiles; there were no grooved rails on the tramway, and although the points were guarded in street tramway fashion, they had large grooves. A tower wagon and flat truck, both hand propelled (or horse-drawn?) were provided for maintenance purposes.

After closure, the final distribution at Little Ness, (entrance doors to rear) was Nos 1, 4, 2 and 11 on the seaward road, Nos 3, 5, 6 and 8 on the next, Nos 7, 15, 9 and 10 on the third road and Nos

12, 16, 13 and 14 on that to landward. In 1951, the writer and others acquired and removed car No 1 for preservation; this vehicle is now (1969) in the Museum of British Transport at Clapham, restored to the authentic crimson and white livery, save that the lettering is in the later D H M D style although stating D S E T. The museum also displays the nameboards from Little Ness and the Whing. The depot track fan was removed to the Crich Tramway Museum in 1960. The depot, and the remaining fifteen cars, were broken up where they stood in the winter of 1951-52.

Fleet List—Douglas Southern Electric Tramways

Car	Motors (2)	Controllers	Truck	Body	Seats	Date
1-6	Westinghouse 12A, 25 hp	Westinghouse 28A	'Lord Baltimore'	Brush	75	1896
7-8	General Electric 800B, 27 hp	General Electric K2	'Lord Baltimore'	Brush	75	1896
9-12	nil (trailers)	nil	'Lord Baltimore'	Brush	75	1896
13-16	nil (trailers)	nil	Brush Trunnions	Brush	76	1897

Nos 7 and 8 were built as trailers in 1896 and motorised in 1897-8.
Nos 3 and 11 exchanged numbers, trucks and equipments in 1909.

East Coast Railways

As late as 1893, the fare from Douglas to Laxey was 8s per horse-drawn car, such a vehicle holding but four passengers; excursion brakes carried seven. Likewise, to Ramsey the alternatives were an earlier-established coach via Kirk Michael, the steam railway (opened in 1879), and the steamers. By the latter years of the century, the Ramsey Steamship Company were running the *Lancelot* and *Fairy Queen* between Douglas and Ramsey making two return trips daily, one starting from Douglas in the morning and one after lunch, with calls at both Laxey and Dhoon Glen. Other facilities were offered by steamers proceeding to or from Glasgow, Belfast or Ardrossan and on cruises round the island.

Meanwhile, schemes for railways were put forward. The first known evidence is a letter of 6 January 1874 from William Lewis to G. W. Dumbell, which proposed an extension from the Douglas—Peel railway, and described the route as following the river Glass to below Glenville, then running north-eastwards up a side valley to Hillberry and down the southern side to the Groudle valley to Port Groudle. Nothing came of this proposal.

On 1 March 1882 there appeared the Douglas, Laxey & Ramsey Railway Co Ltd, with a capital of £130,000 in £5 shares. Of the eight subscribers, three were Manxmen, four hailed from Manchester and district, and one from Flint. The engineer appears to have been Daniel Cregeen. A manuscript of 1883 exists on the costs of working a line to Laxey, followed in 1885 by an elegantly written manuscript estimate of working expenses for the same Douglas, Laxey and Ramsey Railway, the detailed costing even including lamp oil! Agreement had been reached with the I M R for the joint use of Douglas station and for a station and junction at Quarter Bridge, the other intended stations being at Ballaquayle, Falcon Cliff, Summer Hill, Onchan, Ballameanagh, Glen Gawne and Laxey; those from Douglas to Onchan were rated suburban. New articles of association were drawn up on 22 August 1885 and a prospectus issued by Chadwick, Boardman & Co of 64 Cross Street, Manchester, on 17 November 1885, but the scheme failed for lack of support.

George Noble Fell undertook surveys during 1887-8 for an east coast line with the title Douglas, Laxey & Snaefell Railway, though the application lodged was for Douglas—Laxey only. To secure land purchase powers, Fell appeared in November 1888 before a special committee of Tynwald Court, his ambitious proposals involving expert witnesses on an unusual scale. One mile of the eight would have been on viaducts (of Fell's own design), and the land costs were estimated by the court at £62,000 if the line had a separate quay-side terminal, or £37,000 if the line ran into Douglas alongside the I M R. Plans for the Douglas—Laxey section had been lodged in the Rolls office on 19 September 1888, and the enquiry began on 6 November; the chief technical witness was James Whitestone, who had been an articled pupil of W. H. Barlow on the Midland Railway. The line was approved, but work was never started.

A further company, the Douglas, Laxey & Maughold Head Marine Drive and Tramway Company Ltd, was registered on 8 September 1890 with a capital of £100,000 and an address c/o F. Browne, Advocate, of Athol Street, Douglas. All seven sub-scribers had London addresses. Joint working with Isle of Man Tramways Ltd was proposed, though with no details of motive power.

In 1891, Fell's scheme of 1887-8 was revived with a new title, Manx East Coast Railways. A book of lithographed plans survives, showing a line from Douglas to Laxey. Starting at Douglas with a station just north of the I M R locomotive shed, the line paralleled the I M R to Quarter Bridge and then followed the river Glass, crossed the road to Tromode, and climbed by sinuous reverse curves to cross the Glencrutchery stream beyond the then Douglas waterworks. The next station was to be close to Onchan's central crossroads, after which the line descended towards Groudle, crossing the stream by a 44-ft high bridge. A summit height of 325 ft 6 in was reached just over six miles from Douglas, the route thereafter being virtually that of the electric line as built in 1893-4, but ending at the Queen's hotel, Laxey, 150 ft above datum. The total distance was eight miles seven furlongs.

Daniel Cregeen's lithographed plans for the Douglas, Laxey & Dhoon Railway exist in the Manx Museum, and although probably post-1890, are the culmination of much earlier field work dating back at least to November 1883. From a full-scale separate terminus near the North Quay (and fronting the I M R station), it tunnelled under the Peel Road/Athol Street junction to emerge alongside the I M R, which it followed to Quarter Bridge. The line then turned north-east to Ballaquayle Cottage, Glencrutchery and Onchan, with no gradient steeper than 1 in 50 and with bridges at all road crossings, save for a level crossing at Summer Hill Road. After a station at Onchan, close to the centre of the village, the line was to parallel the road to Laxey, crossing the Groudle river by four 80-ft spans with a maximum height of 68 ft. From here, the route followed was that of the later electric line, but with a girder bridge to cross the main Laxey road, a viaduct of three 50-ft spans across Glen Gawne (Garwick), and a summit level of 319 ft, reached after five miles five furlongs. The Laxey station was again just to seaward of the Queen's hotel, on the 150-ft contour line.

The ensuing section was much more dramatic. A seven-arch viaduct 99 ft high with spans of 43 ft was to cross the Laxey valley on a curve of $6\frac{1}{2}$ chains radius, forming a virtually complete semi-circle. A mineral branch to the washing floors was to form a trailing connection just beyond this viaduct. From here until the Dhoon terminus (at 442 ft) the line was to climb at an almost constant 1 in 31. The intended terminus, ten miles from Douglas, was on the southern shoulder of Bulgham Bay, where no doubt railhead development was envisaged.

After part of Fell's 1887-8 survey was used by Saunderson for the electric line in 1893-4, Fell's Snaefell survey was kept alive until 1895 by a separate Snaefell Railway Company, whose office was in Athol Street. The Douglas, Laxey & Ramsey scheme of Cregeen and associates had its office in 1893-4 at 1 Gellings Court, but Cregeen died on 19 April 1894, after a career largely spent with HM Commissioners of Works in London.

The last east coast steam railway proposed was a direct rival of the electric line. On 9 April 1896 a Mr Mylchreest sought leave to introduce into Tynwald a Bill for a railway from Laxey to Ramsey, and a first reading followed on 13 May. His backers were a London syndicate, R. Blackie, J. Templeton Slade and A. T.

Green, with G. Noble Fell as its surveyor. The I O M T & E P petitioned Tynwald on 28 October for leave to present their own
Bill, and by 10 December the steam railway scheme had been
'withdrawn by consent'.

The Ramsey Pier Tramway

The Queen's pier at Ramsey, 2,300 ft in length, is owned by the Isle of Man harbour board and cost £45,000 to build. It was opened by the Lord Bishop of Sodor and Man on

Track diagram, Ramsey Pier Tramway. Tracks A were removed in 1955-6

22 July 1886. As built, it included a 3-ft gauge tramway used to take luggage to and from the steamers : at its landward end two diverging tracks continued into the roadway to permit unloading. There has been no subsequent track renewal, other than points.

In 1899, a new landing-stage was completed at the pierhead, and in August there arrived a low-built manually-propelled passenger car. This brought the rolling stock to nine, the balance comprising seven luggage trucks of two main sizes but differing in details, and a small four-wheeled flat for heavy items. Around 1906, the M E R were apparently acting as consultants in an electrification project, and prepared a drawing of a very small four-wheeled, single-deck saloon tramcar.

The original hand-propelled Ramsey Pier passenger car

At the pierhead, Ramsey Pier Tramway; Planet locomotive and trailer in foreground, Wickham car at the rear

Modernisation came in May 1937, and involved the purchase of Hibberd 'Planet' petrol locomotive No 2037 and a matching bogie 'toastrack' coach, No 2038, with seating for fifteen; both were built by Park Royal Coachworks of London, NW 10. In 1950 a self-propelled Ford-engined, eleven-seat Wickham petrol railcar was added. In 1955-6 a new entrance was built; the old Y-tracks were buried and a straight spur on to dry land laid instead, using rails from the Douglas cable tramway. The pier has seen both Edward VII and Queen Elizabeth the Queen Mother as royal visitors; on the second occasion, 4 July 1963, the Hibberd combination served as the royal train.

The 1899 passenger car survives as a store, still with its internal upholstery, while the rest of the stock—and the pier—are kept in excellent order.

Other Proposed Tramways
(with acknowledgments to Mr W. S. Basnett)

Ramsey, 1882-1899

According to a map of 1882, the 3-ft gauge freight tramway on the future Ramsey pier (built 1886) was originally to have extended into the town, assumedly with horse traction. In 1897, during negotiations for bringing the electric line into Ramsey, the Ramsey commissioners proposed a horse tramway to link the electric line's terminus with the steam railway, and in 1899 the *Courier* was pressing the Harbour Board to build an electric tramway from the pier to the town.

Douglas Head Cable Tramway, 1894

On 19 January 1894, at a public meeting in Douglas on the Upper Douglas tramway question, Douglas draper Robert Archer produced a plan for a cable tramway intended to run to Douglas Head. It began at the Promenade, at a junction with the horse line, proceeded down Victoria Street, then diagonally from the foot of Prospect Hill across the site of the later *Isle of Man Times* printing works into Athol Street at the junction of Upper Church Street. It then turned down Bank Hill, crossing the stone bridge to reach South Quay, where it diverged sharply inland on a course curving through the quarry behind the gasworks, then straight across fields to a terminus on the still residentially undeveloped part of Douglas Head.

Douglas-Kirk Braddan, 1895-7 *(horse traction)*

On Sunday, 4 August 1897, a census recorded 4,118 persons pass Burleigh on foot between 9.30 and noon, and 326 carriages in the same period, all making for the open-air church service at Kirk Braddan originated by Bishop Powys in June 1856. Tramway promoters, represented by Advocates Kneen and Cruikshank of Douglas, had meetings with the Highway Board between November 1895 and November 1897 for inconclusive discussions on widening the road and on the proportion of receipts to be paid over.

*Peel-*M N R *Station,* 1895

With Peel Road M N R station one and a half miles from Peel, the Peel Railway Co Ltd was registered in 1886 to build a connecting steam line; it became inactive by 1890 and was dissolved in 1910. In December 1895, Advocate C. B. Nelson, a notorious background member of the I O M T & E P concern, applied to the Highway Board for permission to lay a tramway (probably horse-worked) along the Poortown Road, and intermittent correspondence ensued until 11 October 1897.

Dhoon Glen, 1895

In 1895, correspondence took place between a Mr Drinkwater and Governor Ridgeway concerning an undefined tramway along Dhoon Glen. It should here be noted that the West Baldwin reservoir line, which was described in the *Journal of the Stephenson Locomotive Society* for May 1963, and subsequently in the *Journal of the Manx Museum,* was considered for retention as a passenger line according to a contemporary Ward Lock guidebook, but this did not occur and the line was removed.

Peel-Port Erin, 1906

Tramway and Railway World for 25 August 1906 reveals proposals for what could have been a stupendous electric line along the cliff from Peel to Port Erin, in the style of the Marine Drive line. A. N. Laughton, High Bailiff of Peel, had offered his land en route free of charge.

Cliff Lifts

Falcon Cliff Lift

Falcon Cliff was developed in the 'eighties as an entertainment complex overlooking Douglas Bay. A lift was constructed in 1887, but by 25 June was not ready for use, as on that date Falcon Cliff was obliged to advertise for tenders for a 'horse car' service to the resort's upper entrance. The 'Patent Tram' lift

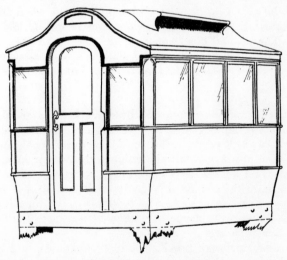

Original car of Falcon Cliff incline railway, drawn as when serving as a kiosk on Port Soderick promenade

had been built by one, T. Cain, and was reportedly first tested on Thursday, 26 May. It was 218 ft long and rose 110 ft, taking 1 minute 25 seconds for the journey. The two tracks were of 4-ft gauge, with flat-bottomed rails 4 in deep, coach screw fastened by their foot to longitudinal timbers about 12 in by 12 in, into which their underfoot fishplates were recessed.

The lift was inspected early in July by P. Nevill of the the IoM Harbour Board. On 23 July the forthcoming opening was announced, but by 30 July buses were again in use and the lift did not begin work until 6 August.

In 1896, the by-then disused lift was sold to the Forrester family who re-erected it at Port Soderick, new cars being provided. The 1887 cars survived as shops on Port Soderick promenade. The Falcon Cliff lift's lower terminus is now built over. It is uncertain whether the 1887 installation was worked by steam, oil or gas engine.

In 1927, a single-car lift was built on a new site at Falcon Cliff by Wm Wadsworth & Sons Ltd of Bolton. This is of 5-ft gauge, with channel section rails set at an angle of 45 degrees. A counterweight runs beneath the track, equal to the weight of the car and up to 50 per cent of its possible load (six passengers). When the lift was built, power was supplied at 400 volts DC to a 6-hp motor driving the twin 1-in diameter cables, but in 1950, when DC supply ceased, power was taken at 415 volts three-phase AC and rectified on site. The lift and hotel are owned by Okell's Brewery, Douglas, and an illustration appears in *Cliff Railways* by C. Body and R. L. Eastleigh. Service was at first year-round, but is now seasonal.

Port Soderick Holiday Beach Lift

Forrester family development here reached its zenith in the construction of an elegant curved promenade, still carrying a datestone inscribed 'Erected by M. & T. Forrester, 1897', and in the construction of a lift to link the beach with the new Marine Drive tramway. This was the 1887 Falcon Cliff lift, re-erected in the same basic form, with 4-in deep Vignoles rails laid to 4-ft gauge on parallel 12 in by 12 in timbers at centres of 4 ft 2 in, 2 ft 9 in and 4 ft 2 in respectively. Some new material was used, the line being longer than at Douglas.

Two new cars were provided, builder unknown, and the drive was now by an oil engine driving a cable of $3\frac{1}{2}$ in circumference. An oddly-shaped corrugated-iron building housed the engine and

The Port Soderick Lift

head gear, still partly *in situ,* and a top loading platform, whose characteristic iron fence and twin gateways also survive. Lower down, expensive timber viaduct construction was involved; the ivy-clad stone pillars remain today. The cars were sloped to match the lift's gradient, and at the bottom end of their run entered a terminal station, later given an all-over roof, built about 1902 to the same slope.

P. Nevill, Harbour Board engineer, gave his inspector's approbation on 9 July 1898 after making six visits. He had reported to the governor on 25 June that he was far from happy with the installation—whilst the cars were new, little else was. The governor's secretary wrote on 11 July 1898 giving final approval for working to commence.

Final closure can be assumed concurrent with that of the Marine Drive tramway in September 1939. In 1946 it was sold with the hotel, and was dismantled between 1947 and 1949. A footpath which offered an alternative way down was later rebuilt. The cars survived into the post-war years as henhouses, until some cattle poisoned themselves by chewing the lead paint from the canvas of their roofs!

Douglas Head Incline Railway

On 21 January 1898 an agreement was concluded between Sir John Goldie-Taubman and R. M. Broadbent for a 'double or single mechanical tramway or lift or railway and lift combined or railway and lift combined with necessary crossings and loops' from a point near the Battery pier to a point to seaward of the Douglas Southern tramway on Douglas Head. Promoted by R. M. Broadbent of Ivydene, Douglas, this took shape in 1900 as a double-track funicular, probably of 4 ft gauge, extending from a lower station at the rear of Douglas Head lighthouse near Port Skillion to a combined upper terminal building and engine house not far from the D S E T terminus, and passing over a footpath en route. The inclination was 1 in 4½ over the entire length of 450 ft, with a bend about one-third of the way up, and the double track (laid in 70-lb flat bottom rail) was close together on the lower section and further apart higher up. Motive power was an oil engine, housed in the basement of the upper terminal. In July 1900, two inclined railway cars (drawing 5072/25) were supplied by Hurst Nelson & Co of Motherwell, and the line assumedly opened later that summer. Operation thereafter was seasonal.

On 7 July 1922, the line was sold by Broadbent and his wife to Douglas Head Incline Railway Ltd, whose office was at the upper station. A Nunnery estate deed of 30 June 1926, includes the requirement to operate from the Friday before Whit Monday until September 30. The lift was closed during the two wars, and recommenced about 1949—the writer used it in 1950—but ran only for the next five seasons, and by August 1954 it lay disused. It was dismantled in October and November of 1955, the rails being relaid on the M E R approaching Ramsey. Little now remains.

The closure was a direct consequence of competing corporation bus service to Douglas Head and the resulting starvation of the ferry service to the foot of the lift. A rather pathetic letter from the proprietors of Douglas Head Ferries Ltd to the town council, dated 22 February 1950, asked that their previous monopoly be left undisturbed for a further period now that two steamers were available, but this met with no response and the buses to the Head ran from 1950. During 1949, the corporation had tried to run a service along the south side of the harbour to the cliff lift. In its heyday, the steam ferry fleet comprised three vessels, *Thistle, Rose* and *Shamrock*; today, the remaining two ferry boats lie decaying at the top end of the harbour.

Laxey Wheel Incline Railway ('Browside Tramway')

This little-known line connected Laxey Wheel with the roadway below. It was built about 1890, and comprised a double track with two twenty-seat 'toastrack' cars having dissimilar diameter wheels. The line was worked on the water counterbalance method, taking water from a cistern filled from the mine tailrace. A braked drum acted as a controlling windlass at the upper end.

The line was initially owned and operated by the Faragher family of Cronk e Chule farm, who later sold it to the mining company. Spasmodic Press advertisements appeared; one of 1895 specifies the return fare as 1d, but another source gives the original fare as 1d up and 1d down, later reduced to 1d up, ½d down. An old employee of the mine, living in 1964 in Laxey, was employed as a 'tout' for the lift and sometimes as 'bung boy' at the lower station, emptying the tank of the car that had just descended.

By 1910 the line had shown itself unprofitable, and it was dismantled; the remains of the head gear still exist.

Douglas Holiday Camp Escalator

Cunningham's Camp had moved from Howstrake Park to Little Switzerland, Douglas, about 1902; in 1914 it became an internment camp. About 1920, an 'escalator', or electric stair, was built up to the camp. This is a unidirectional installation ('up' only) and is a wooden shed containing a fixed staircase and a moving parallel steel chain link belt to which seats are attached, facing the fixed stairs; motive power is an electric motor. In 1938 the escalator was rebuilt, doubling its original capacity. Service was from May to September, and an attendant was stationed at the top and bottom. Campers originally rode free, but paid from 1963; members of the public paid a fare (3d in 1966) and subsequently walked through the camp to the Victoria Road entrance. A somewhat similar installation once existed at Southend-on-Sea, but was replaced in 1912 by a conventional cliff lift; one wonders if it was re-used at Douglas. The lift did not run in 1969.

The *Crellin's Hill Scheme* of 1956 and the *Douglas Harbour Chairlift* project of 1962 both deserve mention as latter-day schemes, as does another 1962 proposal for a chairlift from Fairy Cottage to Laxey beach.

Manx Tramway Tickets
(Contributed by W. H. Bett, FCII)

The subject of ticket and fare-collection systems is a considerable study in itself. Though in the very early days of tramways, fare-collection methods were crude and unstandardised and there were sometimes no tickets at all (though this was commoner on omnibuses than trams), simple tickets torn from a roll or pad soon made their appearance, and later, as an additional check to prevent the fraudulent re-issue of tickets, a registering punch was introduced. This *bell-punch system* was in general use on most tramways in the British Isles from about 1890 to 1940, and is still used on the Douglas horse trams. Bell-punch tickets are on thickish paper and nearly always $1\frac{1}{4}$ in in width; length is usually from about 2 to $2\frac{1}{4}$ in upwards, according to the amount of matter to be accommodated. There is a series for each fare value, and tickets are punched on issue in a numerically-registering punch which rings a bell as it does so. The punch-hole position is usually made significant.

The *Edmondson ticket* is the familiar small stiff card as used by railways.

The *Automaticket machine* issues small tickets about 2 in by 1 in. Holes between adjacent tickets engage with a sprocket wheel in the issuing mechanism flush with the pay counter.

The *Willebrew system* is a patented one whereby pre-printed tickets are cut in a machine in such a manner that the position of the cut indicates the fare paid. The portion cut off remains in the machine.

'*Stock*' tickets are untitled tickets produced cheaply in bulk and held in stock by printers and stationers.

An *'Exchange'* ticket is issued only upon collection of a return transfer or other prepaid ticket.

'Roll' tickets are pre-printed tickets made up in a perforated roll and simply torn off by hand as required.

Unlike most street tramways, on the Manx Electric, tickets are issued at booking-offices before boarding the car. Reduced-fare tickets issued in books and known as 'name tickets' are also a feature. The journey coupons are not transferable and are for the personal use of the holder whose name appears on the cover.

(i) *Isle of Man Tramways & Electric Power Co Ltd—Douglas lines*

On the I O M T & E P Bay tramway, coupon tickets for residents are mentioned as early as 1884. About 1896, the horse-car line was using (in summer) 2d white bell-punch tickets (1)* printed by Foster of Northampton, a long-extinct firm. These showed only 'Victoria Street to Electric Tramway Station' and reverse; there were probably similar tickets for the cable line to Stanley View and its short-lived continuation to the foot of Broadway, where the Act provided for through bookings to the horse cars. Later, a similar 2d horse-car ticket by Williamson of Ashton existed, differing only in minor typographical details. In 1899 the cable line was worked as Victoria Street—Avondale and Broadway—Avondale, 2d up hill, 1d down in each case.

(ii) *Douglas Corporation Tramways*

The earliest tickets seen were 1d green and 2d white (2) each with a red fare overprint, printed by Williamson. These covered both horse and cable routes and were of a characteristic design which remained basically unchanged for many years; on the left were the words 'From VICTORIA PIER to' subdivided into sections worded 'Electric Tram Station' (sometimes 'Electric Railway Station') and 'Stanley View' with a small 'Parcel' section between, and reverse sections on the right, worded 'To VICTORIA PIER from' the same points.

Over the next thirty years minor changes were to be made to the wording, the printer changed (to Auto-Tickets of Birkenhead) and a wider range of fares and colours were introduced.

The present style derives from (2) and originated about 1938, by which time the former Upper Douglas route ticketing had already been incorporated into a wider range of bus route tickets. Of a basic range of 3d (white), 2d (pink), 1½d (brown) and 1d (green)

* See illustration on page 288

tickets, the 3d by 1947 had appeared in lilac, with 'Transport' substituted for 'Tramways' in the title. The all-the-way fare subsequently rose to 4d (lilac ticket) in 1951, 5d (grey) in 1955, 6d (grey) in 1956, 8d (green) in 1961 and 9d (green) in 1963. In 1960 the printer became Bell Punch; this was simply because Bell Punch had absorbed Auto-Tickets, and in fact the 1959 issue, though still bearing Auto-Tickets' imprint, had certain Bell Punch typographical features. In 1962 there was a genuine change of printer—back to Williamson, the corporation's first love.

There appear to have been no intermediate stages in 2d all-the-way days (the 1d mentioned is apparently a half-fare ticket), but by 1928, when the fare was 3d all the way, a 2d ticket appeared for short stages. This was pink with the lower half overprinted with a purple wash, and bore sections 'Victoria Pier and Broadway/and Rosemount' at the head, and 'Broadway and Derby Castle', 'Rosemount and Stanley View' at the foot; title and conditions occupied the centre space. The title was 'Douglas Corporation Trams and Buses', doubtless in view of the already seasonal operation of the cable tramway. In later years there have been separate adult tickets for the stages each side of Broadway, but usually a child ticket common to both; child tickets were not always specially printed for the trams, and sometimes bus 'left-overs' values have been used. The half-way fare has been successively 2d, $3\frac{1}{2}$d, 4d, 5d and 6d, but after the 1965 summer season the half-way fare was abandoned and the full 9d charged for any distance.

During 1956 there was a special issue of souvenir tickets to celebrate the eightieth anniversary of the horse-car service. The set included 4d adult short-stage tickets (3) for each stage separately, 6d all-the-way, and 2d and 3d child.

The corporation has a convenient habit of showing the last two figures of the year of ordering on its tickets.

Less usual tickets include a newspaper contract parcel label (on thin yellow paper, $2\frac{1}{2}$ in square) headed 'Douglas Corporation Tramways, Horse Section'. Passengers on the circular bus route could transfer to the horse cars for part of the journey, using an oversize 'Circular Route Break of Journey Ticket' (pale yellow, $2\frac{5}{8}$ in by $1\frac{5}{8}$ in). There was also an Exchange (normal size, pale yellow, with red overprint 'EXCHANGE TICKET/NO VALUE'), with sections covering various types of bus returns and prepaid tickets on the left, and 'C (circular) R (route) B (break) of Jny (journey) to Horse Cars' on the right.

(iii) *Isle of Man Tramways & Electric Power Co Ltd—Electric lines (including Snaefell Mountain Electric Tramway)*

About 1896 I O M T & E P was using tickets (4) by Foster, of a very remarkable type. These tickets mingled features of typical railway and tramway practice, providing in fact a perfect and unique 'missing link' between Edmondson and bell-punch tickets. The layout of the text was similar to that of the true bell-punch tickets used on the horse cars, with the serial number at the head, and the tickets were the same size (ie, somewhat longer and wider than a standard Edmondson) but they were on stout card nearly as thick as an Edmondson, and were dated on the reverse in a standard railway dating press (incidentally, one using an inked ribbon, as on the mainland, and not the 'dry' type of date-stamp common on the Continent, and now used on the island by both M E R and I M R). The example shown (dated 12 June 1896) has been punched on both outward and return journeys with a large round hole, which is quite unlike the marks by the later M E R hand nippers, but *is* very similar to the large holes made by the earlier 'pistol' type of bell-punch; it seems possible that an actual bell-punch was used, specially modified to take a thicker ticket. Fares quoted for 1895 were Douglas—Groudle 5d, Douglas—Garwick 8d, Douglas—Laxey 1s.

Somewhat later, probably when Williamson first became the printer, a new type of electric-line ticket appeared virtually identical with that used by the M E R to this day but for the company title. These were physically of pure Edmondson type, with serial number at the foot and of standard Edmondson size and thickness, though with a rather un-railway-like layout of the text which is discussed below under M E R.

The Snaefell Mountain line, in this era, also used Edmondson tickets by Williamson, but of standard railway layout and in vertical two-coupon form for returns, unlike the tickets of the coastal line. A Laxey—Snaefell 2s return dated 8 July 1896 and parti-coloured green and white, is illustrated. (5)

(iv) *Manx Electric Company Ltd (later Board)*

The basic design, by Williamson, is that established in the later days of the I O M T & E P as described above. Even the nationalisation of the line in June 1957 has meant no change except the substitution of the word 'Board' for 'Company' in the conditions of issue. Under both regimes the title printed on tickets has usually been simply 'Manx Electric Railway'.

The tickets, though physically Edmondsons of railway type, have the text arranged in a manner much more reminiscent of bell-punch tramway tickets. There is a space for dating at the head, but except in the case of rover tickets, where accurate dating is essential, this is often unused. As with most tram tickets, there are punch-spaces down each side and the title and conditions in a centre column. In some simple cases there is but a single punch-space, the matter in which effectively indicates the validity of the ticket, and the word 'single' or 'return' then usually appears across the head; 'single journey' or 'return journey' on most tickets also appears at the foot, immediately above the serial number. In other cases the punch-spaces are numerous and represent not alternative 'stages' but intermediate points along the line for checking breaks of journey; the validity of the ticket as a whole is then shown across the head, as 'Ramsey—Laxey' or 'Douglas and Snaefell Summit'. (6)

This rather unusual arrangement is necessary as the tickets issued at stations are prepaid tickets which must be invalidated when actually used. Generous break of journey facilities are allowed, and collection of all tickets at the end of the journey is scarcely practicable, although trains approaching Douglas are sometimes boarded by an inspector who collects tickets, or stopped at Onchan for the purpose, consequently fractional cancellations are made by punching when the ticket is first presented. If the passenger is riding through, the conductor gives three or four clips down the side of the ticket from top to bottom; if break of journey is requested he punches the section or sections to be travelled on his car and leaves the remainder to be cancelled by a subsequent conductor. In the case of returns, one side relates to the outward and the other to the return journey. A 'break of journey' ticket (similar in function to the stop-over checks used in the USA) existed at one time, and was used when a passenger changed his mind and decided to leave the car at an intermediate point after his ticket had already been presented and cancelled 'through'. Most tickets issued at offices are white and bear an overprint consisting of (a) '$\frac{1}{2}$' for half-fares, if applicable, (b) a letter or letters denoting which of the three routes radiating from Laxey the ticket covers—'D' for Laxey—Douglas, 'R' for Laxey—Ramsey, 'S' or sometimes 'LS' for Laxey—Snaefell (also 'T' or 'BT' for the former Bungalow—Tholt-y-Will—Sulby Glen

X

bus service), and finally (c) 'S' or 'R' for single or return. Thus a Douglas to Ramsey Return is overprinted DRR, a half-fare Ramsey to Laxey Single ½RS. These overprints are usually in red on singles and *half*-fare returns, but in green on adult returns.

Tickets issued on the cars originally had the fare printed in the text and had stage sections set out 'fareboard' fashion, they were usually plain white or vertically parti-coloured white and blue (7) for single and vertically parti-coloured white and pink for return, without overprints. Today a type bearing an over-printed fare (8) and a standardised stage-array for all values is used, having the letters D-L-R (for Douglas, Laxey, Ramsey) across the head and the names of the principal intermediate points in route order down the sides; both boarding point and destination are punched on issue. Singles are white with fare overprints in various colours; returns are variously coloured, with overprints, and bear additional sections 'break of journey' and 'C' for final cancellation.

At Onchan Head there was a two-unit Automaticket machine for local adult and child single bookings to Douglas, the tickets bearing the word 'Automaticket', the fare and a serial number only. Less standard issues include 'name ticket' coupons in 20-ride booklets and the 3½ x 2½-in book of tickets for a personally conducted day tour including refreshments. (See pp 246)

By 1965, the Board were offering residents winter-fare tickets in 'tens' for the price of eight (the fares themselves were already at half the summer level), and in summer ten journeys for eleven times the winter fare. Boarding-house keepers and hotels were offered distribution of coupon tickets at 25 per cent reduction to Laxey, Ramsey and Snaefell, for their summer guests.

Staff privilege tickets were usually yellow with green overprint, 'Camp B.O.' tickets (parti-coloured dark blue and white or lilac and white) are those formerly sold at a booking office in Cunningham's Camp. Circular tour tickets were white with red circular overprint, or if involving the Bungalow—Sulby bus, yellow with green stripes. 'Rover tickets' are now plain white (some early issues were green) and carry day spaces and a Snaefell section, all selectively punched.

(v) *Douglas Southern Electric Tramways Ltd* and *Douglas Head Marine Drive Ltd*.

About 1899 D S E T used railway-type Edmondsons, bearing no printer's name, dated in a press and in horizontal two-coupon form for returns. These included Douglas Head to Port Soderick single, brown; Port Soderick to Douglas Head single, primrose (9), adult return left-half blue, right-half pink; child return left-half white, right-half green. Both the above returns have the Port Soderick—Douglas Head half on the right.

By the 'thirties, tickets were roll issues by Williamson, of normal bell-punch size. These included single Douglas Head to Port Soderick, green (1s 3d); single Port Soderick to Douglas Head, yellow (1s) (10) (later reduced to 10d); 6d single covering either Douglas Head—Little Ness or Little Ness—Port Soderick, in either direction, grey; all the way adult return, lilac, 2s (later reduced to 1s 6d); half-fare return, blue (1s). In 1938 there was also an evening excursion return (lilac with red stripe) for 1s; and for 2s a combined excursion ticket (13) from Douglas to Port Soderick beach and back, including 'Douglas Steam Ferry' 'Douglas Head Cable Lift', 'Marine Drive Electric Car', and the 'Port Soderick Cable Lift' down at the other end. This, illustrated, was buff with a red stripe. Some sections were apparently cut out, the operators retaining the clippings as vouchers to be produced when claiming their share of the proceeds.

(vi) *Cable Inclines and the Ramsey Pier Tramway*

By the 'twenties, the Douglas Head incline railway followed the practice, not uncommon on funiculars, of having returns and no singles. Upon collection of (nominally single) fares a roll ticket by Williamson was issued, bearing no fare but worded 'This ticket is available for RETURN journey FREE on day of issue only'. The title of the line and a heading 'RETURN TICKET' also appeared; and across one end, the day of the week. Colours were changed daily; a Tuesday issue in pinkish buff (11) and a Thursday issue in bright green with blue stripe, are typical. They were torn in two on the return journey.

The Port Soderick Holiday Beach Lift's tickets by 1938 were of Automaticket machine type (but apparently issued manually, as all seen are roughly torn off). They were 1d white, and 2d blue, headed 'Port Soderick Holiday Beach' on the face with the fare on each half; on the reverse the word 'LIFT' appeared diagonally across each half together with some fancy decoration.

The Falcon Cliff hotel, Douglas, electric lift has only one fare (3d up or down, but formerly 3d up, 2d down) and surprisingly, in the 'thirties, used titled 'Willebrews', usually associated with

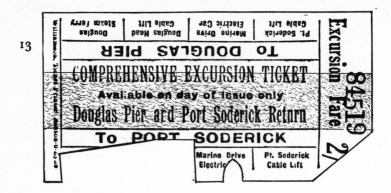

undertakings having a large range of fares. These tickets (14) (plain white and titled as above) were considerably shorter than most Willebrews (3¼ in by 1⅝ in) and bore large sections '3d up' '2d down' all along one side with analytical categories 'Weekly Resident', 'Season Resident', 'Daily Resident' and 'Privilege' along the other. These designations apparently referred to various classes of hotel guests etc, entitled to use the line free. In recent years stock roll tickets, by Williamson, have been used, punched in a bell-punch (latterly unpunched). There have been various colours for both 2d and 3d values and apparently attendants on different shifts have differently coloured tickets. Colours seen include 2d pink, brown, salmon, lilac; 3d grey, red, green. The tickets show nothing but a serial number, the fare, and Williamson's imprint.

The Queen's Pier tram (IoM Harbour Board) at Ramsey was long a user of similar stock roll tickets in conjunction with a bell-punch. Properly titled tickets suddenly appeared in their stead about 1961. These were perforated at one end and made up in pads, and worded ISLE OF MAN HARBOUR/QUEENS PIER TRAM ADULT 2d (12) (or CHILD 1d). The adult's ticket was white, and the child's blue. About 1963, fares were doubled and similar tickets at 4d adult, 2d child, came into use. They are now issued unpunched, or sometimes clipped with a non-registering hand-nipper; some have appeared with no fare stated.

The Douglas Holiday Camp Escalator offers 'up' service only, and originally used titled Automaticket issues (the 2d was violet), but later stock Automatickets (1d child, salmon, 2d adult, blue) were used, almost identical with those used by the Manx Electric Railway at Onchan. Titled tickets were reintroduced when the fare rose to 3d (adult or child) in 1965; the 1968 4d ticket was blue. The Escalator went out of use after 1968.

No tickets from the Laxey Wheel Cliff Lift are at present known.

Notes on Illustrations

Numbers in parentheses in Appendix 5 text refer to these

1 Early Foster bell-punch ticket of I O M T & E P Co for horse-car line.
2 Earliest type of Williamson 2d ticket of Douglas Corporation (horse and cable lines).
3 1956 4d ticket, Derby Castle—Broadway or vice versa, of eightieth anniversary commemorative set, Douglas Corporation horse tramway.
4 Foster ticket, intermediate in character between bell-punch and Edmondson, of I O M T & E P electric coastal line, 1896 (Derby Castle to Groudle return).
5 Edmondson ticket of Snaefell Mountain Electric tramway, Laxey to Snaefell (summit) and return, 1896.
6 Manx Electric Edmondson ticket, Douglas to Snaefell Summit and return, dated 18 August 1931.
7 Manx Electric conductor's ticket of earlier type, for various 2d fares. Note section Douglas to Port Jack; the latter is not now an official outward stop.
8 Manx Electric conductor's ticket of later type with over-printed fare and standardised stage-array (Half-single and issued for Douglas to Fairy Cottage).
9 Douglas Southern Edmondson single, Port Soderick to Douglas Head, c. 1898.
10 Roll ticket for the same journey c. 1930 when the tramway was operated by Douglas Head Marine Drive Ltd.
11 Free return ticket of Douglas Head Incline Railway, Tuesday issue.
12 Isle of Man Harbour Board Queen's Pier tram (Ramsey) 2d adult ticket, c. 1961.
13 Combined excursion ticket Douglas Pier to Port Soderick Beach and return, by steam ferry, electric car and two cable inclines (1938).
14 Willebrew ticket of Falcon Cliff Hotel Electric Lift (cut up for 3d cash fare).

Route Maps—Manx Electric Railway

These maps are based on the original parliamentary and other plans, but with buildings and field boundaries corrected as far as possible to the present day. The map sections coincide with those of the gradient profiles in Appendix 7. A solid bar across the line indicates a car stop observed in both directions; unidirectional stops are shown by a bar to the left (northbound) or right (southbound), former stops by a white bar. S after a stop name indicates occasional use only (secondary status). Other standard symbols are : CR (Crossover), FP (Feeder Point), P (Pillar box), T (Telephone access point) and WB (warning board). Detailed plans of Derby Castle, Laxey and Ramsey stations appear in Chapters 3 and 7, and of Douglas and Laxey depots in Chapter 10.

Electrical Feeder System

Feeder points are shown by FP on the maps and are numbered serially from Douglas. Some are pole-mounted switch boxes, usually associated with overhead feeders, and others are the older I O M T & EP ground pillars, which serve for underground feeders. Both types of feeder are normally left bridged across the section breakers in the trolley wires, but are interrupted by switches between these breakers; this allows maximum localisation of faults. Most ground pillars have pull-out (fused) connections, but some contain switchgear and more elaborate internal connections, especially if linked to the trolley wires at feeder points. Their external appearance is the same, with a lifting lid to give access to the pull-out connections and a side door to the lower interior.

At Feeder Points 16 and 34 there is only a pole-mounted switch, at Feeder Points 1, 3, 8, 9, 10, 11, 12, 13, 17, 18, 27, and 29 there is only a ground pillar, and at Feeder Points 2, 4, 6, 7, 14, 19 to 25, 28, 30, 31, 32 and 33 there are both. At Feeder Points 01, 02, 5, 15, 26, 32 (partly) and 35, the switchgear is in adjacent buildings. Section breakers are at Feeder Points 1, 3, 5, 9, 11, 13, 15, 22, 24, 26, 28, 31 and 33 (bridged) and telephones at Feeder Points 01,

02, 1, 5, 15, 17, 18, 23, 24, 26, 28, 30, 31, 32, 33 and 35. A replacement feeder runs overhead from 26 to 27 to take the place of the underground feeder from 26 to 30, now disused. The underground feeder runs overhead from 16 to 17, and the overhead feeder runs underground from 15 to 16, with a feeder from point 15 to the Snaefell line overhead in Laxey station. The Snaefell DC underground feeder passes through one pole switch and two standard pillars (no longer connected to the wires) to reach the section gap at the former power station; on this line, the trolley wires are connected by cross wires.

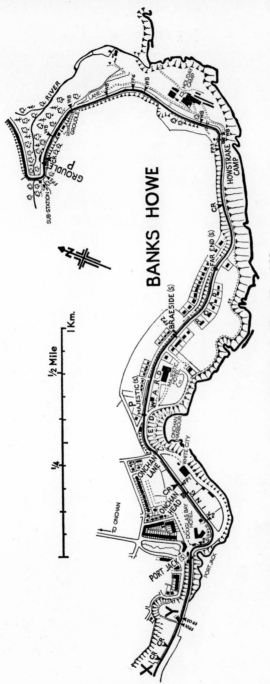

BANKS HOWE

See area plans for details at X and Y

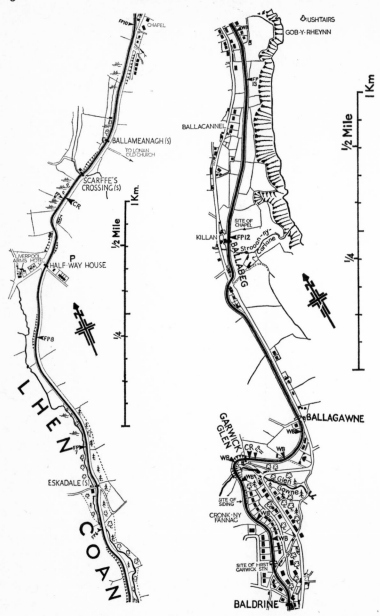

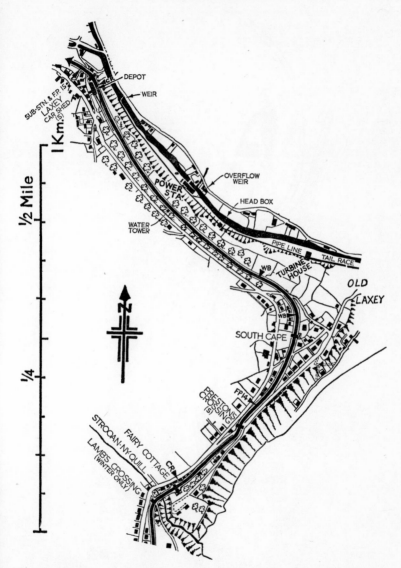

For northwards continuation, see p 167 in conjunction with map on following page

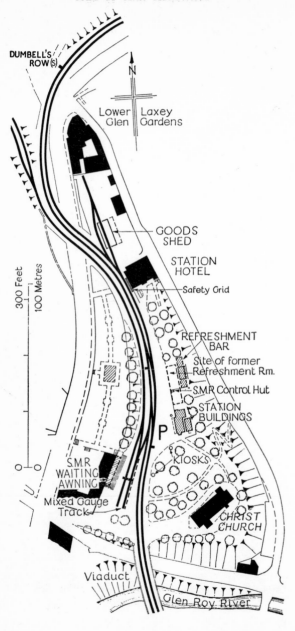

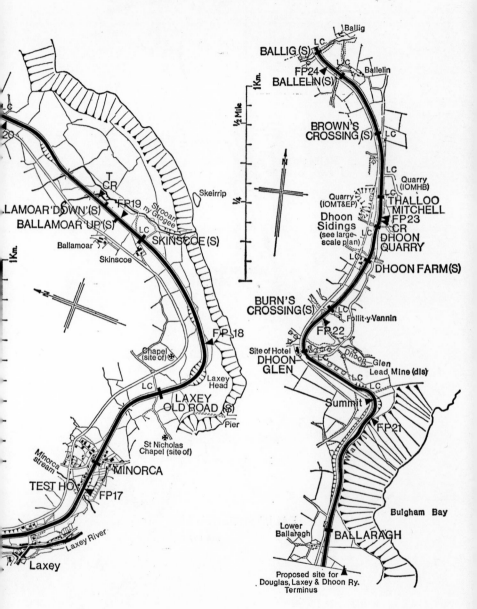

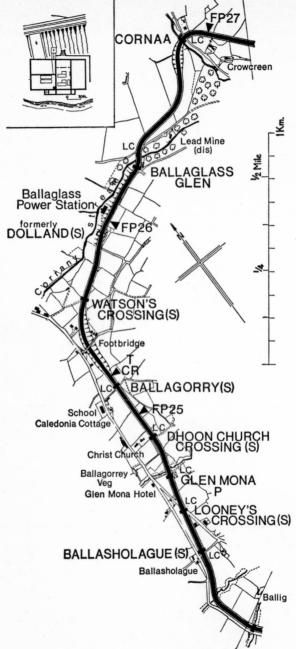

CORNAA

FP27

LC

Crowcreen

LC

Lead Mine
(dis)

BALLAGLASS
GLEN

Ballaglass
Power Station

formerly
DOLLAND(S)

FP26

WATSON'S
CROSSING(S)

Footbridge

T
CR

LC

BALLAGORRY(S)

School
Caledonia Cottage

FP25

LC

DHOON CHURCH
CROSSING (S)

Christ Church

LC

Ballagorrey
Veg

GLEN MONA

P

Glen Mona Hotel

LC

LOONEY'S
CROSSING(S)

BALLASHOLAGUE (S)

LC

Ballasholague

Ballig

1 Km.

½ Mile

¼

Inset: plan of power station at Ballaglass

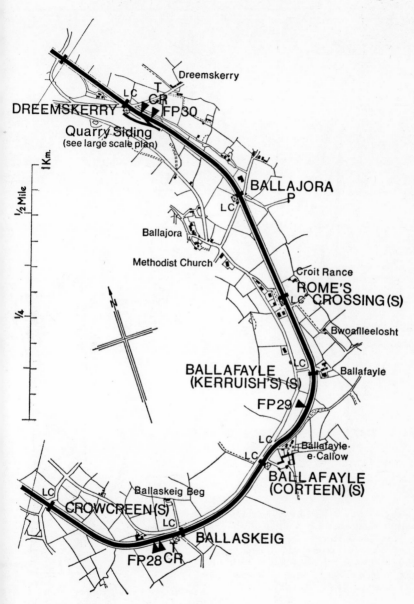

Dreemskerry

DREEMSKERRY   LC   T   CR   FP30

Quarry Siding
(see large scale plan)

1 Km.

½ Mile

BALLAJORA
P

LC

Ballajora

Methodist Church

Croit Rance

ROME'S
LC   CROSSING (S)

¼

Bwoaflleelosht

LC

BALLAFAYLE   Ballafayle
(KERRUISH'S) (S)

FP29

N

LC   Ballafayle
LC   e·Callow

BALLAFAYLE
(CORTEEN) (S)

Ballaskeig Beg

LC

CROWCREEN (S)

LC

BALLASKEIG

FP28 CR

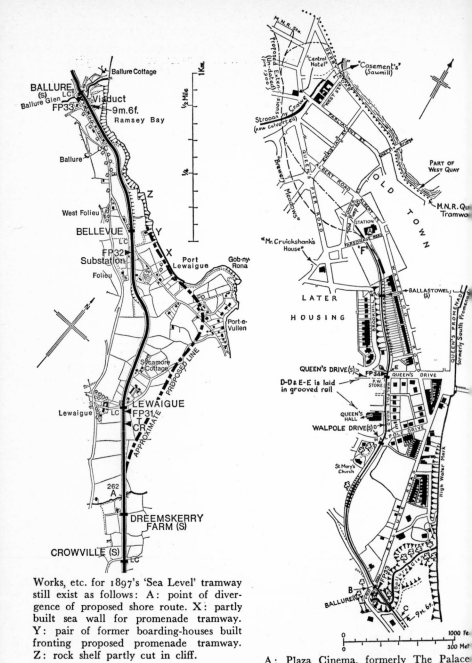

Works, etc. for 1897's 'Sea Level' tramway still exist as follows: A: point of divergence of proposed shore route. X: partly built sea wall for promenade tramway. Y: pair of former boarding-houses built fronting proposed promenade tramway. Z: rock shelf partly cut in cliff.

A: Plaza Cinema, formerly The Palace B: road crossing with traffic lights. C: site of 1898 depot. F: 'Mr Cruikshank' garden' (see 1899 text). (Extension proposals shown here are pre-1900).

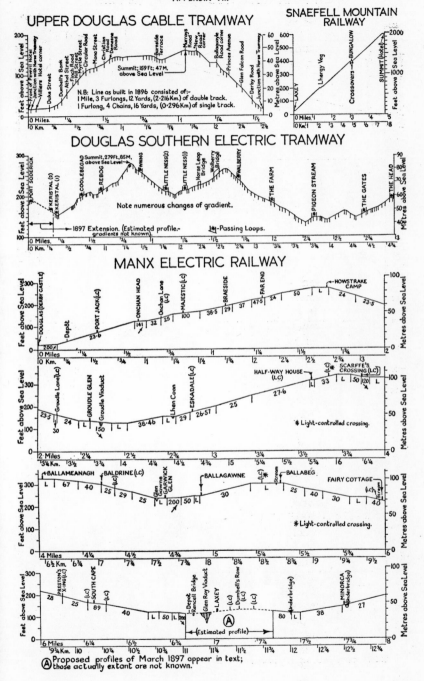

UPPER DOUGLAS CABLE TRAMWAY

SNAEFELL MOUNTAIN RAILWAY

N.B: Line as built in 1896 consisted of:-
1 Mile, 3 Furlongs, 12 Yards, (2·216 Km.) of double track.
1 Furlong, 4 Chains, 16 Yards, (0·296 Km.) of single track.

DOUGLAS SOUTHERN ELECTRIC TRAMWAY

Note numerous changes of gradient.

1897 Extension. (Estimated profile-
gradients not known).   ⌊◆⌋-Passing Loops.

MANX ELECTRIC RAILWAY

✱ Light-controlled crossing.

✱ Light-controlled crossing.

Ⓐ Proposed profiles of March 1897 appear in text;
those actually extant are not known.

MANX ELECTRIC RAILWAY (continued)

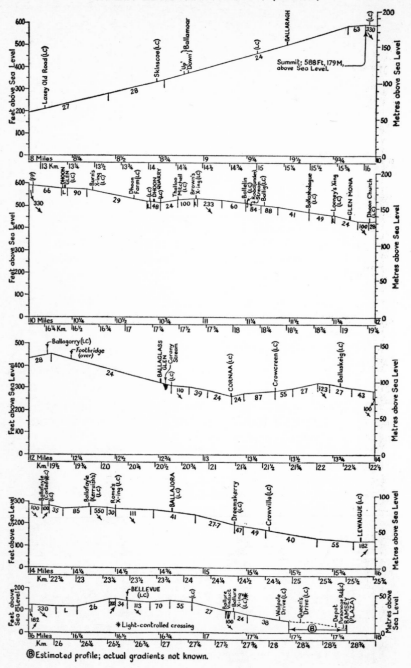

BIBLIOGRAPHY AND ACKNOWLEDGMENTS

The basic research for a great deal of this book was undertaken some eighteen years ago, and outline histories of the horse and electric lines by the writer appeared in 1954-6 in *Modern Tramway, Tramway Review,* and in the brochure issued by Douglas Corporation to mark the seventy-fifth anniversary of the horse tramway. Apart from these, few published accounts exist of the lines described in this book and the writer is thus more than usually grateful to all those who have assisted. They have been grouped under the subjects dealt with, but it is a considerable exercise of memory to recollect all who have helped and the author here asks the understanding of any whose names have inadvertently been omitted.

Douglas horse and cable tramways
The late S. G. Alder, Mrs M. Corkhill, W. Cowin, the late J. D. Craine, J. E. Cull, W. Davie, successive Douglas Corporation Tramway Committees, Inspector J. Dugdale, Mrs A. M. de A'Echevarria, the late Alderman J. C. Fargher, D. Halsall, A. Hampton, the late G. E. Lace, J. S. Quayle, R. L. Quayle, J. Quine, E. C. Shimmin, A. J. Teare, MBE, R. Temmerman (Brussels), J. S. Webb, the late C. F. Wolsey, the Royal National Lifeboat Institution, the Musées Royaux d'Art et d'Histoire, Brussels.

Manx Electric lines
A. Callister, A. R. Cannell, the Lady Chorley, D. Clayton, the late R. C. Drinkwater, W. Duggan, B. Barraclough Fell, Professor H. B. Fell, L. Gale, H. Gilmore, F. Henry, the late W. E. Kerruish, D. Kinnell, A. McMullen, A. W. Morley, the late H. Quayle, the late T. A. Quilleash, J. Rowe, M. Saunderson, Miss Ida Shaw, C. Taylor, Mrs E. Tollemache, R. Ward, J. F. Watson, the *Electrical*

Review, the Librarian of the Institute of Electrical Engineers, Mather & Platt Ltd, Post Office Records Dept, station, depot and engineering staffs of the M E R Board, and successive boards and their several chairman.

Douglas Southern Electric Tramway

R. C. W. Brown, W. A. Camwell, S. H. Davenport, R. Elliott, Messrs J. & J. Knox, W. T. Lambden, the late Mrs M. Marshall, B. R. S. Megaw and the then staff of the Manx Museum Library, M. J. O'Connor, the late Reginald Orton and members of his family, B. Y. Williams, W. E. Vick. the manufacturers of cars, equipment and bridgework (especially Messrs Bellis & Morcom), C. Anderson (formerly borough electrical engineer, Douglas) and the IoM Highway and Transport Board.

Assistance in general

Government Office, Douglas, the Isle of Man Harbour Board, the Isle of Man Highway & Transport Board, the Isle of Man Tourist Board, the Rolls Office, Douglas, Miss C. E. Baron, W. S. Basnett, G. Body, L. Bond, W. Bond, J. I. C. Boyd, G. B. Claydon, the editor of the *Courier*, T. Cowley, B. E. Crompton, A. M. Cubbon, R. L. Eastleigh, the Right Rev the Bishop of Montreal, F. R. G. Farrell, Mr Godwin (Isle of Man Holiday Centre), Major F. C. Harris, Miss Ann Harrison and colleagues at the Manx Museum. P. G. Hislop, W. G. S. Hyde, the editor of the *Isle of Man Times*, D. W. K. Jones, Rev Bertram G. Kelly, F. W. Killip, F. W. Ladds, J. B. Matthews, J. H. Meredith, Ramsey B. Moore, D. Odabashian, R. B. Parr, G. R. Peake, J. H. Price, J. N. Slater, A. Tranter, W. J. Wyse.

The main sources used in compiling this work, other than personal interview and correspondence, have been the Manx Press, the transport and technical Press, and official reports. The first comprise *The Courier* and its predecessor *The Ramsey Courier, The Isle of Man Examiner, The Isle of Man Times, The Manxman,* and *Mona's Herald,* the second *The Engineer, Electrical Review, The Electrician, The Light Railway and Tramway Journal, Modern Tramway, Railway Magazine, The Street Railway Journal,* and *Tramway and Railway World* (formerly *Railway World*). The reports consulted are those of Douglas Corporation, the Select Committees of Tynwald, and the Manx Electric Railway Board, and use has also been made of papers held by the M E R Board.

the Isle of Man Railway Company (via W. T. Lambden and B. E. Crompton), Douglas Corporation Transport Department, the Rolls Office, Douglas, Government Office, Douglas, the British Museum Newspaper Library, the Public Record Office (London), the Companies Registry of the Board of Trade, and those at the Nunnery, Douglas, by kind permission of the late Captain J. W. L. Fry-Goldie Taubman.

The tickets accompanying Appendix 5 were supplied by Mr W. H. Bett, and photographed by Mr F. Roland Whiteside, FRSA. Other specialised help in photographic work is acknowledged to Messrs J. T. Chapman Ltd, S. R. Keig Ltd (Douglas), Mr D. W. K. Jones and Mr R. B. Parr. Measurements used in the preparation of the car drawings were taken by Messrs P. Hammond, S. Basnett, J. N. Slater and the author.

In conclusion, I would express personal appreciation of the exertions of my editor, J. H. Price. The volume of work undertaken by Mr Price in this capacity approaches that involved in compiling the original manuscript, to which he had already made major research contributions over the past years.

F. K. PEARSON

Author's Supplementary Note

The reference to the Marine Drive's Whing—Keristal section on p 307 (lines 33/34) should read '. . . . was being extended to. . . .'. This is then compatible with the remarks on DHMD finance on page 317: both statements derive from contemporary reports but those regarding the first statement are ambiguous.

Also, references in this chapter to the 'entrance gates' and to the 'Toll Gates' refer to the same structure—both titles were used at different periods. The map (p 308) shows this as 'The Gates', the name commonly used by tramwaymen.

Since this book was completed the Suspension Bridge Co and the Marine Drive have been the subject of more detailed studies by the author. The reader is thus referred to the *Journal of the Manx Museum*, Nos 85 and 86, for further information on these subjects.

Index